I0425471

ClusterPhuck:
Leading at the Speed of Stupid

Money   Power   Politics   Leadership

Dr. Gregory L. Cotton

Copyright © 2019 Dr. Gregory L. Cotton

All rights reserved.

DEDICATION

This book is dedicated to my late mother and father who made the decision, prior to their marriage, to make whatever sacrifices they needed to for the good of their children. It was as if their primary business in life was to take care of us. Imagine that.

CONTENTS

ACKNOWLEDGMENTS

I would like to first thank my beautiful wife Deana, who has put up with me all of these years, along with my boys Scooter, Chris, James, and Nate. I would also like to acknowledge my brothers and sisters, and my wonderful mother and father-in-law. Dr. Avella deserves thanks for leading me through the doctoral process and instilling the value of good research. Lastly, a special thanks to all of the good, bad, and great leaders that I have either worked for, worked with, or had the opportunity to experience their leadership actions within the military and in the private sector.

Chapter 1

Leadership, Speed, & Stupidity

For those of you that have not been exposed to the term ***ClusterPhuck,*** go to "Google", or pretty much any search engine, and you will find definitions like "…a derogatory term used to describe a system or operation that has been totally hosed up by a group of managers who couldn't leave well enough alone." Or perhaps, "Chaos. Anything that occurs haphazardly."

Still, there are other definitions, such as ***"…used to describe a situation that has gone horrendously wrong. Almost always involves a large group of people that are disorganized: where the leader has failed,"***

or ***"…currently used in popular culture to describe any situation in which: extremely poor decisions are made for the purpose of very tired and predictable personal gain, without consideration for how decisions impact others, and an overall sense of intimidation due to a lack of competence and personal responsibility by the aggressor."***

As a ClusterPhuckologist, which is the comprehensive study of ClusterPhucks; this book is primarily focused with:

1. Determining the root cause of a ClusterPhuck.

2. Examining the decision path leading to the creation of a ClusterPhuck.

3. Determining both the short-term and long-term ramifications associated with a ClusterPhuck.

4. How ClusterPhucks affect you and your family.

5. Eliminating or Reducing the impact of a ClusterPhuck.

6. Leadership styles utilized during various ClusterPhucks.

Leadership Decisions and 2nd & 3rd Order Consequences

Have you ever made a decision that you thought, at the time, would yield positive results, but ended up costing you money, your reputation or your job? Well, you are not alone. Every decision has second and third order consequences to that decision. What that simply means is that there are outcomes that are different than the first desired outcome, but are directly related to the initial decision.

For example, one might think that working in The White House or say perhaps a company that claimed to have devised a breakthrough blood testing technology, would be a good career decision. However, as you will see, predicting 2nd and 3rd order consequences can be easy for some and tough on others.

In April 2018, the manager of a Philadelphia Starbucks called the police on two black men who were told to buy something or leave. The two men were waiting for another person to arrive for a business meeting. The police came in and arrested the men for trespassing. They spent about nine hours in jail, and were released without charges.

The entire incident was recorded by an onlooker, and within days had been viewed close to 11 million times. The incident sparked protests and calls for boycotts of the coffee chain due to what many thought was clearly racial bias. One white woman told the media that she and her friends frequent Starbucks and do the exact same thing the black men were accused of and nothing ever happened to them. To make matters worse, Starbucks does indeed have a policy that allows people to remain in its cafes without making a purchase.

Clearly, whether it was racism or just plain stupidity, it was the managers initial decision (**first order** consequence), to call the police that started the ClusterPhuck. The **second order** consequence from the managers initial decision, resulted in the arrest of two black men that had every right, according to Starbucks policy, to sit there for as long as they wanted. The bad publicity associated with the second order consequence, leads us to the third order consequence, that had to be handled by the CEO of the company.

The CEO announced that Starbucks was going to close more than 8,000 stores for employee racial-tolerance training. Experts believed that this could cost Starbucks millions of dollars in lost revenue. The CEO also apologized directly to the two black men very quickly, as well as going on national television to apologize and calling the incident "reprehensible.".

Keep in mind that Starbucks does pride itself on diversity and inclusiveness. How much so? In 2013, founder and CEO Howard Schultz addressed an investor at their annual shareholders meeting in Seattle, who argued that the company's support for gay marriage was bad for business.

Schultz replied that Starbucks's endorsement of marriage equality wasn't about making money, but about the principle of diversity. He went on to state:

"If you feel, respectfully, that you can get a higher return than the 38 percent you got last year, it's a free country. You can sell your shares of Starbucks and buy shares in another company. Thank you very much."

As of 2017, Starbucks employs 238,000 people and operates 27,339 locations worldwide. It took just one manager in one location to not only hurt their reputation, but their profit margin as well.

Starbucks isn't the only one apologizing to the two men and to the public. The Police Commissioner, Richard Ross, who is black, apologized to the two men only after he previously staunchly defended his police officers for their handling of the incident.

Ross stated that he "failed miserably" in the messaging around the arrests. He went on to say that the police department did not have a policy for dealing with this kind of situation in the past, but now has one. You could say that Police Commissioner Ross displayed a **Pragmatic Leadership** style during this controversy. How?

Pragmatic leaders "focus on the processes behind any task, initiative, or goal. Their top priority is to figure out how the team is going to get things done." He admitted that he "failed miserably" in the messaging, which is a failure in situational awareness. However, he did admit his mistake and immediately took action by implementing a policy that covered a situation like occurred at Starbucks.

The manager that started the mess, showed **Incompetent Leadership**, due to his lack of knowledge for something that the average employee should know. Walmart, for example, has a policy for Recreational Vehicles or RV parking that states:

"While we do not offer electrical service or accommodations typically necessary for RV customers, Walmart values RV travelers and considers them among our best customers. Consequently, we do permit RV parking on our store lots as we are able. Permission to park is extended by individual store managers, based on availability of parking space and local laws. Please contact management in each store to ensure accommodations before parking your RV."

What if a Walmart manager would have called the police department on those parking at a Walmart...or turned RV owners away because he or she failed to check the policy or made a call to a regional manager for guidance? There is probably a good chance, if it resulted in Walmart receiving negative publicity, the manager would be moved or terminated for incompetence. Or, in other words, creating a needless ClusterPhuck.

***

Dr. Gregory L. Cotton

Root Cause Analysis of a ClusterPhuck (CP)

Have you ever initially assigned blame to a person, employer, or organization because it seemed logical or because people pointed to them as the cause of the problem? Well, this book is designed not only to uncover who **really** started the problem CP, but also to determine how and why people knowingly and unknowingly create them.

This book also examines how and why seemingly good leaders within the swirling winds of a potential ClusterPhuck not only tend to miss the signs that they are heading directly into a storm, but often make things considerably worse. Yes, there are ways to reduce or eliminate a ClusterPhuck, which we will get into later. Let's first however take a closer look at what a **root cause** is and what role it plays in determining the true culprits behind a ClusterPhuck.

Root Cause Analysis

A Root Cause Analysis (RCA), is a method of problem solving that tries to identify the root causes of faults or problems. The practice of RCA tries to solve problems by attempting to identify and correct the root causes of events, as opposed to simply addressing their symptoms. One of the main goals is to correct root causes in order to prevent a problem or a ClusterPhuck from recurring in the future. Let's take a root cause analysis look at the Challenger Space Shuttle disaster as an example.

Challenger

The Space Shuttle Challenger broke apart 73 seconds into its flight, leading to the deaths of its seven crew members on January 28, 1986. The Presidential Commission on the Space Shuttle Challenger Accident, also known as the Rogers Commission, was formed to investigate the disaster. It found that the Challenger accident was caused by a failure in the O-rings sealing, which is a joint on the right solid rocket booster.

The contributing causes of the accident, according to the investigative report, was the failure of both NASA and Morton Thiokol to respond adequately to the danger posed by the deficient joint design. Rather than redesigning the joint, they came to define the problem as an acceptable flight risk. The report found that managers at Marshall had known about the flawed design since 1977, but never discussed the problem outside their reporting channels with Thiokol, which was a flagrant violation of NASA regulations.

Even when it became more apparent how serious the flaw was, no one at Marshall considered grounding the shuttles until a fix could be implemented.

Marshall managers went as far as to issue and waive six launch constraints related to the O-rings. The report also strongly criticized the decision-making process that led to the launch of Challenger, saying that it was seriously flawed.

Suppressing Red Flag Leader Actions

Allan J. McDonald, rocket engineer, and Roger Boisjoly, a booster rocket engineer at NASA contractor Morton Thiokol, were two, what I refer to as Red Flag leaders, attempted unsuccessfully to stop the launch. McDonald felt so strongly that the launch should be cancelled that he refused to sign a piece of paper recommending that NASA launch the space shuttle Challenger, despite enormous pressure from his employers and NASA. His supervisors in Utah overruled him and faxed a signature to NASA indicating the company, if not McDonald, approved the launch.

Earlier, Boisjoly wrote a memo in July 1985 to his superiors concerning the faulty design of the solid rocket boosters that, if left unaddressed, could lead to a catastrophic event during launch of a Space Shuttle.

In his book, **Truth, Lies and O-Rings**, McDonald wrote, "Roger and I already felt like lepers, but when we returned to Utah following the May 2nd session our colleagues treated us as if we had just been arrested for child sexual abuse."

Unfortunately, Red Flag leaders will always take a lot of heat for standing up for what is right, even when they have the data to back up their concerns. The problem with the Challenger disaster was that the decision makers that overruled Mr. McDonald, were not Red Flag leaders.

Imagine if Mr. McDonald had the overall authority to cancel the launch, would he have been fired? Perhaps, but after the accident NASA's Space Shuttle fleet was grounded for almost three years. If Red Flag leadership would have been allowed to take the decision making lead, the O-ring issue would have been fixed, and the seven crewmembers would still be alive.

McDonald and Boisjoly did their utmost to avoid this ClusterPhuck, but due to incompetent leadership at the top, their efforts were in vain.

Pressure, Stress & Decision Making

In her book, **The Challenger Launch Decision: Risky Technology, Culture, and Deviance at NASA**, author Diane Vaughan investigated the series of events leading to the Challenger launch decision. She first describes NASA's space shuttle Challenger's launch schedule, which was originally scheduled to launch on

January 22, 1986, and outlined how the inclusion of an elementary school teacher, Christa McAuliffe, which made it a special mission.

She also rejected the theory that pressure from the media had influenced the decision to launch. The Presidential Commission, by the way, found no evidence of any political pressure from the White House. Vaughan believed that NASA's political environment forced the space agency to compete for scarce financial resources, which led to "production pressure", leading to the risky launch decision.

NASA, in a move to save money, decided to cut costs on safety testing, which was a divergence from the earlier Apollo Program. The Covert Report (Eugene Covert, Department of Aeronautics, MIT) concluded that the key components may not have been tested sufficiently and certification of components required more time than that given by NASA, leading to problems with the main engine. Economic constraints and the success of the program was heavily dependent on the success of its business model, which was based on maintaining high frequency of launch to meet financial goals.

Vaughan introduced two structural factors. First, Culture of Production, and second, Structural Secrecy, which she found was essential to understanding the environment in which NASA engineers and managers were operating.

In the formative years of NASA, the culture was shaped by a pure technical mentality, where "can do" attitude was a part of the self-image. It slowly became structurally more complex and bureaucratic, and later budgetary constraints transformed it into a 'technical production system."

Vaughan argued that the decision-making was affected when initial technical culture of NASA became entangled with the bureaucratic and political accountability, leading to the structural source of the disaster.

The working group was conforming to a set of cultural beliefs, which included using the paradigm of acceptable risk, belief in redundancy, and in the need to continue production in spite of evidence suggesting problems, that they had formed, and continuing to recommend launch. This conduct was culturally approved and conforming to the established norms and practice.

By Structural Secrecy, Vaughan is referring to *"the way that patterns of information, organizational structure, processes, transactions, and the structure of regulatory relations systematically undermines the attempt to know and make decisions, in an organization."* She examined the sources of structural secrecy and traced their effect on information and its interpretation.

Information that reached higher levels was filtered, and people high up in the line of command were, more often than not, unaware of the "nitty-gritty" of the details and discussions that went on pertaining to several technical issues which were dealt with and resolved or categorized as *acceptable risk* by engineers.

She concluded that the decision making was rule based, and the launch decision resulted not from managerial wrongdoing, but from structural factors that were deep rooted, resulting in a tragic disaster.

As you can clearly see from this example, ClusterPhucks can be formed because of deep rooted beliefs that have been cultivated over a span of years, but it's not the only way. Individuals that are poorly vetted or fraud their way into influential positions, increase the risk of a ClusterPhuck.

Keep in mind that there will always be controversy as to the root cause and severity of a ClusterPhuck. As you will see, people are generally self-serving when it comes to taking the blame. However, some leaders have admitted to miscalculating the outcome of what turned out to be a devastating ClusterPhuck.

Take the attack on Pearl Harbor on the morning of December 7, 1941, which was a complete surprise to the United States and led to World War II. 2,402 Americans were killed and 1,282 wounded. The attack was intended to neutralize the U.S. Pacific Fleet, and hence protect Japan's advance into Malaya and the Dutch East Indies, where it sought access to natural resources.

In order to reduce the number of potential casualties and end the war, the United States unleashed atomic bombs on the cities of Hiroshima and Nagasaki, resulting in the deaths of 90,000–166,000 people in Hiroshima and 60,000–80,000 in Nagasaki, with roughly half of the deaths in each city occurring on the first day. During the following months, large numbers died from the effect of burns, radiation sickness, and other injuries, compounded by illness.

On August 15, six days after the bombing of Nagasaki, Japan announced its surrender to the Allies, signing the Instrument of Surrender on September 2, officially ending World War II. There has been several articles and studies written about the leadership response from both Japan and the United States. Many believe that Japan did not need to attack Pearl Harbor in order to realize its dreams of dominating the South Pacific.

The rationale that it needed to take out the American fleet in order to have a free hand in the Pacific was, in the end, a flawed assumption. Few Americans wanted a war with Japan, and almost no politician in Washington was willing to risk American lives. Japan created this ClusterPhuck and threw away its empire all because it overestimated both America's willingness to contest her expansionist plans, and the real threat it posed to those plans.

Over the last four decades, different arguments have gained and lost support as new evidence has become available, and as new studies have been completed regarding the use of the atomic bomb on Hiroshima and Nagasaki. The primary focus has been on the role of the bombings had in the U.S.'s justification for them based upon the premise that the bombings precipitated the surrender.

American historian, J. Samuel Walker wrote, "The fundamental issue that has divided scholars over a period of nearly four decades is whether the use of the bomb was necessary to achieve victory in the war in the Pacific on terms satisfactory to the United States."

Supporters of the bombings generally assert they caused the Japanese surrender, preventing massive casualties on both sides, and thought Japan would not surrender unless there was an overwhelming demonstration of destructive capability. Those who oppose the bombings argue there were already fierce conventional air raids on Japan and, therefore, "…militarily unnecessary, inherently immoral, a war crime, or a form of state terrorism."

Deadly Miscalculations or Leader Stupidity?

On November 28th, 2018, Boeings fast-selling plane, the 737 Max 8, crashed into the sea moments after takeoff in Indonesia, killing all 189 people on board. Fast forward to March 10th, 2019, when another 737 crashed shortly after takeoff, killing all 157 people on board. It was the second fatal accident involving a Boeing 737 Max 8 jet in five months.

A preliminary report suggested that "Faulty sensor data" led to a series of events that caused pilots of an Ethiopian Airlines to lose control of the airplane before the crash. On April 10th, 2019, a lawsuit was filed in a Chicago courtroom alleging that Boeing misled investors by hiding problems with its 737 Max 8 jet, in order to push its shares higher.

Would a company, that had revenue of over $100 billion in 2018, risk the lives of hundreds of passengers? Well, apparently they did just that. It was revealed that the company knew there was an issue with a warning system in the 737 Max 8 jet, but didn't share that information until after the second crash.

Remember the "Challenger" disaster and the culture around "acceptable" risk? It would be like sending troops into battle, knowing that some of the weaponry was subject to failure during times of sustained conflicts…and not providing this information to soldiers on the ground.

It has been estimated that settlement of claims that will without be filed by family members of the 737 Max 8 disasters, will reach $1 billion. So, as you will see, there are people out there that will take "acceptable" risks with other people's lives, though it may costs them billions in lost revenue, settlements with family members of the victims, as well as months, or even years, marred in ClusterPhuck hell.

The size of an organization does not matter when it comes to creating "acceptable risks" that increase the likelihood of a catastrophic ClusterPhuck. James Smalley, a quality assurance engineer at PMI Industries near Rochester, New York, allegedly forged the signatures of an inspector on reports for rocket parts that were sold to California-based SpaceX. The charge carries a maximum sentence of 10 years in federal prison.

When one of his bosses asked him why he allegedly did this, Smalley said that "he wanted to ship more product for the company." The 35 employee company was making $200,000 per month from SpaceX. They have since cancelled their contract with PMI, which forced them to close, and now 35 people are without jobs.

It took just one person to initiate a ClusterPhuck that shutdown an entire business. How would you feel if suddenly your whole world changed in an instant? You have a mortgage, children, car payment, medical bills, etc. By the way, one third of the people in Rochester live in poverty…so what are your chances of finding a comparable employment opportunity?

Some of you may look at the potential for the millions of dollars that could have been lost if the parts turned out to be faulty. However, what if the faulty parts caused the rocket to veer off course and landed, let's say, in San Francisco? Smalley would be looking at a lot more than 10 years.

Of course, Smalley led stupidly…but what if one decision you made collapsed an entire government?

The Nazi Partnership & Political Calculus

Political Calculus refers to *"…calculation or reasoning of a specifically political nature and means to make evaluations and decisions which are primarily based upon politically expedient considerations, rather then and as opposed to all other considerations (i.e., reality, principle, moral, ethical)."*

Sebastian Kurz has been the Chancellor of Austria since 18 December, 2017. Kurz came to power through a coalition between his center-right People's Party and the far-right Freedom Party. The 32 year old Kurz is widely seen as the **"conservative golden boy of Europe"**.

Rather than forge a grand alliance with center-left Social Democrats, he opted for a partnership with the Freedom Party, which was formed by neo-Nazis. All of that ended when Freedom Party leader and Vice Chancellor, Heinz-Christian Strache, who resigned after he was caught on video promising government contracts in return for donations from a woman posing as a wealthy scion of a Russian oligarch family, which she was not.

Additionally, he wanted the woman to acquire a controlling stake in Austria's largest tabloid, Kronen Zeitung, and support the anti-immigrant Freedom Party. To put simply, Strache was caught on tape selling out his country to Russia.

Just being curious, I searched for what dog breeds would most likely turn on their owners. The list included the Great Dane, Tosa Inu, Fila Brasileiro, Wolf hybrid, Siberian Husky, Rottweiler, German Shepherd, and American Pit Bull Terrier. I can honestly tell you that I didn't know any of that until I researched it.

I bring this up because there is a lot of information out there on the Freedom Party and the Nazis. Why would you partner with a group that most rational thinking people would try to avoid?

Even before this current scandal, there were other controversies. Kurz was forced to denounce a racist poem written by a Freedom Party official that likened immigrants to "rats", and suggested that cultures destroy themselves when they mix. A party campaign poster, which depicted a fair-haired white couple surrounded by a sea of "sinister-looking foreigners", drew comparisons to Nazi propaganda.

After the video of Strache was publicized, every single minister of the Freedom Party resigned, making this a full blown crisis. Kurz, in the meantime, has called for "snap elections." On the 27th of May, Kurz was ousted by parliament in a no-confidence vote, paving the way for a new election.

With all of that being said, does it mean that Kurz is done as a politician? Of course not. He still has popular support, and has vowed that he and his center-right People's Party would return to power with increased strength. His political calculus may turn out to be right in the end. Why? Because the ramifications associated with a ClusterPhuck, as you will find out, are not always equal. Take Virginia Governor Ralph Northam.

On February 1, 2019, images from Northam's medical school yearbook were published on a far-right website. The photos showed an unidentified person in blackface and one person in a Ku Klux Klan hood. The photos were on his yearbook page, so Northam figured that he had to be the person in blackface. Northam, a democrat, issued a statement saying:

"Earlier today, a website published a photograph of me from my 1984 medical school yearbook in a costume that is clearly racist and offensive. I am deeply sorry for the decision I made to appear as I did in this photo and for the hurt that decision caused then and now. This behavior is not in keeping with who I am today and the values I have fought for throughout my career in the military, in medicine, and in public service.
But I want to be clear, I understand how this decision shakes Virginians' faith in that commitment. I recognize that it will take time and serious effort to heal the damage this conduct has caused. I am ready to do that important work. The first step is to offer my sincerest apology and to state my absolute commitment to living up to the expectations Virginians set for me when they elected me to be their Governor."

Any **Crisis Leadership** expert would have advised Northam to make the statement. However, there were still immediate calls coming from across the country for Northam to resign, but he resisted.

In a confusing turnabout, Northam privately told several people that he did not believe that he was either of the men depicted in the photo. After a couple of really awkward press conferences, and keeping his head down, a months-long investigation could not "conclusively" determine who was in the photo, or even how the image ended up there.

So Northam created this ClusterPhuck on his own when he assumed that he was indeed one of the people in the photo. He didn't make things any better during one of his press conferences when he stated that he once put "a little shoe polish" on his face when he was younger to imitate Michael Jackson at a dance contest.

But how has this affected his standing with voters…especially in the African-American community? A February, 2019 Quinnipiac University poll showed that 48 percent of Virginia voters said Northam should not resign over the scandal, while 42 percent said he should.

Perhaps even more important for his political future, 56 percent of black voters said Northam should remain in office, while 31 percent said he should step down. White voters were evenly split on the issue at 46 percent. There was a time when there would have been no doubt about Northam stepping down due to the relentless pressure one receives in a very short period of time.

However, we now live in a 24-7 news cycle in which a story like Northam's can be knocked off the front pages by a President that does or says something controversial seemingly every single day. So, as I stated before, ClusterPhucks are NOT created equal, and it seems Northam's political calculus to weather the storm was correct.

***

Fake Leaders in Real Positions

Laura Callahan was a former senior director at the United States Department of Homeland Security (DHS), who resigned in 2004 after an investigation revealed that she had received her doctorate from Hamilton University, an unaccredited school, or what is commonly known as a diploma mill.

There was outrage, of course. People questioned how an individual could rise up the ranks within arguably the most important department in the United States, with a phony doctorate degree. This prompted an investigation by the General Accounting Office (GAO).

The GAO conducted their investigation from July 2003 through February 2004. They searched the Internet for nontraditional, unaccredited, postsecondary schools that offered degrees for a relatively low flat fee, promoted the award of academic credits based on life experience, and did not require any classroom instruction.

They requested that four such schools provide information on the number of current and former students identified in their records, as federal employees. They also requested the amount of money that was payed to the fake schools by the federal government. In addition, posing as a prospective student who was employed by a federal agency, their investigator contacted three unaccredited schools to obtain information on how he might have a federal agency pay for a degree.

Three out of four unaccredited schools responded to their requests for information and provided records that identified 463 students employed by the federal government. Two of the four schools provided records that federal agencies paid them $150,387.80 for the fees of federal employee students. Yes, that's your taxes paying for fake degrees.

Eight government agencies reported that 28 senior-level employees had degrees from diploma mills and other unaccredited schools. Follow-up interviews with six of the senior-level employees and their managers, told the GAO that experience, rather than educational credentials, was considered in hiring and promotion decisions concerning these employees. The fact that managers attempted to rationalize as to why they promoted an employee with a phony degree, has shown us what true leadership incompetence looks like.

Unfortunately, the GAO stated that it is extremely difficult, if not impossible, to determine the extent of unauthorized federal payments for degrees issued by unaccredited schools. The data they received from both schools and federal agencies understated the extent to which the federal government had made such payments. Additionally, the way in which some agencies maintained their records of payments for employee education made such information inaccessible.

One of the most disturbing things about the report was that the employees listed on the phony degree list included three management-level Department of Energy (DOE) employees who had emergency operations responsibilities at the National Nuclear Security Administration (NNSA), and security clearances.

Due to employer expectations, Americans with college degrees has rapidly increased in the past several decades. Employers believe, in some cases, that applicants should have, at a minimum, a postsecondary degree. Meanwhile, rising education costs have made obtaining postsecondary and graduate education difficult and too costly for many.

As a result, the allure of obtaining credentials quickly and inexpensively can prove too good to resist. Diploma mills are only part of the problem. Even those who don't buy fake degrees may falsify or exaggerate their resumes.

Many organizations have learned the importance of verifying employees' degrees the hard way. For example:

- In 2018, Melissa Howard, an aspiring legislator out of Florida, who liked posing for pictures with guns and flags, lied about graduating from Miami University in Ohio as she claimed, forcing her to drop out of her campaign, after originally calling it "fake news."

- In 2018, Amanda La Bell, 41, dropped out of Oregon's race for House District 54 following false claims about her college education.

- A Manassas City, Virginia, principal resigned and lost his teaching license in 2014 after it was discovered that he falsified most of his educational credentials, presenting himself as having college degrees he never earned.

- In 2012, it was discovered that Scott Thompson, the then CEO of Yahoo, had not earned the computer science degree he claimed, but instead had a degree in accounting.

- David Tovar, Walmart's former vice president for corporate communications, stepped down in 2014 after it was discovered that he was never awarded the degree that he claimed he received.

- Herbalife's CEO, Gregory Probert, was forced to resign in 2008 after it was revealed that he did not have the MBA he claimed.

- In 2008, The Wall Street Journal reported that J. Terrence Lanni, the former CEO of MGM Mirage, did not receive an MBA he stated on his resume.

New technology, the Internet, and advertisements appearing in major news outlets, have made it easier to both sell and obtain false credentials, such as a high school diploma, bachelor's, Master's, or even a doctorate degree. According to the New York Times, there are 3,300 diploma mills selling degrees to anyone willing to pay. More than 50,000 Ph.Ds. are purchased from diploma mills every year, which surprisingly exceeds the quantity legitimately awarded.

Retired FBI agent Allen Ezell, stated that a **Butcher's Almeda** degree is one of at least 220,000 fake degrees he's discovered that are all connected to a Pakistan company called **Axact**, which may be the world's biggest diploma mill.

Obviously, it is a failure of leadership when fake degrees make their way into the system, due to a lack of due diligence or laziness. Yes, your boss sitting in the big office barking out orders to you and giving you a mediocre evaluation, could have gotten to that position with a couple of fake degrees.

But what about the people that do have real legitimate education credentials, but are placed in leadership positions that they are unqualified for? Now imagine that these unqualified individuals are left in charge of, let's say, a large-scale disaster.

Lawyer of Disaster

Think back to 2005 and Hurricane Katrina. The Director of the Federal Emergency Management Agency (FEMA), was a lawyer. He had absolutely no training in emergency management. He resigned from FEMA, under pressure, after his controversial handling of Katrina.

Michael Brown was appointed to the position by President George W. Bush. This is not the first, and will not be the last time a President appoints a person to a position for which they have zero technical or real world expertise or experience (See Trump administration).

How many people, regardless of our training, education, or experience would turn down a presidential appointment? Presidential appointments can of course lead to more high-profile positions and a higher level of social inclusion.

There are a lot of people, with legitimate college degrees, causing ClusterPhucks and leading stupidly every single day. Does the fact that you have a degree in, let's say criminal justice, mean that you are going to be a good police officer? Meaning, that once the bullets start flying, are they guaranteed to function effectively under extreme pressure? Of course not.

Unfortunately, we live in a society that is built on paper. PhDs, MBAs, and certificates for *this* or *that*, is how the vast majority of people are viewed with regards to their value or expertise. Now, things are even worse because the world is filled with hundreds of thousands of fake degrees, along with the people bent on faking their way into a top position in order to make themselves more competitive in the job market, increasing their public profile, and, of course, knowingly or not, increasing the probability of creating a ClusterPhuck.

The Price of Leading Stupidly

Five years ago the drinking water source for Flint, Michigan was switched from Detroit's water system to the Flint River, creating one of the biggest ClusterPhucks in the country. When all was said and done, 12 people would die, and more than 80 were sickened as a result of two waves of a deadly Legionnaires' disease outbreak in Flint.

Nick Lyon, the director, was charged with involuntary manslaughter, for ***"willful neglect of duty and misconduct in office"*** for the deaths of two men. He was accused of ***"failing to alert the public"*** about a Legionnaires' outbreak when he had noticed that "another outbreak was foreseeable and ... conducting an investigation of the Legionnaires' outbreak in a grossly negligent manner."

Fourteen other Michigan state officials were also charged in connection with the water crisis, which includes such charges as obstruction of justice and lying to an officer. As you will see throughout this book, a lack of preparation and research are two vital components leading to a ClusterPhuck…however, sometimes it's just purely stupid decision making.

***

There is this saying in the Army that a soldier could go from "sugar to shit" after a decision he or she made that went sour or created a ClusterPhuck. Imagine being the "Golden Boy" that could do no wrong in the eyes of his superiors, but a fatal misstep, typically something that they could have controlled, knocked them from the ranks of the chosen. One could argue that former New Jersey Governor Chris Christie could be one of the top ten candidates recruited for the "sugar to shit" poster.

Christie was once a star in the Republican Party with a nearly 80% approval rating. He was viewed by many across the aisle as a "…tough straight-talker." Christie showed some strong leadership during Hurricane Sandy in 2012, and his approval rating increased into the high 70s resulting in a landslide reelection in 2013. However, things started going south pretty quickly with his party due to his working relationship and the praise he heaped on President Obama during Sandy just days before the presidential election between Obama and Mitt Romney.

Speed matters in a time of crisis, and the usual business processes and decision velocities need to be suspended and decisions should be made in a way that reassures stakeholders (citizens) , that they are taking steps to address the problem. President Obama and Governor Christie showed tremendous leadership during Sandy, and the world witnessed that it was indeed possible for Democrats and Republicans to work together and actually get some things done once you set aside politics for the greater good of the people.

Even though Christie was showing strong **Crisis** and **Situational Leadership** traits, it didn't sit well with most Republicans. A few days after Hurricane Sandy, Christie found himself in the middle of a political storm with the Republican Party. Apparently, his "embrace" of President Obama so close to the presidential election tilted the election in Obama's favor. Rupert Murdoch, head of News Corporation which includes Fox News, tweeted that Christie might be responsible for Mr. Obama's re-election.

Christie reportedly told Murdoch that New Jersey needed friends during the crisis, no matter their political party. Christie was right, but it was the trigger that started his downward spiral.

In 2013, two of Christie's senior officials were sentenced to prison for a scandal known as **Bridegate**. They ordered the closure of two lanes on the New York-New Jersey George Washington Bridge for several days, paralyzing the town of Fort Lee. An investigation concluded that Christie's office ordered the closures to basically punish a Democratic mayor who did not support Christie's reelection.

Christie was not criminally charged in the scandal and refused to resign, even though his aides and federal prosecutors said that he was indeed aware that his top officials were involved in the plot. His popularity started to take a dive and continued due to some flawed or just plain stupid decisions.

Christie surprised both parties and his own constituents, given his unpopularity, when he announced his bid for the Republican presidential nomination in June 2015. During his eight-month campaign, he abandoned his identity as a moderate, moving right on several key issues, including immigration. He eventually dropped out of the race after winning just 7% of Republican primary voters in New Hampshire in mid-February 2016.

Two weeks after dropping out of the race, he endorsed Donald Trump for President, which prompted six New Jersey newspapers, in a joint editorial, asking Christie to either resign as governor or be pushed out. They stated:

"We're fed up with his opportunism, we're fed up with his hypocrisy."

They were "disgusted" with his endorsement of Donald Trump after he spent months on the campaign trail trashing him, calling him "unqualified by temperament and experience to be president." A week after Christie's endorsement, his approval rating dropped from 33% to 27%.

After his endorsement of Trump, he reportedly played a significant behind-the-scenes role in the presidential campaign, helping prepare Trump for debates and liaise with policy experts, donors, and other potential allies. He was apparently trying to position himself to be the attorney general. However, he lost favor with Trump and was pushed out of the campaign.

By June 2017, Christie's approval rating stood at just 15%. One would think that you couldn't get any lower in terms of popularity, but Christie found a way. During a state-wide government shutdown, over the fourth of July weekend no less, Christie was photographed, with his family, lounging on the beach outside of the governor's seaside residence in Island Beach State Park.

To say that New Jerseyans were outraged is not a strong enough statement. His actions were seen as selfish, thoughtless, and stupid. He will, like a few ambitious politicians, attempt to rehabilitate his image as a strong leader instead of the incompetent or unethical leader he is perceived to be by many at this stage of his professional life. He is not the only governor or elected official that has led stupidly…there are many more.

Before leaving office, Mississippi Governor Haley Barbour pardoned 203 people.

When all was said and done, it would be revealed that 16 of those pardoned had murdered someone, while others had rape and burglary convictions. Four of the murderers received full pardons even though they were serving life sentences. One state official rationalized that, "It is at any governor's discretion."

As you can probably imagine, the relatives and people throughout the state and the country, were rightly upset with Haley's stupidity or utter incompetence. Haley stated that he was *"very comfortable"* with his decision to release the prisoners. He went on to say that people in the state of Mississippi are predominantly Christian and believe in forgiveness.

The New York Times wrote that a disproportionate number of pardons were granted to applicants from wealthy families and those with personal or political connections. However, the Mississippi Supreme Court upheld the pardons, which had been challenged based on the argument that many of them did not follow a requirement in the state constitution to publish notices in newspapers for 30 days.

The Court wrote, "we are compelled to hold that – in each of the cases before us – it fell to the governor alone to decide whether the Constitution's publication requirement was met." The court went on to say that it could not overturn the pardons because of the constitution's separation of powers of the different branches of government.

Barbour had contemplated a run for president but decided against it. Nationally, this was not playing well. What percentage of the female vote do you think he would have captured in a national election when it was revealed that eight of the murderers he pardoned killed either their wives or girlfriends?

Given his explanation, it would seem that Mr. Barbour was the root cause of this ClusterPhuck. But how closely did he really look at the people he released? Is it possibly that a list of names were provided to him by trusted staff members and he signed off on them without proper due diligence? It really doesn't matter, does it?

Even if a staff member was the perpetrator, the ultimate responsibility to ensure that the pardons wouldn't create, in all likelihood, the end of his presidential aspirations, was his. If he blames it on a staffer he looks incompetent. Instead he rationalizes it in a way that did more harm to his legacy and his future in politics. The only way he could have avoided this ClusterPhuck was to pardon those individuals that were truly deserving of being released.

Throughout this book you will come to see that there is a lot of unexplainable stupidity virtually everywhere around the world. It does not matter what a person's education, gender, experience or wealth happens to be at the moment they initiate a ClusterPhuck.

Brock Turner, a former Stanford University swimmer, was convicted of sexually assaulting an intoxicated and unconscious 23-year-old woman in January 2015. Turner was given only a six-month jail sentence by Judge Aaron Persky. Judge Persky stated that he gave Turner, who served only three months of his sentence, was concerned of the "severe impact" prison would have on Turner.

Persky also stated, "California law requires every judge to consider rehabilitation and probation for first-time offenders," and adding that he previously "fought vigorously for victims" as a prosecutor. However, it was a little too late, because on June 5, 2018, Judge Persky's was recalled by close to 60 percent of voters, and replaced by Cindy Hendrickson, a prosecutor.

ClusterPhucks, whether intentional or unintentional, starts with someone making a decision. But why recall the judge? It's about **Social Order Punishment.**

Social Order Punishment

Social Order has been studied within the social sciences such as philosophy, anthropology, law, and sociology. Some theorists believe that social order is guided by natural forces, while others believe that social order is created and shaped by the social norms, laws, or common beliefs that exist within a society.

These norms and laws, often arising from social institutions such as government and religion, provide people with guidelines or directions of how they themselves should behave in various social contexts and also how other people ought to behave in the same situations. While social
order is achieved when people follow and behave in accordance
with the social norms in place, it is disrupted when people violate these social norms.

The court, for example, legitimately handed out social order justice when it convicted the individuals that were responsible for some of the most heinous crimes known to man, only to be undone by Barbour. So where is the social order justice for the families that lost their loved ones? Where is the social order punishment for Governor Barbour?

People generally have a preference for balance in social order and will seek to maintain social order at its balanced state whenever possible and restore disrupted social order when needed. For instance, there were efforts to undo pardons granted by Barbour, but to no avail. Punishment has been identified as a key means to restore social order, however, there is research that suggests that in some instances individuals will vary the level of punishment delivered to a norm violator in an effort to achieve order.

Anthony Weiner, former member of the United States House of Representatives from New York City, was involved in two sexual scandals related to sending explicit sexual material by cell phone. The first one led to his resignation as a congressman in 2011. The second, during his attempt to return to politics as candidate for mayor of New York City, involved three women Weiner admitted having sexted after further explicit pictures were published in July 2013.

Weiner used the social media website Twitter to send a link of a sexually suggestive picture to a 21-year-old woman. After several days of denying media reports that he had posted the image, he admitted to having sent a link to the photo, and also other sexually explicit photos and messages to women both before and during his marriage.

A second scandal began on July 23, 2013, after Weiner returned to politics in April 2013 by entering the New York City mayoral election, when more pictures and sexting by Weiner were released. Although called on by the **New York Times** editorial board, among others, to leave the mayoral race, he remained in the race until the end, when he took fifth place in the Democratic primary, with 4.9% of the vote. Although Weiner led early in the race, the fact that he continued his sexting exploits after he resigned from Congress was too much for voters to forgive.

Interestingly enough, Eliot Spitzer, who served as the 54th Governor of New York from January 2007 until his resignation on March 17, 2008, because of a prostitution scandal, ran as a candidate for New York City Comptroller. Like Weiner, Spitzer lost in his bid bounce back from a CP. However, he did only lose by 3.5% to the Democratic nominee, which may indicate that at some point he may get the opportunity to get back into the political arena. After all, the former Governor of South Carolina, Mark Stanford, won a special election on May 13th, 2013, to again become a member of Congress. This was after he resigned after he publicly revealed that he had engaged in an affair with María Belén Chapur.

When it comes to law and criminology, defense counsel will occasionally use the argument that an accused should not be punished for his or her behavior because of an experience realized earlier in life such as extreme poverty, parental abuse, and domestic violence. However, there are times when there is no extreme life experience to point to and it really comes down to an individual leading stupidly, like Montana Judge G. Todd Baugh.

All he did was sentence a 54 year old former teacher to 30 days, yes, 30 days in jail for raping a 14-year-old girl who later committed suicide. He stated that the victim was *"...as much in control of the situation"* as the teacher, and referred to the victim as "...older than her chronological age."

Needless to say, his sentence and comments created outrage around the world. The judge, under extreme pressure, tried to shift some of the blame to the prosecution because, according to him, they did not immediately raise objections to his actions. He even attempted to submit documents to get the convicted rapist two years. The Montana Supreme Court on blocked the judge from his resentencing efforts because there was already an appeal pending designed to overturn this ClusterPhuck. Eventually, the Montana Supreme Court ordered another judge to resentence Rambold the rapist, to a 10-year prison term.

Judge Baugh retired at the age of 73 and was given a life time achievement award from his local bar association. The Board statement read, ***"While we recognize that Judge Baugh made a very public mistake in the Rambold case...as a Board, we feel his more than 30 years of service to our community and our profession is worthy of recognition."***

Often times people in leadership positions attempt to adjust, modify, or correct an obviously stupid decision after the cluster has hit the fan. A kid falls in a hole in the middle of a park and we are outraged as to why the city didn't fix it earlier. Of course the hole gets fixed after the media gets a hold of the story.

Sure, there were always people passing by the hole commenting on the potential danger, but it wasn't a *real* problem because no one got hurt. This type of **Reactive Leadership** approach to solving problems that are right in front of our face is more common than you can imagine.

The Role of Leadership

Any Army Officer or Non-Commissioned Officer (NCO), can tell you that *leadership* is at the center of absolutely every activity within the U.S. Army. Everything, and I mean EVERYTHING, is about leadership. The Army made it very clear that while in a leadership position, you are responsible for everything that happens or fails to happen.

The Army defines leadership as:

"...influencing people by providing **purpose**, **direction**, and **motivation** while operating to accomplish the mission and improving the organization."

Purpose: gives subordinates the reason to act in order to achieve a desired outcome.

Direction: is providing clear direction, and involves communicating how to accomplish a mission: prioritizing tasks, assigning responsibility for completion, and ensuring subordinates understand the standard.

Motivation: supplies the will to do what is necessary to accomplish a mission.

As you will see throughout this book, an individual's leadership style goes a long way in determining his or her effectiveness and whether they are prone to starting or preventing ClusterPhucks.

Chapter 2

Leadership Styles & Effectiveness

Whether you are a college student, employee, employer, business owner, teacher, politician, or in the military, you have witnessed some positive and negative leadership styles. Prior to studying leadership styles at the doctoral level, I could perhaps name only a couple of styles that I picked up while attending Army leadership schools. I did however know when I was around good leaders and bad leaders and how their decisions affected the unit. More than likely they used one or more of the following leadership styles:

Charismatic/Transformational	Transactional
Situational	Adaptive
Crisis	Contingency
Servant	Ideological
Pragmatic	Authentic
Ethical	Spiritual
Shared/Distributed	Integrative Public
Toxic	Passive/ Laissez-faire
Divisive	Operational

Forceful	Reactive
Proactive	Strategic
Enabling	Destructive
Narcissistic	Unethical

We can all pretty much guess what **bad leadership** entails and how it has affected your job or career promotion prospects. But just how bad is bad?

Professor Barbara Kellerman, in her book ***Bad Leadership: What It Is, How It Happens, Why It Matters***, wrote that bad leadership falls into two basic categories: bad as in ***ineffective*** and bad as in ***unethical***.

Kellerman also subdivided the two categories into seven groups, which are:

1. **Incompetent leadership:** the leader lacks the will or skill (or both) to sustain effective action. He or she does not create positive change.

2. **Rigid leadership:** the leader is stiff and unyielding. Although competent, he or she is unable or unwilling to adapt to new ideas, new information, or changing times.

3. **Intemperate leadership:** the leader lacks self-control and is unwilling or unable to self-correct.

4. **Callous leadership:** the leader is uncaring or unkind. The needs, wants, and wishes of most members of the group or organization, especially subordinates, are ignored or discounted.

5. **Corrupt leadership:** the leader is willing to lie, cheat, or steal. To a degree that exceeds the norm, he or she puts self-interest ahead of public interest.

6. **Insular leadership:** the leader minimizes or disregards the health and welfare of "others", that is, those outside his or her own group or organization.

7. **Evil leadership:** the leader commits atrocities. He or she uses pain as an instrument of power. The harm done to men, women, and children is severe rather than slight. The harm can be physical, psychological, or both.

Speaking of Bad Leadership

On November 5, 2009, at Fort Hood near Killeen, Texas. Nidal Malik Hasan, a U.S. Army major and psychiatrist, fatally shot 13 people and injured more than 30 others. It is the worst shooting ever to take place on an American military base. A Senate investigation faults the Army and FBI for missing warning signs and failing to exchange information that could have prevented the massacre.

Officials failed to recognize signs that Major Hasan was becoming increasingly radical before the 2009 shooting. Additionally, the FBI failed to share information with the Army, including emails that Hasan exchanged with a suspected terrorist. A Pentagon review also found that several officers failed to intervene in Hasan's career as an Army psychiatrist despite widespread signs of his radicalization and shortcomings as a soldier. So who is more at fault, the FBI or the Army Officers that had direct contact with Hasan? What is the root cause of this leadership failure?

Hasan joined the United States Army immediately after high school in 1988 and served eight years as an enlisted soldier while attending college. He graduated from Virginia Tech in 1997 with a bachelor's degree in biochemistry. If you look at it from that standpoint, the Army had access to his performance records before he was radicalized. However, he gained admission through a selective process for medical school, earned his medical degree, and completed his internship and residency in psychiatry at Walter Reed Army Medical Center.

It wasn't until his senior year of residency that a Red Flag presented itself. Hasan reportedly made a presentation titled ***The Quranic World View as It Relates to Muslims in the U.S. Military***, which reportedly was not well received by some attendees.

He suggested that the Department of Defense should allow Muslim Soldiers the option of being released as conscientious objectors to increase troop morale and decrease adverse events. He went on to say that adverse events could be refusal to deploy, espionage, or killing of fellow soldiers.

Before being transferred to Fort Hood, Hasan was promoted from captain to major. He received a poor performance evaluation from supervisors and the medical faculty. Despite these concerns, his former Army supervisor graded his performance as "outstanding", which was revealed when he was cross-examined during Hasan's trial.

Hasan was investigated by the FBI after intelligence agencies intercepted at least 18 emails between him and Anwar al-Awlaki, a major influence on radical English-speaking jihadist internationally, between December 2008 and June 2009.

In one of the emails, Hasan wrote that he couldn't wait to "join you" in the afterlife.

Hasan also asked al-Awlaki when *jihad* is appropriate, and whether it is permissible if innocents are killed in a suicide attack. In the months before the shooting, Hasan increased his contacts with al-Awlaki to discuss how to transfer funds abroad without coming to the attention of law authorities.

A Joint Terrorism Task Force operating under the FBI was notified of the emails, and its Defense Criminal Investigative Service personnel reviewed the material. Army employees were informed of the emails, but amazingly did not perceive any terroristic threat in Hasan's questions. Instead, they viewed them as general questions about spiritual guidance with regard to conflicts between Islam and military service, and judged them to be consistent with his legitimate mental health research about Muslims in the armed services. They therefore determined that the material did not call for a larger investigation.

Defense Department high ranking officials revealed that they were not notified of the investigations before the shootings. In October 2008, US Undersecretary of Homeland Security for Intelligence and Analysis, warned that al-Awlaki strategically targeted Muslims within the United States with radical online lectures encouraging them to conduct terrorist attacks.

Additionally, Hasan was about to be deployed to Iraq, he was reportedly suffering from some of the same stresses that he was trained as an Army psychiatrist to treat. According to his family, Hasan had hired a lawyer to get him out of the Army.

An Army doctor testified that a month before the attack, Hasan told her that "they will pay" if the military forced him to deploy to the Middle East He was later ordered to deploy to Afghanistan, and began plotting his attack.

An Army study concluded that Hasan's supervisors "sanitized his performance appraisals" and praised him despite knowing he was chronically late for work, saw few patients, disappeared when he was on call and confronted those around him with his Islamic views.

Then Defense Secretary Robert Gates released an internal Pentagon review that found several unidentified medical officers failed to use "appropriate judgment and standards of officership" when reviewing Hasan's performance as a student, internist and psychiatric resident. Actually, this was a simply a case of very bad leadership. The Army Officers involved were corrupt and incompetent, which led to this unfortunate ClusterPhuck.

Hasan was clearly unfit and could have been discharged if the right leadership actions were taken. However, was his supervisors the only culprit here? Of course not. A report made public in 2012 on events surrounding the shooting spree found that the FBI's anti-terrorism officials failed to act on email traffic between Major Hasan and terrorist figure Anwar al-Awlaki.

The 173-page report described how FBI policies and procedures failed to prevent the shooting spree. The report also said there was no clear system in place to determine which office would follow up on a particular lead and to make sure leads would be followed in a timely manner.

The FBI acknowledged "shortcomings in FBI policy guidance, technology, information review protocols and training." The FBI said it had reviewed 18 recommendations in the report and had "already taken action to implement them." If that is the case, why did the Parkland high school shooting occur?

Leaving The Window Open

According to officials, numerous red flags were missed on the February 14, 2018 massacre at Parkland high school in Florida. Neighbors raised concerns about Nikolas Cruz as early as age 9. As a teenager he showed a propensity for violence toward small animals, expressed enthusiasm about guns and knives and even began introducing himself as "a school shooter."

Deputies with the Broward County Sheriff's Office were alerted to Cruz's behavior many times over the years, and the FBI received two tips about Cruz and the potential threat he posed to schools, but the bureau never chased the leads far enough. That being said, is the FBI to blame for not chasing the lead, or is it the Broward County Sheriff's Office who was in close proximity to Cruz?

On the 16th of February, 2018, the FBI sent the following press release:

FBI Statement on the Shooting in Parkland, Florida

On January 5th, 2018, a person close to Nikolas Cruz contacted the FBI's Public Access Line (PAL) tip line to report concerns about him. The caller provided information about Cruz's gun ownership, desire to kill people, erratic behavior, and disturbing social media posts, as well as the potential of him conducting a school shooting.

Under established protocols, the information provided by the caller should have been assessed as a potential threat to life. The information then should have been forwarded to the FBI Miami Field Office, where appropriate investigative steps would have been taken. However, It has been determined that the protocols were not followed after the information was received by the PAL on January 5th. The information was not provided to the Miami Field Office, and no further investigation was conducted at that time.

FBI Director Christopher Wray stated:

"We are still investigating the facts. I am committed to getting to the bottom of what happened in this particular matter, as well as reviewing our processes for responding to information that we receive from the public. It's up to all Americans to be vigilant, and when members of the public contact us with concerns, we must act properly and quickly.

"We have spoken with victims and families, and deeply regret the additional pain this causes all those affected by this horrific tragedy. All of the men and women of the FBI are dedicated to keeping the American people safe, and are relentlessly committed to improving all that we do and how we do it."

***

Imagine that your home was burglarized. Typically, your first reaction is to call the police. Your second response is to call your insurance company and file a report and pray that you are covered. Your third response is to get a home security system. You had of course been thinking about doing it for years, but put if off. So now you have a fantastic system. If anyone tries to break into your home you will be notified and so will the police.

However, you forgot to close the window leading to the basement and your home is burglarized again. My point simply is that you can have all of the processes and systems you want in place, but if leadership does not ensure compliance or fails to constantly update their technology, bad things are sure to happen.

Systemic Technological ClusterPhucks

High profile hacks happen on a regular basis. You may recall that the notorious "dating" or "cheating" site, **Ashley Madison,** was hacked and some 32 million user profiles were made public. Some people were stupid enough to sign up using company and government work email addresses, making them especially easy to positively identify. There were 6,904 addresses linked to the Canadian and American governments, plus another 7,239 in the U.S. Army, 3,531 in the Navy, 1,114 Marines and 628 in the Air Force.

According to the **Identity Theft Resource Center**, there have been 8,069 data breaches between January 2005 and November 2017. Some of the worst data breaches in history, in terms of resulting costs and the number of records compromised, are from some of the largest companies in the world.

3 billion **Yahoo!** accounts were compromised by a 2013 hack. All Yahoo! users were affected by the breach, but Yahoo! did not determine that this was the case until 2017. **eBay**, in 2014, requested that 145 million users change their account passwords due to a breach that compromised encrypted passwords along with other personal information.

In 2017, credit bureau **Equifax** was breached, putting the data of over 143 million Americans and many people in other countries at risk. At the very least, several hundred thousand identities were stolen.

JP Morgan Chase, Anthem, Target, Uber, Home Depot, and Sony, are just some of the thousands of companies that have compromised hundreds of millions of records. The most disturbing part is that a lot of this could have been prevented. Sony's breach began with a series of phishing attacks targeted at Sony employees. These attacks worked by convincing employees to download malicious email attachments or visit websites that would introduce malware to their systems. This type of attack used social engineering, where phishing emails appeared to be from someone the employees knew, thus tricking them into trusting the source.

Lacking Leadership Initiative

Failures associated with technology projects, such as the upgrading of cyber infrastructure, could be significantly reduced if leadership embraced the idea of implementing an early warning system that identifies and mitigates future risks. Facebook is arguable the epitome of a commercial company that could have benefited from an early warning system given its market dominance.

As of January 2018, Facebook reportedly had more than 2.2 billion monthly active users. Its popularity has led to prominent media coverage for the company, including significant scrutiny over privacy issues. Advertisers do however spend billions of dollars on Facebook promoting their products and services in an effort to influence their buying decisions.

Over the last generation, there has been a sizable shift in the way people find news stories. There was a time not too long ago, that we got our news from the morning newspaper and the nightly news. Now, more and more are now pulling out their smartphones using the Facebook news feeds.

For well over a year, Facebook has faced intense pressure over the amount of fake news, hate speech and depictions of violence prevalent on its services. They are not the only company that has this issue, but they are the most dominant force out there.

A few days after Donald Trump was elected President of the United States, Facebook CEO Mark Zuckerberg was asked about Facebook's responsibility for the election results at a California technology conference, regarding fake news stories on its network. Zuckerberg's response:

"There is a certain profound lack of empathy in asserting that the only reason someone could have voted the way they did is they saw some fake news... Why would you think there would be fake news on one side and not the other?"

Zuckerberg went on to state that Facebook was a "tech company" and "not a media company." He believed, at the time, that Facebook was just a "platform" and thus a neutral channel for helping its users share information with one another.

Well, Mr. Zuckerberg was wrong. The order of posts in the Facebook news feed is chosen by a proprietary Facebook algorithm. This algorithm takes into account a variety of factors, like how close you are to the poster, how many times a post has been shared or liked by other Facebook users, the type of post, etc.

Personally, I would likely click on a news article of interest that involved business, politics, or sports. But what if the news feeds that appeared to be legitimate were fake? For example, what if I clicked on what I perceived to be a real news article that showed *evidence* of racial bias or sexual harassment at a college or university that one of my children were considering as one of their top choices?

And what if there were numerous legitimate looking responses from people who claimed that they were former or current students, or even faculty members that validated the claims...could that influence whether or not you would send your child to that college or university?

Before you answer that question, know that Facebook, in a recent two quarter period, disabled nearly 1.3 billion "fake" accounts. Of all the accounts that have been disabled, there is perhaps only one account that could be considered the trigger that turned Facebooks, along with the political world, upside down, and that is the account of **Cambridge Analytica**.

It took whistle-blower Christopher Wylie to come forward and reveal that Cambridge Analytica had used data that had improperly been *"exfiltrated"* from Facebook. The company promised that they could build psychological profiles of vast numbers of people by using Facebooks data.

This would allow Cambridge Analytica to craft and send appealing messages to potential voters. The thinking was that if you could systematically sift through all of a person's basic information, you could build a decent picture of that person's social world, including a substantial amount of information about their friends.

Having spent several years in military recruiting, I can tell you that the importance of obtaining as much information on a potential recruit as it pertains to their future goals, family member support, education, physical condition, along with the type of people they hang out with, cannot be overstated. Why? To find those handful of individuals that are first and foremost qualified to enlist. Secondly, to influence them to join the Army and not the competition (Navy, Marines, Air Force, Coast Guard).

Cambridge Analytica's approach, according to Christopher Wylie, was " not equivalent to traditional marketing." They instead specialized in *"disinformation, spreading rumors, kompromat and propaganda."* One of the goals of this *microtargeting* approach was to keep minority voters home, and influence white voters to get out and vote.

According to Cambridge Analytica, lead data scientist David Wilkinson, the company advised Trump's campaign to allocate time and resources to rural voters, especially in Florida, Pennsylvania, and Michigan.

As Tony Bradley wrote:

> *"If you were targeted with content from Cambridge Analytica, it's because the data from your Facebook profile indicated that you were part of the key demographic most likely to believe it—no matter how ridiculous or false it was. Did your Facebook data show that you support Fox News, or like right-wing extremist propaganda like Infowars and Alex Jones, or Breitbart, or Rush Limbaugh? Did your Facebook data show that you are anti-LGBTQ or pro-life, or an NRA supporter, or a white supremacist?*

Demographic Targeting

Demographic targeting has been a core function of advertising for decades. Media outlets gather as much information as they can about their audiences so they can effectively target their marketing resources. Have you ever noticed that military recruiting commercials are predominantly aired during televised sporting events? Regardless of how many commercials or images you see that are made to influence your decision, the ultimate decision to buy is up to you…right? Not so fast.

There is, of course, a school of thought that believes that you can't possibly get mad at Facebook or Cambridge Analytica because of your decision to vote for Trump, but there is evidence to suggest otherwise.

Trickery and Credibility

Like it or not, trickery and deception is a common feature of daily social interaction. We lie to, or get lied to frequently. Most lies are trivial; however, 'big lies' in personal (e.g., infidelity), security, corporate, political, and legal settings, can have disastrous consequences if undetected.

According to the Supreme Court of Canada, credibility assessment requires no special tools or training, stating, *__"Credibility is a matter within the competence of laypeople. Ordinary people draw conclusions about whether someone is lying or telling the truth on a daily basis."__*

However, some researchers suggest that credibility assessments hardly seem to be "commonsense" as evidenced by various studies indicating that people rarely perform above chance when detecting deceit. A **meta-analysis**, which combines " the results from multiple studies", in an effort to increase power, found that the average accuracy in discriminating liars from truth-tellers was 54%, with a bias towards classifying individuals as truthful. We simply want to believe what we hear.

While most studies suggest that laypersons and professionals alike are generally poor at detecting deception, some researchers have proposed the existence of deception detection "wizards" who can consistently and accurately detect deception. However, there is evidence to suggest that the detection of high-stakes lies is an inaccurate task, and often go undetected by professional lie catchers.

A study investigated the detection ability of various groups that included Secret Service agents, federal officers, clinical psychologists, college students, and working adults. The results indicated that all groups performed at chance level except the Secret Service agents. It is believed that the enhanced accuracy by the agents was likely due to their greater emotional understanding and focus on reliable non-verbal cues, including emotional facial information. There also is the possibility, according to the study, that wizards may be proficient specifically in detecting powerful emotional lies, relating to crime, for example.

Having spent several years in military recruiting, I can indeed relate to this "enhanced accuracy" displayed by Secret Service agents. How? Recruiting is a numbers game. The more people you talk to the greater chance that you will find a qualified person to enlist. A new recruiter typically interviews a lot of unqualified individuals during their first year, whereas a seasoned recruiter conducts less interviews and is more efficient and effective finding the right people to enlist.

As a supervisor, it wasn't uncommon to quickly make a determination that the person that just walked into the office was potentially unstable or unqualified. On one particular occasion I called a new recruiter into my office to let him know that the man that just sat down for an interview was probably unstable, and likely unqualified. The recruiter gave me a somewhat bewildered look, but before he could respond I explained to him that it would become apparent in about five minutes into the interview.

Six minutes later the recruiter was back in my office and the interviewee was leaving with a few brochures. "How did you know?" the recruiter asked. My explanation could not be summed up in a sentence or two to satisfy his curiosity. I explained that I had been "burned" several times as a recruiter early on, and had wasted a considerable amount of time chasing what law enforcement officials might call dead end leads.

Within those dead end leads that were rife with law violations, medical issues and academic deficiencies, there were compulsive and pathological liars, as well as people who were clearly unstable. According to the National Institute of Mental Health (NIH), mental illnesses are common in the United States, affecting tens of millions of people each year. Their estimates suggest that only half of the people with mental illnesses receive treatment. It therefore stands to reason that having hundreds of personal interactions will not only increase your recruiting numbers, but will also increase your experience level with regards to reading people as it relates to lying, deception, and instability.

That being said, I was by no means a "wizard" with regards to detecting every lie or deception that came my way…regardless of my years of experience in recruiting. Research suggests that "individual differences could facilitate or impair observers' ability to discriminate true and false emotional stories." And that "the potency of the story's emotional content or the emotion of the speaker may interact with the emotional functioning and personality of the observer to influence credibility judgments."

Some of you may remember when then president Bill Clinton stated, "**I did not have sexual relations with that woman, Miss Lewinsky.**" Only to later admit that he did have an "improper physical relationship" with her. This is no different than president Trump stating, several times, that **"I would build a great wall, and nobody builds walls better than me, believe me, and I'll build them very inexpensively. I will build a great great wall on our southern border and I'll have Mexico pay for that wall."** Mexico, by the way, is not paying for the wall, and Trump is pushing Congress to provide the funding.

In both of these situations both Clinton and Trump displayed the kind of "potency" and "emotion" that helped influence whether or not you believed that the "speaker" was credible. You've probably seen it before…the finger pointing, facial contortions or hand waving by speakers doing their best to convince you to believe what is coming out of their mouths.

We All Can Be Persuaded

Most of us have more than likely fallen prey to some kind of product or service only to find out later that it didn't perform as expected, or that we really didn't need the product or service in the first place. Why does this seem to occur so frequently?

Persuasion is a form of leadership that is a powerful tool for forming both the expectations and beliefs in others. Leadership, often described in terms of influencing people or groups toward goal setting and goal achievement, seems dependent on the leader's ability to persuade in one form or the other.

Remarks from our most admired leaders, such as John F. Kennedy, Dr. Martin Luther King Jr., Winston Churchill and Nelson Mandela, are remembered primarily for their ability to instill courage and inspire confidence.

Leaders are under pressure to inspire, mediate, motivate, and direct change. However, a leaders most important role is influencing other people. **Influence** is the ability **to "persuade someone to think or act in the way you want."** This is the reason why so many people fall for Ponzi Schemes and other fraud related activities that usually have devastating consequences.

Ponzi Scheme

The Security and Exchange Commission (SEC), wrote that a Ponzi Scheme is an **"investment fraud that involves the payment of purported returns to existing investors from funds contributed by new investors. Ponzi scheme organizers often solicit new investors by promising to invest funds in opportunities claimed to generate high returns with little or no risk. In many Ponzi schemes, the fraudsters focus on attracting new money to make promised payments to earlier-stage investors to create the false** *appearance that investors are profiting from a legitimate business."*

The SEC goes on to list the "Red Flags" that unsuspecting investors should be aware of before falling into the middle of a deliberate ClusterPhuck. These warning signs are:

High investment returns with little or no risk. Every investment carries some degree of risk, and investments yielding higher returns typically involve more risk. Be highly suspicious of any "guaranteed" investment opportunity.

Overly consistent returns. Investment values tend to go up and down over time, especially those offering potentially high returns. Be suspect of an investment that continues to generate regular, positive returns regardless of overall market conditions.

Unregistered investments. Ponzi schemes typically involve investments that have not been registered with the SEC or with state regulators. Registration is important because it provides investors with access to key information about the company's management, products, services, and finances.

Unlicensed sellers. Federal and state securities laws require investment professionals and their firms to be licensed or registered. Most Ponzi schemes involve unlicensed individuals or unregistered firms.

Secretive and/or complex strategies. Avoiding investments you do not understand, or for which you cannot get complete information, is a good rule of thumb.

Issues with paperwork. Do not accept excuses regarding why you cannot review information about an investment in writing. Also, account statement errors and inconsistencies may be signs that funds are not being invested as promised.

Difficulty receiving payments. Be suspicious if you do not receive a payment or have difficulty cashing out your investment. Keep in mind that Ponzi scheme promoters routinely encourage participants to "roll over" investments and sometimes promise returns offering even higher returns on the amount rolled over.

The term **Ponzi Scheme** originated from an individual named Charles Ponzi. He conned thousands of New England residents into investing in a postage stamp speculation scheme back in the 1920s. At a time when the annual interest rate for bank accounts was five percent, Ponzi promised investors that he could provide a 50% return in just 90 days. He initially bought a small number of international mail coupons in an effort to support his scheme, but quickly switched to using incoming funds from new investors to pay purported returns to earlier investors.

Eventually, with little or no legitimate earnings, Ponzi schemes collapse when it becomes difficult to recruit new investors or when a large number of investors ask to cash out.

***

It can be said that if someone can't convince people of ideas and concepts, they are probably not a leader. In business, leaders are normally responsible for the articulation of the vision, mission, and goals that inspire others, and build solidarity. They bring with them **valid** facts, conviction of purpose, and a compelling rationale for his or her advocacy of a specific plan of action. Although scam artists are void of any valid facts, they do bring a conviction of purpose and a plan of action that comes in the form of a promise of higher than normal returns on your investment.

Most leadership theorists seldom agree completely on how best to define leadership, but most would agree that leaders are individuals who guide, direct, mentor, serve, motivate, or inspire others. By persuading, the leader shapes expectations and beliefs. In many instances, the leader's ability to connect with people emotionally and convince them of the value and appropriateness of the idea, is what guarantees goal success. However, the concept of persuasion, like that of power, often confuses people and can be destructive when mishandled.

The Wolf of Wall Street

Jordan Belfort was convicted of money laundering and securities fraud in 2003. He received a four-year prison sentence, served only 22 month, and was ordered to repay $110.4 million to a victim compensation fund. In December of 2013, a movie based on his exploits titled, "The Wolf of Wall Street", starring Leonardo DiCaprio, was released.

Stratton Oakmont, at the time a Long Island penny-stock boiler room, Belfort ran in the 1990s, employed more than 1,000 brokers at its peak. Eventually the Securities and Exchange Commission would shut down the company, and by 1998 Belfort would be arrested by the FBI.

He now gives self-deprecating speeches describing how he drove his life into the gutter with greed, drugs and excess, stole millions from people, went to jail for it, and how he reinvented himself as a legitimate businessman. He is by all accounts a *"natural performer"* and despite his tarnished background, audiences appear sincerely moved by what he has to say.

He reportedly gets paid in the neighborhood of $30,000 for a speech, which, by the way, a portion of his income, including what he receives from the movie and the sale of his books, has to go towards repaying the investors whose money he fraudulently lost.

As of May 2018, according to prosecutors, Belfort still owes $97 million of the $110 million he owes some 1500 investors. You can bet that he will likely continue to prosper from his notoriety, but I highly doubt he will ever pay off the victims of his crimes. Unfortunately, his employees, the ones that thought they were working for a legitimate company that is, did not survive the ClusterPhuck that he masterminded.

When Trust Turns Deadly

Although Belfort, and others like him, leave a trail of heartbreak and despair, there are other, seemingly trustworthy individuals, that, due to their actions…or **inaction**, results in death.

I have one kid left in high school. It is a public city school that has a decent reputation for its academics. A few years ago, a drive-by shooting directly across the street from the school left three people dead and several wounded. I always warn my kids to stay in school until I get there. It is not that I feared for them being targeted, but there is always that chance of getting hit by a stray bullet.

Now, the school itself is safer than any suburban school in the area. There are security guards, police officers, and metal detectors. I have been to several suburban schools and have been greeted with a nice elderly woman with a pen in order for me to sign in. There or no metal detectors or a crew of security guards at the point of entry.

Yes, there may be a misconception that "city" schools are more dangerous, but with regards to mass shootings, according to statistics, of the 10 deadliest school shootings in the U.S., all but one took place in a town with fewer than 75,000 residents, and the vast majority of them were in cities with fewer than 50,000 people. In other words, if you live in a "small town or suburban city", you are more vulnerable to a mass shooting.

That being said, I still expect the school to protect my kid. My responsible as a parent is to keep a roof over his head, keep him fed, clothed, up to date on shots and regular physicals, attend his athletic events, and leave no doubt that he is at the center of my world. When I hand him off to the school, they are responsible for his safety until I pick him up. But…sometimes, they Phuck it all up.

On the 4th of June, 2019, Scot Peterson, the former school security officer at Marjory Stoneman Douglas High School, was arrested for neglect of duty related to the mass shooting on the 14th of February, in 2018, that killed 17 students and staff members.

While there was little time for anyone to intervene before 11 were murdered on the first floor at the high school, it was determined that If Peterson had ran into the building, and headed up three flights of stairs within a minute, he might have headed off the shooter and cut short his deadly rampage.

Peterson has been booked into the Broward Main Jail on 11 criminal charges, including child neglect, culpable negligence and perjury. A 15-month investigation showed Peterson refused to investigate where the gunshots were coming from, retreated during the gunfire as victims were being shot, and directed other law enforcement who arrived on scene to remain 500 feet away from the building.

I recall a recent college graduate, with a criminal justice major, boasting how he would be a "damn good" police officer because he now had his degree. I looked him straight in the eyes and told him that I would choose a former military member, with a high school diploma, that has actually come under fire, before I would hire him. I told him that I wanted someone that I could count on when the bullets started flying…and that he has not proven to be that guy…yet. Apparently, neither was Scot Peterson. He could have, allegedly, minimized the ClusterPhuck, but chose not to. Sadly, during the hundreds of mass shootings around the United States, there are always brave students and teachers, that have been injured or killed, attempting to stop a shooter. They were not trained for this type of situation, but Peterson was, but his inaction resulted in casualties. There are others, of course, that fail to act until it's too late.

In 2009, Fisher-Price believed that it had solved the "most puzzling problems for new parents", which was getting babies to sleep. Their invention was an inclined sleeper called the Rock 'n Play. Over the next decade, Fisher-Price would sell 4.7 million Rock 'n Play Sleepers at $50 to $80 each.

However, Fisher-Price developed its product with no clinical research into whether it was safe, and, rather than seeking the advice of pediatricians, consulted just a single doctor, which was a family physician from Texas whose expertise had already been doubted by judges, and who would eventually lose his medical license.

The Rock 'n Play was recalled by Fisher-Price after a series of infant deaths. The Consumer Product Safety Commission (CPSC), said more than 30 babies died in the product after they turned over while unrestrained or "under other circumstances." But regulators did not definitively blame the product for the deaths.

In 2013, a pediatrician, Roy Benaroch, called and wrote an email to Fisher-Price's manager of risk management, warning that he thought the product was unsafe and providing links to various studies. He never heard back from them.

Whether Fisher-Price is eventually found liable for the deaths of the babies remains to be seen. However, it seems clear that their leadership cut corners in order to get their product to market, and kept selling the product even as babies continued to die.

You could deem this **Incompetent Leadership**, but you wouldn't be wrong if you came to the conclusion that it was **Unethical**, **Callas**, or even **Evil** Leadership at play. This ClusterPhuck was preventable, or at the very least could have had the risk of injury or death reduced, with the proper testing.

Like all ClusterPhucks, someone had to make the decision to cut corners, perhaps not fully understanding the ramifications. There are however others in leadership positions that understand exactly what they are doing, and fully aware that people will die due to their actions.

Recently, a Brazilian doctor was charged with killing seven patients (**Evil – Callas Leadership**), to apparently free up beds at a hospital intensive care unit. Prosecutors said Dr. Virginia Soares de Souza and her medical team administered muscle relaxing drugs to patients, then reduced their oxygen supply, causing them to die of asphyxia. Three other doctors, three nurses, and a physiotherapist who worked under De Souza have also been charged with murder. There is evidence to suggest that as many as 300 people may have been murdered.

If you think this type of leadership is rare, think again. This type of killing goes on throughout the world. The larger question is why did it take so long to catch them? Where was the oversight?

Pseudo Doctors & Scientists

Scientific Misconduct is *"the violation of the standard codes of scholarly conduct and ethical behavior in the publication of professional scientific research."* A 2009 systematic review and meta-analysis of survey data found that about 2% of scientists admitted to falsifying, fabricating, or modifying data at least once.

Dr. Andrew Wakefield may be familiar to some of you. An investigation published by the British medical journal BMJ, concluded that Dr. Wakefield, ***"misrepresented or altered the medical histories of all 12 of the patients whose cases formed the basis of the 1998 study."*** Wakefield's fraudulent study concluded that vaccines caused autism.

Although Wakefield was stripped of his medical license, as BMJ stated, "the damage to public health continues, fueled by unbalanced media reporting and an ineffective response from government, researchers, journals and the medical profession."

Wakefield's discredited paper panicked many parents and led to a sharp drop in the number of children getting the vaccine that prevents measles, mumps and rubella. Vaccination rates dropped sharply in Britain after its publication, falling as low as 80% by 2004, and measles went up sharply in the ensuing years.

For those of you that may not be familiar with how scientific studies are conducted, you are required to show how you came up with your conclusions. You must keep all of your notes. To put it simply, researchers must provide a roadmap, so that other researchers can also get to the same place. Not only did other researchers fail to match Wakefield's conclusion, Wakefield, facing relentless criticism, wasn't able to reduce his own conclusions.

The United Kingdom's medical regulator, General Medical Council, stated that Wakefield acted with ***"callous disregard for the distress and pain the children might suffer."***

Since its publication, measles outbreaks have exploded in Europe, Australia, and the US in communities where people refuse or fear vaccines. Vaccine refusal has become such a problem that some countries in Europe are now cracking down, making vaccines mandatory for children and fining parents who reject them. In 2019, the World Health Organization called vaccine hesitancy one of the "top threats" to global health.

So not only do prominent people lead stupidly, the ramifications can last for years. Meaning, parents are still, to this day, preventing their children from vaccines, due to a study that was proved to be faked!

Wakefield is not the only scientist to fake data however. Joachim Boldt, a high-profile anesthesiology researcher, had 94 fake papers retracted. His fake data concluded that heart surgery was safer than it actually was. A 2011 analysis found that more than 6,500 patients had received treatments in studies later retracted for fraud.

As you will see in this book, academic fraud isn't purely an academic issue. Think of all those patients that suffered due to some fraudulent researcher that ClusterPhucked lives for his or her own benefit. However, as Dr. Max Wiznitzer, a pediatric neurologist, stated, "Unfortunately, his core group of supporters is not going to let the facts dissuade their beliefs that MMR causes autism."

The question you may be asking is why, after all of the schooling and research, would you risk it all to fake your conclusions?

Cristy McGoff, the Director of the research integrity office at the University of North Carolina at Greensboro, stated:

"I think that while competition plays a part in the quest for funding, ego can be a large barrier to ethical conduct of research in these instances, I think that the self-perception of being respected, and all-knowing can lead someone to "push the envelope." They might think that since they are an expert in their field at such a great level, that no one else would even understand the manipulations they attempt to hide. Many researchers also see the research integrity efforts of an institution as a hindrance to their success, but the importance of the role of a research integrity officer is essentially to protect the public from dangerous behaviors based on this self-perception. Of course there is a level of laziness to data manipulation, falsification and plagiarism, but cutting corners is not what I would consider the motivation for the majority of these individuals, especially serial "fraudsters." Although many people would consider the risks involved, I am not sure the risks of engaging in research misconduct enters into their minds. I think it is fleeting if it does, and it is mostly because they are out for themselves."

So, regardless of the risks, people with a lot to lose, still do stupid things. Like, for example, that there are firefighters that actually start fires.

What The Fire Phuck?

Back in the 80's in Southern California, John Orr, a former arson investigator, was uncannily close at hand when fires broke out. His colleagues thought perhaps he had a "sixth sense" of sort. Suspicion fell on Orr when a fingerprint from a half-burnt incendiary device matched his left ring finger.

In 1992, a jury found Orr guilty of setting fire to three stores in the San Joaquin Valley, and convictions in other arsons followed. Orr was ultimately suspected in more than 1,000 fires, leading an F.B.I. analyst to call him "probably the most prolific American arsonist of the 20th century."

A journalist, who conducted jailhouse interviews with Orr for a book, said of Orr: "He totally got off on setting fires, and then watching, being in control of it. That was his big deal."

Yes, believe it or not, there are firefighter arsonists, which are people who put out fires, and are then accused of starting them. Firefighters from Vermont, Iowa, New York and Oklahoma have been in court for allegedly setting fires. An estimated 100 firefighters are reportedly arrested for arson each year.

Researchers have been working for years to learn what drives firefighters to become arsonists, or whether these are actually cases of arsonists drawn to be firefighters. Learning what drives a firefighter to set fires has become a dedicated field of study.

According to one study, firefighter arsonists are generally 17 to 25 years old. Those individuals that have an unhealthy love of fire is actually pretty rare. More commonly, the offenders see their actions as helping the community. In their mind they are providing chances to train and have some fun, and typically target grasslands or empty buildings.

In a majority of the cases studied, at least two firefighters at the same department were involved in the fire-setting. In Louisiana, authorities discovered that several firefighters from two rural districts were setting dozens of fires each year. Although the fires were mostly grassland, the thinking was that eventually they would move to setting fires to buildings.

I, like many of you, grew up thinking that doctors, firefighters, and others who are sworn to keep us safe and healthy, would never do anything to compromise the public's trust. Some of you probably also think that you could never be deceived, tricked, or influenced by a series of fake news articles, smooth talking investment sharks, or the general **"bullshit"** you hear on a daily basis.

However, let's take a look at some possible evidence that just may…wait for it…influence your thinking on this issue.

Conspiracy Theories, Storytelling, and Bullshit

The Oxford English Dictionary defines bullshit as, simply, "rubbish" and "nonsense", which, some have pointed out, does not get to the true nature of bullshit.

In 2005, philosopher Harry G. Frankfurt, published what was originally an essay, into a book titled **On Bullshit**. His book analyzed the applications of bullshit in the context of communication. He determined that bullshit is speech intended to persuade without regard for truth.

The liar, he states, cares about the truth and attempts to hide it, while the "bullshitter" doesn't care if what they say is true or false, but rather only cares whether or not their listener is persuaded.

President Obama made clear early on that he was a Christian. However, nearly a third still believe to this day that he is a Muslim. Donald Trump launched onto the political stage claiming that President Barack Obama was not a U.S. citizen. Regardless of the fact that Obama produced his birth certificate certifying his birth in Hawaii, 59 percent of registered Republican voters still doubt President Obama's citizenship, and so do 20 percent of the Democrats.

By the way, in September of 2016, Trump finally admitted that President Obama was born in the United States, after claiming for five years that he wasn't. He also blamed the whole Obama "birther" movement on the Hillary Clinton campaign, which too was untrue.

Although, *"some Republicans deliberately, and consistently, vacated all sense of shame and decency by pushing the "birther" conspiracy – claiming President Obama was illegitimate"*, the American people still gave him the popular vote in 2008 and 2012. However, Trumps claim still resonates with some voters and helped him get elected. That being said, it wasn't the only thing that influenced the elections.

Russia Russia Russia

James Clapper was the longtime Director of National Intelligence. In May of 2016, he announced in a speech that the Russian government was targeting the U.S. presidential campaigns with cyberattacks.

He wrote that the Russians were running an enormous scheme that was *"unprecedented, aggressive, multifaceted,"* using "cyber-theft and cyber espionage, propaganda across the broadcast spectrum and all of the largest social media platforms, and an influx of Russian money at least for buying advertisements, perhaps even laundered and funneled into campaigns."

Clapper also wrote that Putin not only wanted to throw the race Trump's way, but that the Russians' broadest objective was *"to undermine the foundation of democracy"* in the United States. Russia, according to Clapper, even published fake medical records claiming Clinton suffered from dementia.

To sum this up clearly, Clapper stated, ***"Again, Russia's aim wasn't to get anyone to actually believe the crazy stories they were publishing…The point of their influence operation was to overwhelm facts, to sow doubt that facts were even knowable."***

Although The House intelligence committee's Republican majority has cleared Trump, his inner circle and the campaign of any wrongdoing, which was fraught with incompetence and infighting, the Senate Intelligence Committee, which is Republican led, determined that ***"The Russian effort was extensive, sophisticated, and ordered by President Putin himself for the purpose of helping Donald Trump and hurting Hillary Clinton."***

***

Back in my Army recruiting days one particular incident awakened me to the realization of just how far some people would go to influence an individual to join their branch of service.

A young man that was looking at all of the military services for possible enlistment, revealed that one service recruiter turned him off completely due to his barrage of negativity towards the Army.

I will not mention the branch of service because I am sure the guy is long gone, and it wouldn't be fair to the recruiters that are currently recruiting for our nations fighting force. Apparently, this recruiter had created a binder with all negative stories about the Army. At that time there was no Google, Facebook, etc. But there were, and still are, magazines that cater specifically to each military service. These magazines are filled with positive and negative stories.

If you bought an Army specific magazine, you could easily cut out all of the negative stories like soldiers complaining of too many deployments, sexual harassment allegations, and the number of soldiers reduced in rank for this or that crime. However, you could do that with any of the service related magazines. This recruiter however, was focused totally on the Army, according to the applicant, since it was apparently his biggest threat.

His secretary, that had no great love for this particular recruiter, acknowledged that the binder did exist. What turned the applicant off was not that he showed him the binder…but that his biggest selling point was bashing the Army. The applicant wanted to hear what each service offered so that he could make an informed decision, but all he got was how bad the Army was as a service.

How many applicants were influenced by the **binder** to stay away from the Army? How many years did Republicans shout from the mountains that they were going to **repeal and replace** Obamacare? To this day, there has not been a repeal or replacement, and the premiums are set to go up $2,000 to $4,000 for people 60 or older in 2019.

So, if you did believe the whole repeal and replace "bullshit", you are not alone. Remember, a majority of us out there want to trust what we read or have been told…but this can also lead to heartbreak, confusion, anger, as well as some violent interactions.

Malicious Lying and Dangerous Bullshit

On Dec. 4, 2016, 29 year old Edgar Maddison Welch, a father of two by the way, drove across state lines armed with an AR-15 rifle, a pistol and a shotgun, to investigate the "internet rumor" that a pedophile ring was operating out of the Comet Ping Pong pizza restaurant.

The conspiracy theory, known as "**Pizza gate**", emerged during the 2016 presidential campaign and alleged that Democratic nominee Hillary Clinton's campaign chairman, John Podesta, had emails with coded messages that referred to human trafficking at a number of restaurants. Welch, through text messages, tried to recruit some of his friends to help him. Court records showed that Welch watched YouTube videos at length about the alleged child sex ring. His girlfriend and a friend tried to stop him from doing **"something stupid"**, but to no avail.

Some of us have heard stories where a friend, colleague, or relative, exaggerates about everything from how many sexual conquests they've had, to just missing on catching that 50 pound fish. However, that kind of exaggerated "bullshit" we tend to let pass because it is amusing and really doesn't hurt anyone…but this is stupidly different.

Welch walked into the restaurant's kitchen and shot open a lock and found nothing but cooking supplies. He pushed open another door and found an employee bringing in fresh pizza dough. Welch, by the way, did not find any captive children in the basement of the restaurant…since they didn't have a basement in the first place.

The Federal Judge that sentenced Welch to four years in prison and ordered him to pay more than $5,000 in restitution, stated that although he didn't harm anyone, his "unsound actions" left a "psychological wreckage."

Welch apologized for his actions and told the judge that he "cannot undo or change what already happened." Imagine if Welch would have proceeded in a logical manner? Meaning, perhaps place a call to the local authorities or the FBI to check out the restaurant. That being said, Mr. Welch wasn't the only person that believes in conspiracies.

Research tells us that belief in conspiracy theories is a widespread societal phenomenon. Large portions of ordinary citizens believe that influential and harmful events such as economic crises, natural disasters, and wars, are caused by evil conspiracies of powerful individuals or groups.

A march 2018 Monmouth University poll showed that Seventy-four percent of the respondents said the deep state, which some define as *"a group of unelected government and military officials who secretly manipulate or direct national policy" "definitely"* or *"probably"* exists.

President Trump's Deep State conspiracy targets career federal government officials, particularly in intelligence and national security agencies, who, he says, are actively working to undermine the administration's policy priorities. This, of course, is his way to create doubt in the many investigations that are taking place that could end his presidency. Will it work? There will always be people that will believe whatever President Trump says, regardless of how much evidence there is to the contrary.

Perhaps some of you may remember the 2018 class valedictorian graduation speech given by Ben Bowling at Bell County High School in Pineville, Kentucky. In his speech he read this quote, "…Don't just get involved. Fight for your seat at the table. Better yet, fight for a seat at the head of the table." He went on to say that the quote was from Donald Trump.

The article states, "The audience erupted. Bowling's fellow students and their parents clapped, while a few folks whistled. Some even screamed." Bowling then stated, "I'm kidding, I'm kidding…that was Barack Obama."

The crowd went quiet. One man let out a low "boo", and a few people just laughed. Bowling said that he used the quote because he thought it was a "really good" quote, and attributed it to Trump because, "It is southeastern Kentucky after all." Indeed. Trump pulled in 82 percent of the vote from that county in 2016. Did the folks go quiet because they felt duped by Bowling…or because they were so attached to Trump that everything Obama stood for was bad?

In a 2017 Monmouth University poll, Six in 10 people who approve of President Donald Trump, say they can't think of anything Trump could do that would make them disapprove of his job as President. This is the same person, who as a candidate, stated, *"I could stand in the middle of Fifth Avenue and shoot somebody and I wouldn't lose any voters."*

Now, I wouldn't go as far as to say he wouldn't lose 'any voters', but there would likely be some staunch supporters that would justify his actions as self-defense, or part of some conspiracy to make Trump look guilty. Rudy Giuliani, who went from "America's Mayor" after the 9-11 terrorist attacks, to looking at times incoherent and unstable, put forth the idea that President Trump is above the law in every imaginable scenario.

The majority of you reading this are probably thinking that no person is above the law. That does not however mean that you can't be influenced to believe that some deep state conspiracy was *really* responsible for whatever crime the President committed.

Of the 5645 people who answered the item, *"I am convinced there is a conspiracy behind many things in the world"*, 1618 people (weighted 26.7%), endorsed the conspiracy belief item. Now, what if we took that same 26.7% and applied the same method to the 137,125,040 that voted in the 2016 Presidential Elections? That would mean, statistically, that over 36 million voters would endorse the conspiracy item.

The claim that Hillary Clinton was part of a human trafficking ring started in a Facebook post, spread to Twitter, and then went viral with the help of far-right platforms like Breitbart and Info-Wars. The Info-Wars host, Alex Jones, was reporting that Hillary Clinton was sexually abusing children in satanic rituals in the basement of a Washington, D.C., pizza restaurant.

According to a sample of tweets with Pizza Gate or related hashtags provided by Filippo Menczer, who is a professor of informatics at Indiana University, Pizzagate was shared roughly 1.4 million times by more than a quarter of a million accounts in its first five weeks of life.

Some cross-referencing showed that the most frequent Pizzagate tweeters with a list of 139 handles, were associated with Trump campaign staffers, advisers and surrogates. As unethical as this may seem to some, it is not illegal…apparently. But what about inducing panic?

Inducing Panic is when *"a person causes the evacuation of any public place, or otherwise cause serious public inconvenience or alarm."* That would be, for example, "Initiating or circulating a report or warning of an alleged or impending fire, explosion, crime, or other catastrophe, knowing that such report or warning is false."

Other examples would be "threatening to commit any offense of violence or committing any offense, with reckless disregard of the likelihood that its commission will cause serious public inconvenience or alarm."

Although laws governing inducing panic vary from state to state, wouldn't you think that promoting and circulating a false human trafficking story that caused a man to fire shots in a restaurant sending people running towards the exits, constitute "serious public inconvenience" or alarm? Shouldn't some of the creators and distributors of this garbage have to be accountable as well?

On December 14, 2012, twenty children and six adults were killed by 20-year-old Adam Lanza at Sandy Hook Elementary School in Newtown, Connecticut.

Alex Jones, yes, the same person that helped to spread the Hillary Clinton human trafficking lie through his media platform, along with some of his associates, are defendants in a lawsuit initiated by the families of four students and two educators who died, along with one FBI agent who responded to the shooting.

The lawsuit states, "Jones is the chief amplifier for a group that has worked in concert to create and propagate loathsome, false narratives about the Sandy Hook shooting and its victims, and promote their harassment and abuse."

The legal complaint stated that Jones does not believe the shooting was a hoax, but nevertheless has repeatedly accused Sandy Hook families of faking their family members' deaths.

The complaint also stated that Jones and his associates would "concoct elaborate and false paranoia-tinged conspiracy theories because it moves product and they make money."

Google, Facebook, and other media platforms make their money primarily off companies paying for advertising. How much money? In 2017, Google's ad revenue amounted to almost 95.4 billion US dollars. Could it be because they averaged a net share of 74.54% of the search engine market? How often do you use Bing, Yahoo, or other search engines over Google? Facebook, with its more than 2 billion monthly active users, brought in $39,942,000,000 in 2017 in digital advertisements.

The reason why advertisers spend so much on the Google and Facebook platforms is simply because of the billions of eyeballs that search and interact with family members daily. Who wouldn't want a couple of billion people glancing at your ad? Imagine if just 10% of them decided to buy your product or service.

Now, while Google and Facebook have grabbed a large share of the advertising market, there are those media platforms, like Alex Jones, that resort to outlandish and conspiracy focused content to get you to their site. The complaint also reveals that the "The Alex Jones Show" is broadcast on more than 60 radio stations, and has a YouTube channel that boasts more than 2.3 million subscribers and almost 8 million unique visitors per month.

On 1 October 2017, Stephen Paddock took up a position in a Las Vegas hotel room and opened fire on a concert crowd below that would kill 58 people and injure hundreds more. It would be the deadliest mass shooting in modern United States history.

I did not think for a moment that the media or some shadow branch of the government faked the shooting. My thoughts were with the families that lost loved ones, and with the countless others that would be scarred for life. But not for Alex Jones…he saw this as another marketing opportunity to sell his products.

Jones told one of his callers, "Vegas is as phony as a three dollar bill or as Obama's birth certificate." Jones would be enabled by "amateur sleuths" that congregate and dissect eyewitness testimony and find "proof" of a conspiracy.

Jones is just one of many conspiracy theorists that practices this type of **Callous Leadership** style. Meaning, they could care less who it hurts as long as they can make money from it and increase their audience size.

One survivor of the shooting was forced off of social media due to the relentless amount of abuse and harassment he faced after the shooting. He was forced to relive the trauma over and over again by people who claim that moment never happened and that he was some "actor" employed by the government.

Misinformation gains traction and spreads when people like then-NBC News anchor Megyn Kelly invites people like Jones in for an interview. Critics condemned the network for giving Jones a larger platform for "spreading dangerous lies". The simple truth is, when you repeat a lie often enough, people may start believing it as truth.

As Brian Resnick stated:

"Psychological science consistently finds when a lie gets repeated, it's slightly more likely to be misremembered as truth. It's called the "illusory truth effect." It's a tendency the whole news media — as well as consumers of news — should be wary of. And it's a reason not to give notorious

bullshitters such a substantial spotlight. Especially bullshitters whose lies hurt others and whose lies have a track record for virality."

By the way, in March of 2019, Jones claimed in a sworn deposition that a "form of psychosis" caused him to believe that the Sandy Hook massacre was staged, but now believes it was NOT a hoax. Simply put, Jones was doing this for the money. However, wasn't NBC leading just as stupidly by inviting him in for an interview? Of course! They did it for the exact same reasons that Jones did…for ratings and money.

Unfortunately, President Trump shares many of the same conspiracy related views as Alex Jones and others as it relates to President Obama's birth place, the 9-11 attacks, and other conspiracies that have been thoroughly debunked over the years.

Is it so shocking that conspiracy theories have become mainstream given the rise of the many social media outlets that allows for virtually anyone to say what they want about anyone they want without much of a backlash?

The Lost Art of Civility

Civility, according to the Institute for Civility in Government, *"is about more than just politeness, although politeness is a necessary first step. It is about disagreeing without disrespect, seeking common ground as a starting point for dialogue about differences, listening past one's preconceptions, and teaching others to do the same. Civility is the hard work of staying present even with those with whom we have deep-rooted and fierce disagreements. It is political in the sense that it is a necessary prerequisite for civic action. But it is political, too, in the sense that it is about negotiating interpersonal power such that everyone's voice is heard, and nobody's is ignored."*

Perhaps some of you may remember the 2012 hotly contested Massachusetts senate race between former Senator Scott Brown and Elizabeth Warren. Warren's background had been the subject of debate during the race, with Brown supporters calling on her to provide documented proof of her alleged Native American ancestry.

Apparently, in order to drive their point home, five of Senator Brown's staff members and supporters are seen on video mocking Native Americans with "hoots" and "gestures" as a means of taunting Elizabeth Warren. The participants in the video were later identified as Senator Brown's Deputy Chief of Staff, his constituents services counsel, his State Director for Massachusetts, his special assistant and a Massachusetts State Republican political operative.

Whether this stunt had anything to do with Brown's seven and a half point defeat is up for debate. However, a strongly worded statement by the Principal Chief of the Cherokee Nation couldn't have helped the campaign, when he released the following statement:

"The Cherokee Nation is disappointed in and denounces the disrespectful actions of staffers and supporters of Massachusetts Sen. Scott Brown. The conduct of these individuals goes far beyond what is appropriate and proper in political discourse. The use of stereotypical "war whoop chants" and "tomahawk chops" are offensive and downright racist. It is those types of actions that perpetuate negative stereotypes and continue to minimize and degrade all native peoples.

The individuals involved in this unfortunate incident are high ranking staffers in both the senate office and the Brown campaign. A campaign that would allow and condone such offensive and racist behavior must be called to task for their actions.

The Cherokee Nation is a modern, productive society, and I am blessed to be their chief. I will not be silent when individuals mock and insult our people and our great nation.

We need individuals in the United States Senate who respect Native Americans and have an understanding of tribal issues. For that reason, I call upon Sen. Brown to apologize for the offensive actions of his staff and their uneducated, unenlightened and racist portrayal of native peoples."

A press release by his spokesperson stated, "Senator Brown has spoken to his entire staff - including the individuals involved in this unacceptable behavior - and issued them their one and only warning that this type of conduct will not be tolerated."

This despicably racist act was committed by the individuals who were in top leadership positions within Brown's organization. Are we to believe that Senator Brown had nothing to do with setting the tone of what is acceptable behavior within his organization?

Corporate & Political Psychopaths

A corporation or political organization's reputation is based on their behavior, communications, symbolism, and how logically they are projected to the stakeholders involved via the employees and managers who oversee these activities. Psychologists agree that a major influence on an organization's reputation is the behavior of the personnel within it.

The individual character of those employees and managers influences their behavior and how they communicate with others. If some of these employees and managers are corporate or political psychopaths then this will adversely affect their organizational behavior.

How psychopaths in leadership positions think, act and behave affects the organization and its reputation in various ways. Their lack of care for others can be expected to negatively influence levels of organizational social responsibility and through this, levels of an organizations reputation.

As personalities, they tend to be extroverts and their sociability makes them appear trustworthy, as people tend to assume that sociable people are trustworthy. This helps them get into organizations in the first place and helps them to create political spheres of influence which help them ascend the organizational ladder.

They care nothing about anything other than themselves, and so it may be expected that if they are in influential corporate or political positions then they will create an organization marked by a poor reputation and by low levels of perceived social responsibility. The levels of job satisfaction, employee withdrawal and absenteeism and other markers of a good organizational reputation, such as having good internal training and good internal communications, are depressed.

If you wanted to find the perfect modern day "poster boy" to represent what a psychopath in a leadership position looks like, you need look no further than the former Environmental Protection Agency (EPA) chief, Scott Pruitt, who was asked to resign by President Trump in July 2018. Just how bad was he? Pruitt was is in a league of his own when it came to creating ClusterPhucks and leading stupidly, as you will see from the many

The EPA inspector general (IG), probed Pruitt's travel practice do to reports that Pruitt would frequently travel home to Oklahoma on the taxpayers' dime. The IG twice expanded the probe, first as the agency acknowledged Pruitt used both a private plane and military jet to travel four times instead of flying commercial, at a price of $60,000.

A couple of top Pruitt aides, who spoke with House Oversight Committee investigators, detailed how Pruitt enlisted them for personal tasks, including attempting to find a job for his wife with the Republican Attorneys General Association.

Pruitt lived for about six months in a Capitol Hill condo owned by a health care lobbyist, whose husband has lobbied EPA, and paid below the market rate.

Pruitt spent $43,000, of taxpayer money, to purchase and install a soundproof booth in his office that violated the federal spending law, according to the Government Accountability Office. The EPA was required to notify Congress before spending more than $5,000 on office improvements. Pruitt told Congress that the booth had not been "certified" as a Sensitive Compartmented Information Facility, backtracking from his previous lie during his testimony.

What took so long to get rid of Pruitt? Conservatives loved Pruitt because he was pursuing Trumps anti-regulatory, federalist agenda, that wasn't worried about global warming. Most Cabinet level picks would have been long gone in any other administration, but Trump donors wanted him to continue on.

Pruitt, who clearly had a disdain for the EPA and was perhaps the absolute worst person to pick for the position, could have still taken the position, kept his head down, and did his job. However, some individuals just can't seem to take the ethical path when given a clear choice.

As you will see, Pruitt is far from the first high-profile corporate, government, entertainment, or sports industry figure that, through their incompetence, initiated what I call a **Self-Inflicted ClusterPhuck** (SICP).

Self-Inflicted Wounds

Without a doubt, it is always best not to be the cause of a ClusterPhuck, pulled into the middle of a ClusterPhuck, or be part of the collateral damage that a ClusterPhuck causes. An acquaintance took a position as the president of a company and resigned the position within three weeks. Why? He made one statement that summed it all up, which was, ***"They are all going to jail."***

Obviously, he didn't want to be part of the impending fallout. If he would have remained as president and continued to do business as usual, he would have no one to blame but himself.

There are individuals out there that can create a CP that, although limited in scope, can result in dire consequences. There is one ingredient present in all self-inflicted ClusterPhucks, and that is someone had to make a decision.

Timing, along with how your company, organization, and of course the public, views your ClusterPhuck, will always play a major role in determining your survivability. Take golf great Tiger Woods who was ensnarled in reportedly 15 extramarital affairs in 2009, with "porn stars, strippers, escorts and party girls."

He lost endorsements with Nike, Gatorade, Gillette and Accenture, and took leave from golf and entered rehab for sex addiction.

According to a study by researchers at the University of California, Davis, Shareholders of Nike, Gatorade and other Tiger Woods sponsors, lost a collective $5 to $12 billion in the wake of the scandal involving his extramarital affairs.

A few months prior to his fall from grace, Woods was photographed in the Oval Office meeting President Obama, and Forbes named him the first athlete to earn $1 billion. He was considered the greatest golfer of all time, had a beautiful wife and two children, as well as a wholesome image that netted the then 33 year old $110 million in yearly endorsements.

Immediately after the 2009 scandal, Woods endorsement deals declined from $92 million to $70 million per year. Although he has never gotten back to being the world's greatest golfer, he still brings in close to $45 million a year, and television rating soar when he enters a golf tournament. As of 2018, Woods estimated net worth was around $800 million. That is likely to go up since he won the 2019 Masters Tournament, and was awarded the Medal of Freedom by President Trump a couple of weeks later.

Imagine what kind of power, charisma, and international appeal it takes to rake in tens of millions in endorsements after a major scandal. Tiger Woods is an exception to the rule of what happens to most athletes however.

Former Major League baseball Most Valuable Player Ryan Braun came under scrutiny for a disputed testosterone test that he failed in 2011. Additionally, in 2012, he was connected to the Biogenesis of America clinic that allegedly provided performance-enhancing drugs to professional baseball players.

After MLB's investigation following the Biogenesis scandal, Braun was suspended without pay for the remainder of the 2013 season, and would miss 65 games. Braun, as well as the other athletes caught up in the many performance-enhancing drug scandals, have found it difficult to capture sponsorships.

Athletes are like CEO's of a corporation. Think about it....Ryan Braun signed a contract in the neighborhood of 100 million dollars. Like any business, your performance and reputation are critical elements to the overall success of your firm.

Braun not only lost over $3 million due to his suspension, but the potential for countless millions in endorsements. Why? Because he adamantly denied that he had ever used PEDs and pointed the finger at the person that handled his urine sample, which in the eyes of some onlookers, is even worse than his PED use.

Seeking to capitalize financially through endorsements and personal appearances is what a lot of athletes count on to supplement their income. This is especially important for those athletes that are in less popular sports who can't afford any missteps when it comes to tarnishing their brand.

However, that didn't stop Voula Papachristou from creating her own ill-timed ClusterPhuck. Papachristou, a triple jumper, was kicked off Greece's 2012 Olympic team for her comments on Twitter mocking African immigrants and expressing support for a far-right political party.

Papachristou wrote: ***"With so many Africans in Greece, the West Nile mosquitoes will be getting home food!!!"*** Her tweet prompted thousands of negative comments that moved quickly through social media outlets. The Hellenic Olympic Committee responded quickly to the controversy and released a statement that Papachristou was "placed outside the Olympic team for statements contrary to the values and ideas of the Olympic movement."

After the comments and the ensuing uproar, the Hellenic Olympic Committee announced that it had banned all Greek athletes from using social media to express any personal opinions not related to the Olympics and to the preparation for their competitions.

Papachristou's initial reaction to the negative comments was to tweet: "That's how I am. I laugh. I am not a CD to get stuck!!! And if I make mistakes, I don't press the replay! I press Play and move on!!!"

Although she attempted to apologize, the ClusterPhuck had taken hold and she was left out of the Olympic Games. Greece's track and field federation, SEGAS, applauded the decision to exclude Papachristou from the Olympics, and announced she would face a disciplinary panel. Papachristou has also had her financial benefits suspended by SEGAS.

As a popular figure in Greece, attractive, and a national champion, Papachristou was picked out as one of five athletes on the team to be part of an advertising campaign during the build-up to the London Olympics. By all accounts, her self-inflicted ClusterPhuck cost her corporation millions of dollars.

You would think that people would learn from Papachristou's actions, especially an executive in the business of public relations. At the close of 2013, Justine Sacco, at the time the head of corporate communications at the media company

IAC, tweeted, *"Going to Africa. Hope I don't get AIDS. Just kidding. I'm white!"* IAC, which operates the websites The Daily Beast, About.com, CollegeHumor and Match.com, fired her within hours of the tweet going viral.

Yes, actions and words can lead to a catastrophic ClusterPhuck, even if you intended for it to be a joke. Comedian Gilbert Gottfried, who was enjoying a pretty good career as the voice of the Aflac duck, tweeted a few insensitive jokes about the 2011 tsunami in Japan. He was fired shortly after his tweet. Why? My guess is that it was because 70% of the revenue generated by the company came from Japan.

Chances are, Mr. Gottfried was not attending to do any harm with his ill-timed joke. That being said, not all ClusterPhucks are created equal, whether it is a government/political ClusterPhuck, or in the commercial world.

Weiner created several micro-cps's that were ill-timed and stupidly repeated. Spitzer, who earned the nickname the *"Sheriff of Wall Street"*, led the prosecution of two alleged prostitution rings, but was paying for the services of a prostitute. Ellen Yaroshefsky, director of the ethics center at Yeshiva University, summed it up best when she stated:

"How stupid. How sad. He's always exhibited high standards of ethics in terms of his public pronouncements and his zealous approach to unethical and illegal behavior when he was prosecutor."

Then there are those individuals that say things that are so utterly stupid you have to question their grasp on reality, like Todd Akin. Akin, a Republican from Missouri, who at the time was running against incumbent Democratic Senator Claire McCaskill, was asked whether he believed that abortion was justified in cases of rape.

Akin replied that rape did not result in pregnancy, and went on to state:

"It seems to be, first of all, from what I understand from doctors, it's really rare. If it's a legitimate rape, the female body has ways to try to shut the whole thing down."

Immediate backlash ensued, with Republicans urging Akin to drop out of the Senate race. But he chose to stay in, vowing that he was around "for the long haul." Six months after he lost the race by more than 15 points, he stated, "I misspoke one word in one sentence on one day, and all of a sudden, overnight, everybody decides, 'Well, Akin can't possibly win'."

Prior to Akins comments, he was leading McCaskill in most polls. The speed in which he plunged in the polls has a lot to do with how social media outlets (Twitter, Facebook, YouTube, etc.) have change the way ClusterPhucks are received around the world.

Akin stated, "…from what I understand from doctors…" Did he actually consult with any doctors? Where was his campaign staff with some statistics defending his claim? A simple Google search would have revealed both a federally funded National Women's Study, along with an analysis by the American Journal of Preventive Medicine. The evidence concluded that among rape victims aged 12 to 45, per year pregnancies ranged between 25,000 and 32,000.

Akin and his staff should have known this. He will always be known as the male candidate that used the term "legitimate rape" to make a disgusting claim about women that had no basis in reality.

During Mitt Romney's 2012 presidential campaign run against President Obama, he was secretly recorded from a serving table at the edge of a room where he was addressing an audience of 40 or 50 people at a $50,000-a-plate fundraising event in Florida. Mr. Romney stated:

"There are 47 percent of the people who will vote for the president no matter what…All right, there are 47 percent who are with him, who are dependent upon government, who believe that they are victims, who believe the government has a responsibility to care for them, who believe that they are entitled to health care, to food, to housing, to you-name-it. That that's an entitlement. And the government should give it to them. And they will vote for this president no matter what."

Romney went on to state, "And I mean the President starts out with 48, 49 percent … he starts off with a huge number…These are people who pay no income tax. Forty-seven percent of Americans pay no income tax. So our message of low taxes doesn't connect. So he'll be out there talking about tax cuts for the rich. I mean, that's what they sell every four years. And so my job is not to worry about those people. I'll never convince them that they should take personal responsibility and care for their lives."

Unlike Akins "legitimate rape" claim, Romney's assertion actually had some research to back him up. According to a 2011 analysis by the Urban Institute-Brookings Institution Tax Policy Center, 46 percent of tax filers paid no income tax, vs. about 54 percent of tax filers that did have some federal income tax liability. In 2009, the Tax Policy Center estimated the proportion who paid no taxes was 47 percent. About half of the people who don't pay income taxes are simply poor, and the tax code explicitly exempts them.

In an interview, Romney stated, "That hurt. There's no question that hurt and did real damage to my campaign."

Writing off the votes of half the country had indeed negatively impacted his chances of being president. It played directly into the stereotype of Romney as an out-of-touch rich guy, and would, due to there being a video, be played over and over again.

Of course, Mr. Romney didn't know that he was being recorded, and politicians are known to tailor their speeches toward the crowd that is in front of them. His statement, *" I'll never convince them that they should take personal responsibility and care for their lives"* may have hurt him the most.

Being lectured to by a "rich guy" doesn't sit well with people that are forced to work two jobs to keep food on the table and a roof over the heads of their family members. The ***Great Recession*** cost millions of people their homes and jobs, and were forced to take whatever jobs they could to survive. Hearing a presidential candidate question your "personal responsibility" over and over again can only lead to negative feelings towards that individual.

Party affiliation doesn't matter when it comes to making ill-advised recorded statements that can be dissected and played over and over again via various social media outlets. Hillary Clinton, during her 2016 presidential campaign, stated:

"You know, to just be grossly generalistic, you could put half of Trump's supporters into what I call the basket of deplorables. Right? The racist, sexist, homophobic, xenophobic, Islamaphobic -- you name it. And unfortunately there are people like that."

Clinton did apologize the next day, after much criticism, for being "grossly generalistic" about "half" the Trump supporters being part of the "basket of deplorables."

The current "First Lady", Melania Trump, proved that sometimes you don't have to say a word to self-inflict a wound that will likely go down historically as the most callous, unthinking, or uncaring gesture ever displayed by any first lady in the history of the presidency.

The First Lady, as she boarded a plane to visit detained immigrant children in Texas, wore a jacket that on the back read, ***"I Really Don't Care, Do U"*** jacket.

Mrs. Trump, an immigrant herself, was heavily criticized not only for her perceived insensitivity, but also calling out Congress to "find a solution" for the migrant crisis, rather than her husband and his administration.

Her spokeswoman would later state, "It's a jacket...there was no hidden message." The notion, by some, that this was a "nothing" story is simply a way to deflect from the controversy. Although the position of the First Lady is not an elected one and carries only ceremonial duties, first ladies have held a highly visible position in American society.

First and foremost, she is the hostess of the White House. She organizes and attends official ceremonies and functions of state either along with, or in place of, the President. It has become common for first ladies to select specific causes to promote.

For example, Lady Bird Johnson pioneered environmental protection and beautification. Pat Nixon encouraged volunteerism and traveled extensively abroad. Betty Ford supported women's rights, while Rosalynn Carter aided those with mental disabilities.

Some of you may remember Nancy Reagan's "Just Say No" drug awareness campaign. Barbara Bush promoted literacy and Hillary Clinton sought to reform the healthcare system in the United States. Laura Bush supported women's rights groups, and encouraged childhood literacy.

More recently, Michelle Obama became identified with supporting military families and tackling childhood obesity. Melania Trump, by wearing the jacket to and from the visit to the immigrant children detainment center, demeaned the office of the First Lady. Keep in mind that she previously stated that she wanted to use her position to help children, work for the prevention of cyberbullying and support children whose lives are affected by drugs.

If Mrs. Trump would have worn that jacket to a baseball game or golf outing, she would have received a much different response. Understanding your surroundings or utilizing a **Situational Awareness** approach, is a leadership trait that can greatly enhance a leaders ability to avoid getting caught up in similar situations. Unfortunately, some people just can't grasp the whole situational awareness thing, and it can end up costing them billions...or at least their reputation.

Following Stupidity

Perhaps some of you have followed a person of questionable character that resulted in the loss of money, credibility, or perhaps a stint in jail. There are some dark alleys out there that I just will not go down. Sure, it's a short cut, but sometimes I get that queasy feeling that this may be the one time I get mugged.

Many of you may have heard of North Korean leader Kim Jong Un. He may perhaps be the most ruthless dictator on earth. His people are starving and he kills his own relatives, military personnel, and others, it appears, due to his insecurities.

In 2013, former 5-time NBA basketball champion, who earned the name "bad boy" due to his many antics on and off the court, visited the authoritarian state to promote what he called "basketball diplomacy." Apparently, the dictator was a big fan of the Chicago Bulls basketball team back in the 90's when Rodman was a player.

At the conclusion of his visit, Rodman had high praise for the dictator, calling him "friend for life" and a "great guy." In 2014, Rodman, along with some retired NBA players, led the crowd gathered to watch a game between North Korean players and the players he brought, in singing happy birthday to the dictator.

This did not go well for Rodman and the players…especially when it appeared that Rodman bowed to the dictator. According to one of the players, Cliff Robinson, the players agreed to put on a basketball clinic and exhibition game. It wasn't until they landed in the capital of Pyongyang that they discovered they would be performing for the country's supreme leader, Kim Jong Un, as a birthday gift.

Robinson stated, "We thought we were going to do something good. We heard some of the backlash right away from our family back home. The range of emotions (among the players) were crazy. We're thinking, 'What are we doing here?' It was definitely a trying four days."

Some of the players felt that they were misled by Rodman. Robinson did also state, "I'm not going to blame Dennis because I went on the trip knowing there was going to be some fallout…" and he "… looked at it as a chance to touch people through basketball and visit a country that doesn't allow a lot of people in." He did admit that mention of the birthday made things "uncomfortable".

Rodman, with some of the players in the background, was interviewed by CNN about the controversial visit. Rodman appeared "confused and defensive" and later admitted he had been drinking before going on camera. His agent, Darren Prince stated, "It's no secret Dennis has been struggling on and off with alcoholism the past 17 years."

Yes, Dennis Rodman had a history of questionable behavior and alcohol related issues that were widely known. So why would a group of ex NBA players follow a person that is prone to creating or landing in the middle of a ClusterPhuck?

Keep in mind that the players were thinking basketball and not about the controversial brutal dictator. Again, some of the players felt that they were "misled" by Rodman, but that is a lame excuse. They blindly followed someone that had issues and additionally failed to research North Korea and their dictator.

When People Just Can't Shut The Phuck Up

We've all been there. Meaning, we failed to shut up about some particular topic and said some things that would have been better unsaid. Maybe it was getting something off your chest to your boss, co-worker, or friend, and you thought it had to be said. The problem is you strayed off topic and headed down that rat hole that had nothing to do with what you were upset about and said some things that won't soon be forgotten.

Perhaps your boss appreciated your initial honesty…but then again, he or she may have thought you were being rude and disrespectful and may seek to retaliate against you in the future. A co-worker or friend may just shut you out altogether. A persons response may also depend on how many people were in the room at the time of your outburst. If it happened to be a higher ranking military or executive in front of employees, your days are likely numbered.

Stupid Employee Social Media Behavior

Social media has given everyone a voice to post whatever tasteless, racist, offensive, stupid, homophobic, sexist or pretty much any inappropriate thing that comes to mind. A few years ago I recall a blond female, back to the camera, throwing puppies into a river…obviously with the intent of drowning them.

This type of senseless cruelty would of course be repeated countless times. Some people have been bold enough to show their stupidity to their employers. Recently, six HSBC bankers in Birmingham, England, were fired over re-enacting a mock ISIS, terrorist group, beheading.

One of the employees wore an orange jumpsuit as he kneeled in front of his five colleagues, who wore black tracksuits and balaclavas. The clip, which was reportedly made during a work-sponsored team-building exercise, circulated online and embarrassed the company, which forced them to take action on the stupidity.

There is a fine line between funny, insensitive, and stupid, as the bank employees found out. Social media has made it possible for people to tell jokes that, in their mind, wouldn't offend anyone. Take Michael Allred, a Maryland state statistics official and police liaison who had only been on the job for a few weeks when he wrote on his Facebook page, "Visiting the prisons... haven't been groped this much since the flight on the honeymoon... and this is just the guards."

He was probably joking about the thoroughness of the guards regarding their search techniques. However, like most people, he may have considered the back story as it relates to the prison. Meaning, what if they were under investigation for mistreatment of prisoners or having inappropriate relationships? Have you ever been in an organization that is undergoing some kind of intense investigation and some outsider makes a joke about it? Stupidly, he tagged his boss as well as the exact prison he was visiting. What would you like to bet that his boss received an angry response from prison officials?

So, funny to YOU, does not mean funny to THEM, like when former major league pitcher turned radio personality Mike Bacsik had a Twitter meltdown after his basketball team was beaten. Bacsik wrote, "congrats to all the dirty Mexicans in San Antonio." He was immediately suspended and then fired.

After his firing he stated in an interview, "Obviously, I made a terrible mistake. It was very bad and stupid on my part...When you tweet like I did, you can't see the sarcasm. It's not a good joke. You can't tell if it was pure hate or sarcasm."

Back in 2013, Jack Clark was hired as a sports talk host on a St. Louis radio station. At least twice during the show's first week, Clark accused Los Angeles Angels baseball player, and no doubt future hall of famer, Albert Pujols of using performance-enhancing drugs (PEDs), while Pujols was with the Cardinals.

Pujols responded by threatening Clark and WGNU with a defamation lawsuit, and vehemently denied that he had ever used PEDs. Keep in mind that major league baseball has cracked down on the use of PED's and Pujols has NEVER failed a drug test. Clark was fired from what may have been the shortest career as a sports talk show host in history.

Eventually, Clark apologized and retracted his accusations against Pujols, stating that he had "no knowledge whatsoever" that Pujols ever used PEDs.

All radio and television personalities will not survive without sponsors. And, sponsors have a keen eye on how many people are listening or viewing their investment. Sex, violence, and controversy sells, and without one of those three ingredients you will likely fail to attract viewers and listeners. Have you ever noticed how news programs lead with one of these big three areas? Shootings, politicians with alleged affairs, or some controversial court case verdict, does attract your attention.

Now, is this a stupid way in which to attract people? Perhaps not...unless you're a respected media personality that embellished or outright lied in an attempt to seem more interesting.

In 2015, NBC Nightly News anchor Brian Williams was suspended for six months without pay for "misremembering" a military incident while reporting overseas. It all started when Williams attended a New York Rangers game with a soldier who helped guard him and other American soldiers while a convoy of military helicopters they were flying on was forced to land on a desert in Iraq in 2003.

Williams said the helicopter he was on had been hit by enemy fire and forced down. However, other veterans from the convoy challenged Williams' story, by the way, he repeated on Facebook. He eventually recanted the story, but the damage to his credibility had been done.

Williams was the leader of the NBC Nightly News program that averaged about 9 million to 10 million viewers a night, ahead of competitors ABC's World News Tonight and CBS Evening News. So why risk your reputation and credibility? Williams would later state in an interview, "It had to have been ego that made me think I had to be sharper, funnier, quicker than anybody else." Williams did make it back to television, but not as the NBC Nightly News anchor. He now hosts a show on MSNBC...at 11 PM.

Why would Williams think that he could get away with a story like that with so many others on the same helicopter that knew better? He should have learned from Hillary Clinton's embellishment of her trip to Bosnia in March 1996. In a 2008 speech Clinton stated:

"I remember landing under sniper fire. There was supposed to be some kind of a greeting ceremony at the airport, but instead we just ran with our heads down to get into the vehicles to get to our base."

Photographs and video of the arrival ceremony, combined with news reports, tell a very different story. Then Army secretary Togo West stated that Bosnia was not "too dangerous" a place for President Clinton to visit in early 1996. In fact, President Clinton was the first Clinton to visit the Tuzla Air Force base.

Additionally, Clinton made no mention of "sniper fire" in her autobiography "Living History," published in 2003, but did say there were "reports of snipers" in the hills around the airport.

Unfortunately, for prominent figures like Williams and Clinton, these stories never go away because they tend to stay in the public eye. And, there will always be people lurking in the background, to remind you and others when you lied about this or that.

***

An **Internet Troll** has been defined as *"a person who starts quarrels or upsets people on the Internet to distract and sow discord by posting inflammatory and digressive extraneous, or off-topic messages in an online community (such as a newsgroup, forum, chat room, or blog) with the intent of provoking readers into displaying emotional responses and normalizing tangential discussion, whether for the troll's amusement or a specific gain."*

There are millions of trolls around the globe, which for the most part do their damage anonymously, and move on to their next target. However, there are others that try to be as provocative as possible in order to attract viewers and national coverage. The truly stupid trolls work in government, education, or some kind of high profile position that will usually lead to them being fired or resigning under pressure.

Perhaps you may remember Elizabeth Lauten, who was the communications director for Republican Rep. Stephen Fincher of Tennessee. She decided to write an open letter on Facebook to the daughters of the President of the United States, chiding them for looking bored during the annual White House turkey pardoning ceremony. Her letter read as follows:

"Dear Sasha and Malia, I get you're both in those awful teen years, but you're a part of the First Family, try showing a little class. At least respect the part you play. Then again your mother and father don't respect their positions very much, or the nation for that matter, so I'm guessing you're coming up a little short in the 'good role model' department. Nevertheless, stretch yourself. Rise to the occasion. Act like being in the White House matters to you. Dress like you deserve respect, not a spot at a bar. And certainly don't make faces during televised public events."

Representative Finch's office received thousands of calls for Lauten to be fired. Although Lauten apologized and was then forced to resign, the real question is why would you create such a ClusterPhuck in the first place when you know that it would create a backlash AND initiate inquiries into your own background?

In an expanded version of her self-inflicted ClusterPhuck, it was reported that when Lauten was 17, just a year older than the president's eldest daughter Malia, she was caught stealing from a Belk department store in her hometown. Social media continued the expansion of the ClusterPhuck by bringing up George W. Bush's daughters on twitter, making statements such as, *"The Bush twins used fake ID's to get into bars, & Jenna Bush stuck out her tongue at the press. Is that classy?"* and "Did you forget that Jenna bush got photographed at the age of 19 knocking someone over at a FRAT party? good lord."

Again, this was a communications director, in a leadership position, for a congressman, creating this mess. However, she isn't the only "staffer" that has made their boss look bad. During Donald Trump's campaign, his former butler Anthony Senecal, made a series of racist Facebook posts that threatened President Barack Obama, which subjected him to a Secret Service investigation.

In 2015, then Republican Rep. Aaron Schock, who was already facing questions about his spending and decorating, was caught off guard when his communications director, Benjamin Cole, had some of his racist posts uncovered. He made disparaging comments about African Americans, saying "The closing of the National Zoo has forced the animals to conduct mating rituals on my street." Cole, a former pastor, took the Lauten route and ultimately resigned.

Many of you may remember celebrity chef Paula Deen, who had a habit of making racial slurs. She lost deals and contracts with the Food Network, Smithfield Foods, Walmart, Target, QVC, Caesars Entertainment, J.C. Penney, Sears, Kmart and her then-publisher Ballantine Books.

Any type of racist behavior, especially if you are the face of the brand, is just incompetent leadership. As of 2018, Nielsen ratings show a 4.7 percent decline in viewer households for Food Network, and in ad-supported cable viewership. Restaurants by famous chefs have been closing around the country as consumer tastes have changed. Add a racist or sexist rant to the mix and your brand will decline even faster than the industry norm.

Rapper Kanye West, who once stated President George W. Bush "didn't like black people", is a unapologetic Trump supporter, despite his occasional racist rhetoric. West, who has lost a tremendous amount of African-American support, stated:

"When you hear about slavery for 400 years ... For 400 years? That sounds like a choice."

As the outrage of his comments drew condemnation from around the globe, comedian and actor Sinbad gave perhaps the best response to West's multifaceted stupidity, stating, *"If this is where Kanye wants to be, then let him be there. Quit trying to explain Kanye to us. He's doing a pretty good job of telling us who he is and where he wants to be..."*

***

ClusterPhucking a Path to Destruction

There has been an abundance of evidence illustrating people's tendency to persist with losing courses of action. This phenomenon has been labeled *"entrapment"* or *"escalation of commitment."* For example, governments are prone to escalation tendencies, like engagement in a war that has already resulted in a remarkable loss of life. However, further engagement in a war may lead to long-lasting freedom and democracy. Thus, little is known whether people cling to losing courses of action when it is unequivocally clear that a turnaround is unattainable.

Brazil's Eike Batista had a personal wealth estimated at $34.5 billion, making him, at one time, the 8th richest man in the world. In an 18 month period Batista found himself of what may be the largest personal and financial collapse in history. So how does one go about losing close to $35 billion? It starts out with an ill-advised effort to develop a gold mine in Greece that was engulfed in a huge battle with the public over the potential environmental impact. Couple that with mining projects in Russia and the Czech Republic that lost 96 percent of its $1.7 billion value, and you are well on your way.

Batista did, in 2007, successfully secure government offshore oil leases, paying $1.3 billion for 21 blocks. The leases reportedly held 80 percent of Brazil's output, which is perhaps why his company offered double what his chief competitors were offering. His acquisition strategy was basically to pay several times what anyone else was willing to pay for the blocks, which put him in the unenviable position of having to produce extraordinary results in order to recoup his investment, which, combined with other stupid business moves, hastened his downfall.

Just when you think things couldn't get any worse than losing more than $30 billion, in July of 2018, Batista was convicted and sentenced to 30 years in prison on bribery charges.

Although a reluctance to abandon a losing course of action is often a clear instance of irrational behavior, even after receiving negative feedback, it may not seem that irrational as it seems at first sight. One might simply assume that success is more likely after failure. It may be that the devoted effort to attain a goal was insufficient and thus further goal pursuit could lead to a turnaround. It is therefore difficult to know in advance whether discontinuation of a course of action is not too early; sometimes even non-rational de-escalation may be the consequence.

Some researchers believe that control can be exerted by changing the situation actively (primary control), and by restructuring cognitions (secondary control). **Primary Control** can be defined as the *"self as agent, the self's actions or behaviors as the means, and an effected change in the social or physical environment as the outcome"*, and involves such strategies as active coping, planning, and use of instrumental support.

Secondary Control is most often exerted after attempts at primary control were ineffective, and can be defined as when *"people … adjust some aspect of the self and accept circumstances as they are."* Secondary control involves such strategies as use of emotional support, positive reframing, and denial. Batista was very confident in his ability to make an investment work. He was the 8th richest man in the world and had the charismatic skill to attract investors even when it was apparent that the tide was shifting in the wrong direction.

Why do people still use primary coping strategies even when a situation is unchangeable? Research suggests that motivation points to a combination of two components, namely, *"expectancy of success"* and *"incentive value of success."* Expectancy of success refers to a person's belief about being able to do a certain task. Optimistic beliefs about one's own capabilities to attain a certain goal will result in increased goal striving, whereas pessimistic beliefs will result in decreased goal striving, which in turn affects goal achievement.

Incentive value of success refers to a goal's perceived desirability and is positively related to investment of resources to attain the goal. One of **Batista**'s goals was to be the richest man in the world, which was possible if a couple things would have gone in his favor. Expectancy of success and incentive value are theoretically inversely related.

There is a belief that the less likely a goal can be attained, the higher its perceived desirability. For this reason, seemingly unattainable goals might have a greater incentive value than attainable goals in that individuals overestimate the intensity of their experienced emotional reaction to whether they finally attain or do not attain this goal. However, in the quest to attain success, one may disregard warning signs and move forward, often times leading to a ClusterPhuck.

Chapter 3

Money, Power, & Risk Taking

It has been theorized that power transforms individuals, producing systematic effects on thought and behavior. **Power** is defined as ***"the asymmetric control over valued resources by one or more parties in a social relationship."*** It captures the relative state of dependence between two or more parties. The low-Power party is dependent on the high-power party to obtain rewards and avoid punishments, whereas the high-power party is less dependent on the low-power party.

A **High Power Party** would be the equivalent of a business owner, whereas a **Low-Power Party** would be the employee. Whether you are serving in the military or working for a corporation, you are likely familiar with the most important high-power people in your chain-of-command or corporate structure. They are not just the people who write your performance evaluations that can make or break your career, but the people that make the major decisions within the organization.

The freedom afforded by power results in increased illusions of control, optimism, and action. An actor's or leaders control over resources and lack of dependence on others to achieve desired aims lead the powerful to think and act without inhibition and the powerless to think and act with constraint. Think back to Lehman Brothers and how top management (the powerful), continued to take on more risky investments despite the concerns of the risk managers (the powerless), that were paid to limit this type of behavior.

There is a behavioral-approach theory of power that is often invoked to explain this pattern of effects. According to this theory, the effects of power are the result of increased activation of the **Behavioral Approach System** for those in power and increased activation of the **Behavioral Inhibition System** for those who lack power.

The Behavioral Approach System regulates "behavior associated with rewards, such as food, achievement, sex, safety, and social attachment." The Behavioral Inhibition System, in contrast, has been equated to "an alarm system that once activated, triggers heightened vigilance for threats in the environment."

Several years ago there was a 3 on 3 basketball tournament in Flint, Michigan. You were allowed to have four players on a team. I asked four women if they would be interested in playing in the tournament. Having competed in several tournaments over the years, I had a pretty good idea how to develop a strategy that would allow them to compete effectively. Of the four women, only one of them had any college experience. The tallest player on the team was about 5' 5" inches tall. The women were all in their early to middle thirties, and they would be competing in the "open" or top women's division.

Well, after a few good bounces and some luck, the women found themselves in the championship game against the McGee twins. For those of you that haven't heard of them, let me provide you with a little background. The McGee twins, both 6' 3", were part of back-to-back NCAA Championships at the University of Southern California. Both made All-American teams, and Pam played many years as a professional basketball player, and was also a member of the U.S. Women's Olympic Gold Medal team.

At that time, both women were still in prime basketball condition, and had brought along a couple of other highly talented former college players to fill out their four team roster. What I didn't know at the time was that this charity tournament was something that the twins were part of for years…given that they were from Flint. They were literally heroes, and treated as such.

Although the tournament was a primarily an outdoor affair, the championship game was moved indoors to a local high school. I approached one of the tournament coordinators and asked when the team would be playing. His response was, "Oh, your team will be playing in the television game against the McGee's."

Three of the four women on the team stood there in shock. Two women were mumbling something about the McGee twins and the other was concerned about playing in a televised championship. Karen, who had played at a small college in Mississippi, had a smile on her face. She wanted the opportunity to compete against women of this caliber. To her, it was a chance of a lifetime. To the others, it was more about being crushed in front of a pro-McGee crowd and a live television audience.

In the end, the McGee's were much too tall, talented, and strong. They beat us 20 to 12. While the others were visibly intimidated, Karen shined. I believe she scored all 12 points. After Karen hit a couple of shots on her defender, Pam switched to defending her, but Karen continued to play great.

Three of the four players showed Behavioral Inhibition tendencies, in that they were experiencing "distress" and wanted to "withdraw" from this "unfamiliar" situation that had them competing against what they rightfully perceived as superior competition in front of a hostile crowd.

Karen, on the other hand, displayed a Behavioral Approach that was more aligned with the "rewards" that would come if they were to win the championship. She never had the opportunity to play on an Olympic team or get drafted to play professional basketball. She did not shy away from the "stress" associated with this particular "environment", but instead welcomed it.

Deciding whether or not to play in a 3 on 3 basketball tournament presented a low level of risk. You either were going to win or lose the tournament. Sure, there was the possibility of your pride being hurt and perhaps a bruise or two, but there was no money on the line, and no one was getting fired for losing. However, it still didn't stop 3 of the 4 women on the team from withdrawing a bit.

One study suggests that those endowed with power endorsed and pursued risky plans of action, such as expressing a greater willingness to engage in unprotected sex with a stranger, than did those lacking power. The same thing can be said about those seeking to become titans of business, who will stupidly go to any length to fraud their way to **money** and power.

Money Equals Social Inclusion

Social Inclusion is the *"act of making all groups of people within a society feel valued and important."* On the opposite side is **Social Exclusion**, that is, *"being alone, isolated, or ostracized."* Most of us have likely had romantic relationships end, or been ignored at parties or in office conversations. One might think that recent advances in communication technologies and social media would decrease the prevalence of social exclusion, but recent research shows that modern societies have in fact become lonelier in the last 40 years. And then there's money...the great equalizer.

This may not come as a surprise, but there are studies that support the general principle that money operates as a social resource that produces a strong feeling of being able to cope with problems and satisfy your needs. Resources are valued more in times of threat and adversity than at other times, presumably because resources improve one's overall ability to cope.

Think back to the devastation that Hurricane Katrina, and more recently, Hurricane Maria in Puerto Rico caused. People, to this day, are still trying to get their lives back together long after the media has moved on to another story. However, having resources allows you to reduce your pain and suffering because, if need be, you can rebuild rather quickly or move out of the area altogether. Conversely, losing resources makes one more vulnerable, which intensifies suffering.

A study found that both social rejection and thoughts of physical pain led to increased desire for money. It also found that counting money, which presumably evoked the idea of getting and having money, reduced pain. Lastly, remembering having spent money made participants in the study more vulnerable to distress in response to social exclusion and physical pain.

Money has considerable psychological power. So much that it is enough to alter reactions to social exclusion and even to physical pain. There is a growing body of evidence that suggests that the human body's physiological systems for physical pain and trauma respond also to social, interpersonal events.

The thought of an *"abstract"* social resource, like money, produces reactions paralleling reactions to social acceptance and physical pain suggests how deeply the human mind and body are attuned to, and perhaps designed for, functioning in complex social and cultural systems.

The bottom line is that money gives people the ability to control their lives by freeing them from budget constraints, thereby enabling them to select the products, services, and social settings, that best suit their needs and wants.

Humanist psychologist Abraham Maslow, believed that human actions are motivated by the need to fulfill basic needs before moving on to other, more advanced needs. This hierarchy is most often displayed as a pyramid. The lowest levels of the pyramid are made up of the most basic needs, while the more complex needs are located at the top of the pyramid. Needs at the bottom of the pyramid are basic physical requirements including the need for food, water, sleep, and warmth. Once these lower-level needs have been met, people can move on to the next level of needs, which are for safety and security.

As people progress up the pyramid, Maslow believed that our needs become increasingly psychological and social. For example, the need for love, friendship, and intimacy become important. As you move further up the pyramid, the need for personal esteem and feelings of accomplishment take priority. Maslow emphasized the importance of self-actualization, which is a process of growing and developing as a person in order to achieve individual potential.

The five different levels in Maslow's hierarchy of needs are:

1. **Physiological Needs**: These include the most basic needs that are vital to survival, such as the need for water, air, food, and sleep.
2. **Security Needs:** These include needs for safety and security. Security needs are important for survival, but they are not as demanding as the physiological needs. Examples of security needs include a desire for steady employment, health care, safe neighborhoods, and shelter from the environment.

3. **Social Needs:** These include needs for belonging, love, and affection. Relationships such as friendships, romantic attachments, and families, help fulfill this need for companionship and acceptance, as does involvement in social, community, or religious groups.
4. **Esteem Needs:** After the first three needs have been satisfied, esteem needs becomes increasingly important. These include the need for things that reflect on self-esteem, personal worth, social recognition, and accomplishment.
5. **Self-actualizing Needs:** This is the highest level of Maslow's hierarchy of needs. Self-actualizing people are self-aware, concerned with personal growth, less concerned with the opinions of others, and interested in fulfilling their potential.

If we believe in what Maslow's hierarchy of needs suggest, wouldn't money play a vital role in achieving most of our needs? Researchers have found, for example, that preventing consumers' need for social connection leads them to spend strategically in service of affiliation. How many of us have purchased a product symbolic of group membership or tailored our spending preferences to those of an interaction partner, like eating unappealing food favored by a peer for an opportunity to commence social connections?

Our welfare largely depends on the soundness of our financial decisions, such as choosing a mortgage, saving for college, using credit cards, paying for health care, investing in the stock market, and of course retirement. Money serves not only to acquire what one needs, wants, or desires, but also to impress, along with the power to control others.

Motivated By Power

Power Motivation is the extent to which an individual considers possessing power to be his or her primary goal. Research suggests that power motivation **increased risk-taking behavior**. Those placed in high-power roles were less risk taking if they were high, rather than low, in power motivation. They explained these findings by proposing that those high in power motivation acted with greater risk aversion in order to maintain the status quo and preserve the longevity of their power.

Within organizations and institutions, power is seldom an either-or construct. At some points it is perceived as stable and unlikely to be altered and at other points it is conceived as unstable and holding the potential for fluctuation. Let's take Matt Lauer, who was the co-host of NBC's *Today* Show from 1997 to 2017. On November 29, 2017, NBC News terminated Lauer after an unidentified female NBC employee reported that Lauer had sexually harassed her during the 2014 Winter Olympics in Sochi, Russia, and that the harassment continued after they returned to New York.

Variety Magazine reported allegations by at least ten of Lauer's current and former colleagues. Production assistant Addie Zinone stated that although she had a consensual sexual relationship with Lauer, it was "abuse of power" on his part because she felt that turning down Lauer's advances would have hurt her career. Lauer has apologized, saying although some of the accusations were "untrue or mischaracterized", but that "there is enough truth in these stories to make me feel embarrassed and ashamed."

Bill Cosby was once seen as America's favorite dad when he was the star of the sitcom **The Cosby Show**, which aired for eight seasons on NBC from September 20, 1984, until April 30, 1992. The show focused on the Huxtable family, an upper middle-class African-American family living in Brooklyn, New York. The show spent five consecutive seasons as the number-one rated show on television, and all eight of its seasons in the top 20.

On April 26, 2018, that same Bill Cosby was found guilty of three counts of aggravated indecent assault, for drugging and sexually assaulting Andrea Constand at his home in a Philadelphia suburb in 2004. Montgomery County District Attorney, Kevin Steele, stated that Cosby ***"used his celebrity, he used his wealth, he used his network of supporters to help him conceal his crimes."***

Although Cosby did possess the power to influence a career or two, perhaps no other person in the television or movie industry wielded and displayed more despicable leadership than Harvey Weinstein.

On May 25, 2018, Harvey Weinstein surrendered himself to the New York Police Department to face sexual-assault charges. It all started back on the 5th of October in 2017 when The New York Times published a story detailing decades of allegations of sexual harassment against him. Actresses Rose McGowan and Ashley Judd are among the women who came forward. Among the accusations are that he forced women to massage him and watch him naked. He also promised to help advance their careers in return for sexual favors.

Weinstein and his brother Bob Weinstein, co-founded the entertainment company Miramax, which produced several successful independent films. Weinstein won an Academy Award for producing **Shakespeare in Love**, and won seven Tony Awards for a variety of plays and musicals.

After leaving Miramax, Weinstein and his brother founded The Weinstein Company. In March of 2018, unable to survive the allegations of sexual abuse leveled against co-founder Harvey Weinstein, The Weinstein Co. filed for bankruptcy.

Weinstein, Lauer and Cosby are not the only high profile figures that have ruined their reputations, lost their job, and are perhaps facing jail time. Roger Ailes, who has since passed away, and was the former head of Fox News, resigned in July, 2016, after he was accused of sexual harassment. Bill O'Reilly, the once popular host at Fox News, was forced to resign after Fox was discovered to have paid five women millions of dollars in exchange for silence about their accusations of sexual harassment. One of the women was given a settlement of $32 million, and yet Fox signed O'Reilly to a large contract extension shortly after.

Probably the most disturbing allegation of sexual misconduct by a public figure came out a month before the Presidential Elections, when a tape emerged of the candidate Donald Trump telling a celebrity-news reporter, *"And when you're a star, they let you do it. You can do anything. . . . Grab 'em by the pussy. You can do anything."*

At least 15 women have come forward with a wide range of accusations against Trump, ranging from sexual harassment and sexual assault to lewd behavior around women. Of the women, 13 say Trump attacked them directly and two others say they witnessed behavior that made them uncomfortable. All the alleged incidents took place prior to his assuming the presidency. Trump has denied the accusations and has made himself the victim. He has called all of his accusers liars and has threatened to sue them. Despite his damning comment about "*Grab 'em by the pussy*", Trump still was elected President of the United States.

What does that say about us as a society? There were plenty of women defending Trump after his comment and still voted for him. Could it be that he was considered such a powerful figure that voters put their values on hold…or is he just that good of a salesman? There is little doubt, in my mind anyway, that some of these women may feel a bit more powerless, especially since Trump has risen to what many people feel is the most powerful position in the world.

Powerlessness is defined by *"lacking control of valued resources."* Weinstein controlled what actors and actresses got what parts in movies and plays. He also utilized his *valued resources*, as alleged by some women, to have them blackballed or blocked from potential acting roles, which hindered their careers and income potential.

The potential for loss of power (i.e., unstable power) or the inability to gain control over valued resources (i.e., stable powerlessness), will create stress in individuals, and this increase in stress will lead to greater risk taking by these individuals. So, on the one hand you have O'Reilly and Ailes, for example, trying to hang onto power by paying off those accusing them of sexual misconduct, while at the same time you have the women that have come forward, at great personal and professional risk, to take back their dignity and punish the offenders.

As you will see, people will stupidly take a considerable amount of risk to either gain control of "valued resources", or fight to keep the valued resources they already have. They will lie, cheat, commit fraud, threaten people, fire people, defame people, or worse. By the way, gender doesn't matter when it comes obtaining and keeping valued resources.

Theranos: "When There's Blood in the Streets"

Elizabeth Holmes was 19 years old when she dropped out of Stanford University to start her company **Theranos**. Holmes claimed that her technology could take a pin-prick worth of blood from a finger and perform hundreds of laboratory tests. She boldly claimed that her blood testing machine, Edison, would save Medicare and Medicaid hundreds of billions of dollars on an annual basis.

Holmes became a celebrity and the youngest self-made female billionaire in the world. However, the Wall Street Journal uncovered a massive multi-year fraud that duped investors and put unsuspecting patients at risk. In March of 2018, Holmes agreed to a settlement with federal regulators that strips her of voting control of Theranos, bans her from being an officer or director of any public company for 10 years, and requires her to pay a $500,000 penalty. However, it doesn't end there.

On the 15th of June, 2018, Holmes and her chief operating officer and President Ramesh "Sunny" Balwani, were charged with two counts of conspiracy to commit wire fraud and nine counts of wire fraud. If convicted, according to the US Attorney's office, they each face a maximum sentence of 20 years in prison and a fine of $250,000, plus restitution for each count of wire fraud and each conspiracy count.

Investigative reporter John Carreyrou, in his book "**Bad Blood: Secrets and Lies in a Silicon Valley Startup**", stated, "There's no question in mind that she knew there was a risk that she was putting patients in harm's way." Holmes ignored warning signs from employees who raised red flags about the technology's effectiveness prior to introducing it to patients.

With a leadership style that has been described as "tyrannic", Holmes expected participation in elaborate lies. For example, she staged a fake laboratory test to impress Vice President Joe Biden. Carreyrou interviewed more than 150 people, including 60 former Theranos employees, who at times felt like they were under surveillance. In fact, Holmes' administrative assistants connected with Theranos employees on Facebook, and reported back to Holmes what others were posting.

Imagine being told to put on a fake demonstration to deceive the Vice President of the United States…how would you respond? Holmes demanded "absolute loyalty from her employees" and if she sensed that she no longer had that loyalty, they were typically asked to leave the company. The fact of the matter is that her blood testing technology did not work, and she was doing everything she possibly could to keep her valued resources, which before her self-inflicted ClusterPhuck, was worth about $4.5 Billion. She is now worth absolutely zero.

My third oldest son will be heading to college in the fall. He has been working as a bus boy for a local restaurant for the last couple of years between school and football. A week or two ago he confessed to me that while he was bussing tables at the outdoor patio a man walked up to him and said something like his credit card wasn't working and he needed $20 to put in his gas tank to get home. Being the good person that he is, he gave the guy the money.

It wasn't until later in the evening that he pulled me aside and wondered if his good deed had been a scam. I explained to him that "yes, it probably was" a scam. I confessed that I had, while stationed in Naples, Italy, was scammed by what is known as the three-card monte scam, which the "mark", which was me, is tricked into betting a sum of money on the assumption that they can find the "money card" among three face-down playing cards. My nineteen year old self got that queasy feeling when I upped the bet right at the very end, but it was too late.

My son and I discussed how to avoid a scam, like the one he experienced, from happening again in the future. My advice was simply to ask more questions. Why are you here in this city? Didn't you come here to visit friends? Why don't you call your friends? Where is your car? Do you have a driver's license? Typically, a few questions and a little digging will expose a scam. Unfortunately, some pretty smart people failed to do their homework and got duped by Holmes for a lot more than twenty dollars.

Education Secretary Betsy DeVos and her family lost $100 million. The Walton Family heirs lost $150 million, Rupert Murdoch lost $125 million, and the Cox family, of Cox Communications, lost $100 million…among others.

This is not the first time that smart, well-connected people, have been duped by an individual trying to maintain their valued resources at the expense of investors. There have been countless times over the years that seemingly intelligent people have lost millions of dollars to smooth talking individuals, but Bernard Madoff is in a category all by himself.

Madoff: The Significance of Red Flag Blindness

On March 12, 2009; Bernard Madoff plead guilty to 11 federal felonies and admitted to turning his wealth management business into a massive Ponzi scheme that defrauded thousands of investors of billions of dollars. The amount missing from client accounts, including fabricated gains, was estimated by prosecutors to be about $65 billion. On June 29, 2009, Madoff was sentenced to 150 years in prison, which is basically life in prison. The list of people and institutions ruined by Madoff is heartbreaking, but like Elizabeth Holmes, he did not want to lose his wealth and social status.

Harry M. Markopolos, a former securities industry executive and an independent forensic accounting and financial fraud investigator, discovered evidence over nine years suggesting that Madoffs wealth management business, Bernard L. Madoff Investment Securities LLC, was actually a massive Ponzi scheme. In 2000, 2001, and 2005, Markopolos alerted the U.S. Securities and Exchange Commission (SEC) of the fraud, supplying supporting documents, but each time, the SEC ignored him or only gave his evidence a cursory investigation.

However, there is evidence to suggest that Madoff could have potentially been stopped in 1992 by the SEC, when the agency filed suit against a Florida investment firm, Avellino & Bienes, accusing it of selling $440 million of unregistered securities to 3,200 investors. As it turns out, Madoff was the sole manager who took in the Avellino & Bienes money. In a December 1992 interview with *The Wall Street Journal*, Madoff himself explained he didn't know the funds had been raised illegally. The Avellino firm was closed down in 1993, and the money was returned to investors.

Madoff, rightly, should be in prison for the rest of his life…but what about the leadership at the Securities and Exchange Commission (SEC)? Could their leadership inaction be the root cause of how Madoff was allowed to continue his fraud for several years? The SEC was warned several times and stupidly did nothing. Yes, incompetent leadership was in play here, but did any of them pay for it?

Seven employees of the Securities and Exchange Commission were disciplined, but no one was fired. The most severe punishment was one person getting a 30-day suspension without pay and a reduction in pay. Most recently, the SEC's "dysfunction and incompetence" was in full view when Kathleen Furey, a senior lawyer who worked in the New York Regional Office (NYRO), filed a whistleblower complaint. She alleged, among other things, that 20-odd lawyers who worked in her unit at the NYRO were actually barred by a superior from bringing cases under two of the four main securities laws governing Wall Street, the Investment Advisors Act of 1940 and the Investment Company Act of 1940.

Furey stated that her group, from a period stretching for over half a decade through December, 2008, did not as a matter of policy pursue cases against investment managers like Bernie Madoff. She cites statistics that provides evidence that there was, in fact, some kind of policy in place that prevented her group from going after investment advisers.

Imagine if you were a detective and told, by members of your leadership, that you could not investigate murders from, let's say, people that have a net worth of at least $100 million...how would you react when you find out that the person was actually a serial killer?

In 2014, the SEC settled the lawsuit with Furey who was seeking documents related to its failure to uncover the massive Bernie Madoff Ponzi scheme. Although the terms were not released, you can probably figure out how much she was paid based on a lawsuit filed by another attorney, Gary Aguirre.

Aguirre, won a $755,000 wrongful termination settlement against the SEC after he was fired for trying to press an insider trading case against John Mack, who would later become the CEO of Morgan Stanley. The SEC's incompetent leadership did cost thousands of people their life savings or a sizable portion of their investments. Some people paid an even higher price.

A hedge fund manager, Charles Murphy, who was duped by Madoff's Ponzi scheme to the tune of $50 million, and was subsequently sued by investors, jumped from the 24th floor of a New York hotel. A French aristocrat who'd lost $1.5 billion in Madoff's scheme previously committed suicide in 2008. Another investor, a 65-year-old former Army major, committed suicide a year later. Madoff's eldest son, Mark, hanged himself on the second anniversary of his father's arrest in 2010. Unchecked bad behavior can, and does, lead to life ending consequences.

Unlike Madoff, there are those that attempt to amass fortune, fame and power, on a somewhat smaller scale. Meaning, there is some fraud, deception, and of course stupidity involved, but not nearly at the level that will cause people to lose their life savings or commit suicide.

Narcissisms Role in ClusterPhuck Formation

Narcissism has been described as **"...the pursuit of gratification from vanity, or egotistic admiration of one's own physical or mental attributes, that derive from arrogant pride."**

Sandy Hotchkiss and James Masterson's, book titled "Why is it always about you? The Seven Deadly Sins of Narcissism", wrote some damaging arguments concerning narcissism, which includes:

1. **Shamelessness**: Shame is the feeling that lurks beneath all unhealthy narcissism, and the inability to process shame in healthy ways.
2. **Magical thinking**: Narcissists see themselves as perfect, using distortion and illusion known as magical thinking. They also use projection to dump shame onto others.
3. **Arrogance**: A narcissist who is feeling deflated may reinflate by diminishing, debasing, or degrading somebody else.
4. **Envy**: A narcissist may secure a sense of superiority in the face of another person's ability by using contempt to minimize the other person.
5. **Entitlement**: Narcissists hold unreasonable expectations of particularly favorable treatment and automatic compliance because they consider themselves special. Failure to comply is considered an attack on their superiority, and the perpetrator is considered an "awkward" or "difficult" person. Defiance of their will is a narcissistic injury that can trigger narcissistic rage.
6. **Exploitation**: Can take many forms but always involves the exploitation of others without regard for their feelings or interests. Often the other is in a subservient position where resistance would be difficult or even impossible. Sometimes the subservience is not so much real as assumed.
7. **Bad boundaries**: Narcissists do not recognize that they have boundaries and that others are separate and are not extensions of themselves. Others either exist to meet their needs or may as well not exist at all. Those who provide narcissistic supply to the narcissist are treated as if they are part of the narcissist and are expected to live up to those expectations. In the mind of a narcissist there is no boundary between self and other.

Speaking of narcissist, Stephen Calk, a former economic adviser to President Trump's 2016 presidential campaign, was indicted on the 23rd of May, 2019, for allegedly approving $16 million in loans to former Trump campaign chairman Paul Manafort, who is now in federal prison, in exchange for his help seeking a top post in the Trump administration.

Calk, founder, CEO, and Chairman of the mortgage lender Federal Savings Bank of Chicago, illegally used the bank's resources, according to authorities, to curry favor with Manafort. He allegedly ignored internal standards and lied to regulators.

Calk was even bold enough to provide Manafort with a listed ranking of the administrative jobs he wanted… starting with Treasury Secretary. The list also included 19 ambassadorships. Calk faces up to 30 years in prison if convicted of the charge of financial institution bribery.

One would assume, that if you were the founder of a financial institution, valued at almost $300 million, you wouldn't have a need to put yourself in the middle of a ClusterPhucktual quagmire. However, the quest for money and power, often supersedes common sense and ethical behavior.

CEO Capability Cues

Researchers introduced a concept called **Capability Cues**, which are contextual signals that decision makers might reasonably interpret as indicators of their current level of overall ability. They argue that positive cues will induce boldness, while negative cues will induce timidity. Imagine you are that basketball player that hits your first three shots. The crowd is cheering, the coach is happy, and you think it's going to be one of those great games you always wanted.

However, let's say you miss your first three shots…are you as willing to shoot that next shot? The crowd is not cheering and the coach is now giving you that *look* that only players on the team understand. Some players will continue to shoot regardless of how many shots they miss, while other players may be more selective or cautious.

Two studies, the first one focused on the risky outlays by CEOs of publicly owned U.S. companies from 1992 to 2006, and the second , was focused on acquisition premiums paid by CEOs from a sample of U.S. acquiring firms that occurred between the years 2001-2008.

The results of the studies shows us that capability cues generally influence executive risk taking. Highly narcissistic CEOs are much less responsive to recent objective performance than their less narcissistic peers; in contrast, highly narcissistic CEOs are especially encouraged by social praise.

For business executives the role of confidence in risk taking cannot be overstated. The studies also found that executives do not equate business risk taking to gambling. As one executive said, *"my ability to influence whatever goes on after the moment of choice is perhaps more important."*

Beyond referring to their ability to control post-decision events, the respondents also spoke of varying levels of confidence in picking good projects and avoiding bad projects, as well as in their ability to forecast future occurrences such as prices, competitors' actions, and technological trajectories.

Confidence is a major ingredient in executive risk taking. CEOs, for example, make large corporate acquisitions, even though it is well known that most acquisitions destroy shareholder value. CEOs make acquisitions because they believe they have the ability to make better deals and to manage acquisitions better than their peers. Throughout the book you will see examples of how confidence and risk taking lead to the ClusterPhucks that most people typically try to avoid.

The Six Degrees of ClusterPhuckiness

A *burn* is a type of injury to the skin caused by heat, electricity, chemicals, light, radiation or friction. Most burns only affect the skin. Rarely, deeper tissues, such as muscle, bone, and blood vessels can also be injured. Managing burns is important because they are common, painful and can result in disfiguring and disabling scarring.

Burns can be complicated by shock, infection, multiple organ dysfunction syndrome, electrolyte imbalance, respiratory distress, and even death. There are six classifications of burns which begins with your basic first-degree burn, which is usually limited to redness and minor pain. As you progress through the classifications the pain and damage gets worse. For example, a sixth-degree burn occurs when heat destroys the muscles, charring and exposing the bone. These burns are almost always fatal, and if death does not occur, amputation will be required.

With a little bit of imagination you could probably utilize this same *"degree"* system to rank some of the ClusterPhucks that have occurred during your lifetime. Let's take a look at what I consider a first-degree ClusterPhuck.

A First-Degree CP

Perhaps some of you may recall the *Pearson v. Chung* civil case filed in 2005, by Roy L. Pearson, Jr., an administrative law judge, in a dispute with a dry cleaning company over a lost pair of trousers. Pearson filed suit against the owners of Custom Cleaners in Washington, D.C.., initially demanding $67 million for inconvenience, mental anguish and attorney's fees for, according to Pearson, the owners did not live up to the *"satisfaction guaranteed"* sign that was displayed in the store.

The owners of the cleaners presented three settlement offers in the amounts of $3000, $4600, and $12,000, all of which were rejected by Pearson. The owners of the business, South Korean immigrants, were reportedly considering moving back to South Korea. After a public outpouring of support for the owners, a website was set up to accept donations for their legal defense.

Pearson eventually reduced his demands to $54 million in damages rather than

$67 million. Among his requests were $500,000 in attorney's fees, $2 million for **"discomfort, inconvenience, and mental distress",** and $15,000, which he claimed would be the cost to rent a car every weekend to drive to another dry cleaning service. The remaining $51.5 million, according to Pearson, would be used to help similarly dissatisfied D.C. consumers sue businesses.

The trial ended in favor of the dry cleaners, which awarded them court costs, which the owners later withdrew after recovering their costs ($83k), through fund-raising. The owners did so in the hopes of persuading Pearson to stop litigating. However, Pearson continued to pursue appeals until his appeal options were finally exhausted.

An Administrative Law Judge (ALJ), *"…is an official who presides at an administrative trial-type hearing to resolve a dispute between a government agency and someone affected by a decision of that agency. The ALJ is usually the initial trier of fact and decision maker. ALJs can administer oaths, take testimony, rule on questions of evidence, and make factual and legal determinations."* They have, among other things, absolute immunity from liability for their judicial acts and are insulated from political influence.

You don't need a law degree to understand that Mr. Pearson held a very powerful position. I say held because after he created this ClusterPhuck, a panel recommended <u>NOT</u> giving Pearson a ten-year term as an Administrative Law Judge, after his initial two-year term expired in mid-2007. It was widely determined that he demonstrated a lack of judicial temperament.

Mr. Pearson attempted several appeals to get his position back, but to no avail. The owners of the dry cleaners, due to what they called emotional stress and loss of revenue, closed the dry cleaning establishment that was at the center of the lawsuit.

When all was said and done the first-degree classification was justified due to the limited destruction surrounding Mr. Pearson's ClusterPhuck. The owners of the dry cleaners clearly lost money, as well as perhaps a couple of employees due to the closing of the business. I am willing to bet that there were several customers in the area that depended on that dry cleaner over its competitors, and they were forced to look elsewhere.

Over the years there have been literally hundreds of low, medium, and high-level ClusterPhucks in both the commercial and government sectors, that were created by only a handful of individuals. Take for example the Vietnam War, which I consider a sixth-degree ClusterPhuck.

The Vietnam War

The architect behind the Vietnam War was Secretary of Defense Robert McNamara. He served both Presidents Kennedy and Johnson from 1961 to 1968. There was a time that Mr. McNamara felt strongly that the United States would win this very unpopular war. As the years passed, and the casualties mounted, his optimism began to fade. In 1967, he tried to persuade President Johnson to stop sending troops and the bombing strikes. This is not exactly what President Johnson wanted to hear from his Defense Secretary, which eventually led to Mr. McNamara's departure.

Years after Mr. McNamara left the Pentagon he admitted publically that the Vietnam War was a big mistake. He said it was wrong to see Vietnam as a pawn of the Soviets, wrong to believe in the domino theory, which was based on the notion that countries could fall to communism. When all was said and done, the United States suffered over 58,267 casualties and 303, 644 Wounded in Action (WIA). According to the Vietnamese government, over 1,100,000 North Vietnamese Army and Viet Cong military personnel were killed during the Vietnam War. The cost of the war was estimated to be as high as $133 billion.

There is no disputing that the Vietnam War was one of the biggest ClusterPhucks in the history of the United States. It's not as if Mr. McNamara hadn't been groomed for the Defense Secretary position. He was a Lieutenant Colonel in the Army Air Forces (AAF), both a Harvard graduate and professor, and became the first president of Ford Motors from outside the Henry Ford family. He also received much of the credit for Ford's expansion and success in the postwar period.

Despite the fact that he was wrong, McNamara did initially believe in what he was doing. However, you can't change history. Thousands of people died and many more suffered through Agent Orange and Post Traumatic Stress Disorder (PTSD), due in large measure to his leadership actions.

I am not naïve enough to believe that all of you will agree with me with regards to my CLusterPhuck ranking system, simply because our experiences, politics, and how directly the event affected us personally, will undoubtedly dictate our ranking mentality.

College Admissions Scam

So, you want to get your kid into a prestigious college or university. Ok, you have your heart set on sending them to USC or perhaps Georgetown. You, as a parent, do everything you can, early on, to get your kid a leg up on the competition.

You make sure that your son or daughter takes challenging courses, plays a sport or two, volunteers at a local non-profit center, and you spend a few hundred dollars at the local ACT or SAT test preparation centers. You also visit the schools, which may cost you a few nights in a hotel and perhaps a couple of roundtrip plane tickets.

You finally get a letter from the university. All you really need to do is read the first five words that say, "we regret to inform you". After that your mind goes blank, you throw the letter down, run to your room and wonder what happened. After all, you did everything by the book. How could they NOT accept you? Well, perhaps you should have reached out to Rick Singer.

In what Department of Justice prosecutors are calling the "biggest admissions scam in U.S. history", at least 50 people, which includes business people, and celebrities like Lori Loughlin and Felicity Huffman, allegedly bribed coaches and paid for forged standardized tests in a conspiracy to get their children admitted to elite American colleges.

Dubbed **Operation Varsity Blues**, some parents allegedly paid as much as $6.5 million to have someone take the college entrance exam on behalf of their kid, and in some cases, faked photos and athletic achievements to fraudulently get their kids into school. Some of the parents have already plead guilty. Some of the parents have been fired from their companies, while others had television shows and endorsements cancelled.

Some students involved in the scam have either left school voluntarily, or were forced to leave. The coaches involved in the scam have been fired, and are facing federal charges as well. So what degree of ClusterPhuck would you give this? If I were a student, I would feel both embarrassed and would probably feel that I had wasted a couple years of my life. However, how many kids that truly deserved entrance into the school were hurt by the fraud?

Remember, the degree level associated with a ClusterPhuck is based on your own personal experience. Students, both who were fraudulently accepted, and the ones that were rejected, may feel the same degree of ClusterPhuckiness. But what if you were a student that had absolutely no knowledge of the scam, but were forced to leave the school? What about the television shows that were cancelled? How many other actors, actresses, and others, are out of work due to the scam? Again, it depends on your personal perspective.

Vantage Point

On November 24, 2009, Michaele and Tareq Salahi, a then married couple from Virginia, attended a White House state dinner for Indian Prime Minister Manmohan Singh, allegedly without being invited guests. They were able to pass through two security checkpoints, enter the White House complex, and meet

Dr. Gregory L. Cotton

President Barack Obama.

Fallout from the incident included an array of security investigations, legal inquiries, and *"sensationalistic reporting."* This is likely a second-degree ClusterPhuck. However, if the security breach had cost me my job I am pretty sure that I would have placed it a bit higher on the scale.

For example, an **Air Force One** lookalike, the backup plane for the one regularly used by the President of the United States, flew low over parts of New York and New Jersey, accompanied by two F-16 fighters so that Air Force photographers could take pictures high above the New York harbor.

But the exercise was conducted without any notification to the public and caused panic that led to the evacuation of several buildings in Lower Manhattan and Jersey City. By the afternoon the situation had turned into a political nightmare, with New York City Mayor Michael R. Bloomberg and President Obama obviously infuriated by the event.

Depending on your vantage point, you are likely to have very different opinions on what degree of ClusterPhuck (CP) this incident warrants. Mayor Bloomberg may look at it as a six-degree CP, while President Obama may give it a five-degree ranking. Then again, if you live in Los Angles, you may give it a second or third degree ranking, while a person living in Manhattan is likely to give it a solid six-degree ranking. Why? If you were in New York City on September 11th 2001, during the terrorist attacks that left hundreds dead and the world trade center buildings leveled, your perspective and degree level would be quite different.

Sixth-degree CPs, or any level of CP for that matter, can be originated by a single individual or a small group of individuals. The problem is that the individual(s) that are making the decisions that create the CPs, tend to destroy, at times, the lives of millions of innocent people along the way. People in virtually every occupation imaginable have created a CP in this sixth degree ranking system. However, it's that 6th degree ClusterPhuck that is the most troubling…like being responsible for the largest bankruptcy in the history of the United States.

A Handful of Stupidity

Lehman Brothers left a large path of destruction in its quest to maximize profits. Although they had a risk management department, the top decision makers ignored their warnings. As bankruptcy examiners sifted through the mess, there was one internal email that summed up the entire debacle. It stated:

"I am shocked at the poor risk mgmt at the highest levels, and I don't think it started with Archstone. It is unbelievable and I think there needs

to be an investigation into the broader issue of malfeasance. Mgmt gambled recklessly with thousands of jobs and shareholder wealth…"

Lehman Brothers was founded in 1850 and was once well-respected around the world. It took only a handful of executives to destroy everything that was built over the years. The pressure to make money, especially for public companies, is relentless.

What keeps Chief Executive Officers up at night? According to **The Conference Board**, a not-for-profit organization that *"…conducts research, convene conferences, make forecasts, assess trends, publish information and analysis, and bring executives together to learn from one another."* One of their most "CEO Challenge" research reports, ranks the top ten challenges cited by CEOs, chairmen, and presidents that responded to the study.

The Top Ten Challenges in the United States are as follows:

1. Excellence in execution
2. Sustained and steady top-line growth
3. Consistent execution of strategy by top management
4. Customer loyalty/retention
5. Profit growth
6. Government regulation
7. Corporate reputation for quality products/services
8. Speed, flexibility, adaptability to change
9. Stimulating innovation/creativity/enabling entrepreneurship
10. Cash management

In order to meet these challenges leaders must cope with change. As technology and international competition increases, major changes are becoming more and more necessary to survive. Today's successful executive understands the complexities in which he or she has to cope with, and they are able to focus on a handful of issues that allows them to achieve their vision.

Regardless of how complex the issues are, executives are paid to make decisions and to take responsibility for their decisions. Successful executives understand such things as the name of the person accountable for carry out the decision, the deadline for completion, names of the people who will be affected by the decision, and the names of the people that need to be informed of the decision.

It can be argued that executives that face a multitude of demands are under too much pressure to accurately weigh situations when it comes to strategic decision making. Those executives that are under great pressure tend to take mental shortcuts and rely heavily on experiences to search for and interpret information in order to make a decision. Unfortunately, research shows us that this can lead to some bad decisions.

In July of 2018, Papa John's founder John Schnatter resigned as chairman of his company's board after admitting and apologizing for using the "N-word" during a May conference call. Schnatter's conference call came to light after Forbes magazine detailed the incident in an article. Shares of Papa John's fell by as much as 5.9 percent to a new 12-month low of $47.80 a share, which erased $96.2 million in market value.

Some onlookers point out that although Schnatter's "hard charging" entrepreneurial skills assisted him in making his company one of the most successful and most significant in the fast food category, it also hastened his downfall. Meaning, his success took him into the big leagues, but he lacked understanding of what the public wants in a business leader. Being impatient, outspoken, and terse as the leader in a public setting historically does not end well for leaders.

***

A Tale of Five Mayors

In October, 2013, A U.S. judge sentenced former Detroit Mayor Kwame Kilpatrick to 28 years in prison for corruption, which is one of the longest such sentences ever handed to a major U.S. politician. Kilpatrick's racketeering, bribery and extortion worsened the city's financial crisis as part of a conspiracy that spent millions of taxpayer dollars.

He extorted bribes from contractors who wanted to get or keep Detroit city contracts, steering $127 million in contracts to his friend and business partner, at least $73 million of which came from extortion and bid-rigging. At least 18 city officials and 16 other individuals who did business with the city were convicted of corruption offenses from Kilpatrick's tenure as mayor.

Detroit was once a symbol of American industrial power, but now it is the largest city ever to file for bankruptcy protection. The magnitude of the destruction has squarely placed the former mayor as one of the biggest ClusterPhuckers of all time, and deserves a 6th degree ranking.

Then of course there is the first woman mayor of San Diego, Maureen O'Connor, who served the city from 1986 to 1992. She acknowledged in court that she misappropriated more than $2 million from her late husband's foundation to fund a casino gambling habit with which she allegedly won and lost $1 billion over nine years. Another San Diego mayor, Democrat Bob Filner, resigned in august 2013, for a slew of sexual harassment allegations. He eventually plead guilty to felony false imprisonment and two misdemeanor counts of battery involving three women. If you were Filner's former chief of staff or campaign manager, what are your prospects for future employment?

Again, how you rate these CP's are dependent on your own personal vantage point. As a female being sexually harassed by mayor Filner, you are likely going to rank this as a 6th degree CP. Filner, on the other hand would view this as a first degree CP because in his mind he meant no harm.

As a member of the foundation, or as a potential recipient of the money that was gambled away by Mayor O'Connor, there is surely some resentment that may warrant a 6th degree ranking. However, Ms. O'Connor could potentially rationalize the theft as a second degree CP because she had a gambling addiction.

There is no doubt that a great many people will view what mayor Kilpatrick did to the city of Detroit as one of the all-time ClusterPhucks. However, didn't the people of Detroit re-elect him to a second term in office even though he was surrounded by scandal? So, is it possible that the citizens that voted for Kilpatrick enabled him to continue his reign of ClusterPhuckiness?

Robert Bruce Ford, who passed away in 2016, was the sixty-fourth Mayor of Toronto, Canada. During his political career, Ford had been the subject of a number of personal and work-related controversies and legal proceedings, including a conflict of interest trial that nearly removed him from office. In 2013, he became involved in a substance abuse scandal. He initially denied the allegations, but a police investigation led to the discovery of a video showing what was believed to be the mayor using crack cocaine, which he had to finally admit to.

One would think that following his crack cocaine use admission, he would resign from office. However, Ford fully understood that the law prevented him from being removed from office, so he stayed put even though the Toronto City Council removed certain mayoral powers from Ford and granted them to Deputy Mayor Norm Kelly for the remainder of Ford's term. He had become, like the other mayors, an embarrassment to the city.

In 2014, the former mayor of New Orleans, Ray Nagin, began serving a 10-year sentence for taking bribes, free vacations and truckloads of free granite for his family business. You may perhaps remember Nagin during Hurricane Katrina blaming everyone except his administration as it pertains to the preparation, response, and recovery, prior to, during, and after the hurricane.

The lack of a robust evacuation plan and missing simple emergency preparatory steps, such as ensuring that the radio's used during an emergency are charged, was his leadership responsibility, and he failed miserably. And, by the way, according to the investigators, his criminal activities started prior to Katrina and continued until his ultimate arrest and conviction.

Not to be outdone, four of the last seven governors in the state of Illinois have been sent to prison on numerous ClusterPhuck-related charges. However, it is becoming apparent that a group of Cluster Phucker's in powerful positions can create a 6th degree CP so massive that it reverberates around the world…like the Great Recession that began in 2008.

The Financial Meltdown & Greed

Financial Mismanagement can best be described as *"management that, deliberately or not, is handled in a way that can be characterized as wrong, bad, careless, inefficient or incompetent, and that will reflect negatively upon the financial standing of a business or individual."*

The Financial Crisis Inquiry Report, which was created to examine the causes of the worst financial crisis in the United States since the Great Depression. There is a statement in the report that will clear up any misconceptions as to whether the leadership surrounding the crisis should be examined.

It states:

"We conclude this financial crisis was avoidable. The crisis was the result of human action and inaction, not of Mother Nature or computer models gone haywire. The captains of finance and the public stewards of our financial system ignored warnings and failed to question, understand, and manage evolving risks within a system essential to the well-being of the American public. Theirs was a big miss, not a stumble. While the business cycle cannot be repealed, a crisis of this magnitude need not have occurred. To paraphrase Shakespeare, the fault lies not in the stars, but in us."

YES! The catastrophic ClusterPhuck of 2008 was A-V-O-I-D-A-B-L-E! How could that possibly be? The Commission came up with 9 Major Conclusions, which are:

Conclusion One: The Financial Crisis Was Avoidable

The committee concluded that the financial crisis was the result of human action and inaction. Although some on Wall Street and in Washington argue that the crisis could NOT have been foreseen or avoided, there were warning signs, just like other ClusterPhucks, but like Madoff and his Ponzi scheme, the signs were ignored or discounted.

There was a rapid in risky subprime lending, which is a type of loan granted to individuals with poor credit histories. Securitization, which combines mortgages into one large pool, allows the issuer to divide the large pool into smaller pieces based on each individual mortgage's inherent risk of default and then sells those smaller pieces to investors.

The process creates liquidity by enabling smaller investors to purchase shares in a larger asset pool. Using the mortgage-backed security (MBS) example, individual retail investors are able to purchase portions of a mortgage as a type of bond. Without the securitization of mortgages, retail investors may not be able to afford to buy into a large pool of mortgages.

The unsustainable rise in housing prices, widespread reports of **"egregious and predatory lending practices"**, dramatic increases in household mortgage debt, and exponential growth in financial firms' trading activities, unregulated derivatives, were among many other red flags. Little, if any, meaningful action was taken to reduce the threats in a timely manner.

The report uses the Federal Reserve as an example of *"inaction"* as it relates to the financial crisis. They had the power to *"stem the flow of toxic mortgages"*, by setting prudent mortgage-lending standards, but failed to do so. Financial institutions made, bought, and sold mortgage securities they never examined, did not care to examine, or knew to be defective.

Firms depended on tens of billions of dollars of borrowing that had to be renewed each and every night, secured by subprime mortgage securities. Major firms and investors blindly relied on credit rating agencies as their "arbiters of risk", which contributed heavily to the overall development of this ClusterPhuck.

Conclusion Two: Widespread Failures in Financial Regulation and Supervision

More than 30 years of deregulation and reliance on self-regulation by financial institutions, supported by successive administrations and Congresses, and actively pushed by the powerful financial industry at every turn, had stripped away key safeguards, could have helped avoid this catastrophic CP. What this created was less oversight of critical areas with trillions of dollars at risk. Furthermore, the government allowed financial firms to select their preferred regulators, which resulted in firms seeking out the weakest supervisor.

Although the Securities and Exchange Commission (SEC) could have required more capital and halted risky practices at the big investment banks, it failed to do so. The Commission report shows that the financial industry itself played a key role in weakening regulatory constraints on institutions, markets, and products. It was not a surprise that an industry of such wealth and power would exert pressure on policy makers and regulators. For example, from 1999 to 2008, the financial sector expended 2.7 billion in reported federal lobbying expenses.

Conclusion Three: Failures of Corporate Governance & Risk Management

Many of the financial institutions acted recklessly, taking on too much risk, with too little capital, and with too much dependence on short-term funding. They took on enormous exposures in acquiring and supporting subprime lenders and creating, packaging, repackaging, and selling trillions of dollars in mortgage-related securities.

Many of these institutions grew aggressively through poorly executed acquisition and integration strategies that made effective management more challenging. Financial institutions and credit rating agencies *"embraced mathematical models as reliable predictors of risks"*, replacing judgment in too many instances.

For example, AIG's senior management ignored the terms and risks of their 79 billion derivatives exposure to mortgage-related securities. Fannie Mae's quest for bigger market share, profits, and bonuses, led it to ramp up its exposure to risky loans and securities as the housing market was peaking; and the costly surprise when Merrill Lynch's top management realized that the company held 55 billion in "super-senior" and supposedly
"Super-safe" mortgage-related securities that resulted in billions of dollars in losses. These are just some of the examples uncovered by the report.

Conclusion Four: Excessive Borrowing, Risky Investments, & Lack of Transparency

In the years leading up to the crisis, too many financial institutions, as well as too many households, borrowed to the hilt, leaving them vulnerable to financial distress or ruin if the value of their investments declined even modestly. Try to grasp this: As of 2007, the five major investment banks, Bear Stearns, Goldman Sachs, Lehman Brothers, Merrill Lynch, and Morgan Stanley, were operating with extraordinarily thin capital.

By one measure, their leverage ratios were as high as 40 to 1, **meaning for every $40 in assets, there was only $1 in capital to cover losses.** Less than a 3% drop in asset values could wipe out a firm. Much of their borrowing was short-term, in the overnight market, meaning the borrowing had to be renewed each and every day

That is the equivalent of a small business with $50,000 in equity borrowing $1.6 million, with $296,750 of that due each and every day. The leverage was often hidden in derivatives positions, in off-balance-sheet entities, and through what the report refers to as "window dressing" of financial reports available to the investing public.

The kings of leverage were Fannie Mae and Freddie Mac, the two behemoth government-sponsored enterprises (GSEs). For example, by the end of 2007, Fannie's and Freddie's combined leverage ratio, including loans they owned and guaranteed, stood at 75 to 1.

Financial firms were not alone in the borrowing spree: from 2001 to 2007, national mortgage debt almost doubled, and the amount of mortgage debt per household rose more than 63% from $91,500 to $149,500, even while wages were essentially stagnant. When the housing downturn hit, heavily indebted financial firms and families alike were destroyed.

As the mortgage and real estate markets pumped out riskier loans and securities, many financial institutions loaded up on them. Lehman Brothers, in 2007, had amassed $111 billion in commercial and residential real estate holdings and securities, which was almost twice what it held just two years before, and more than four times its total equity.

Within the financial system, the dangers of this debt were magnified because transparency was not required or desired. Massive, short-term borrowing, combined with obligations unseen by others in the market, heightened the chances the system could rapidly unravel.

The multitrillion-dollar repo lending market, which is a form of short-term borrowing for dealers in government securities. The dealer sells the government securities to investors, usually on an overnight basis, and buys them back the following day. Off-balance-sheet entities, which are assets or debts that do not appear on a company's balance sheet, and the use of over-the-counter derivatives were hidden from view, without the protections constructed to prevent financial ClusterBombs of this magnitude. In other words, we had a 21st-century financial system with 19th-century safeguards.

When the housing and mortgage markets cratered, the lack of transparency, the extraordinary debt loads, the short-term loans, and the risky assets all *Clusterfied* at the same time, resulting in panic.

Conclusion Five: Government Not Prepared For Crisis

The key policy makers the Treasury Department, the Federal Reserve Board, and the Federal Reserve Bank of New York, who were best positioned to watch over our markets, were ill prepared for the events of 2007 and 2008. Other agencies were hampered because they did not have a clear understanding of the financial system they were charged with overseeing, particularly as it had evolved in the years leading up to the crisis. A lot of this was due to the lack of transparency in key markets. They believed, for example, that risk had been diversified when, in fact, it had been concentrated.

Policy makers and regulators were caught off guard as the ClusterPhuck spread. There was no comprehensive and strategic plan for containment, because they lacked a full understanding of the risks and interconnections in the financial markets. Some regulators admitted errors by allowing the system to race ahead of their ability to protect it. While there was some awareness of, or at least a debate about the housing bubble, the record reflects that senior public officials did not recognize that a bursting of the bubble could threaten the entire financial system.

The government's inconsistent handling of major financial institutions during the crisis increased uncertainty and panic in the market. How? The decision to rescue Bear Stearns and then to place Fannie Mae and Freddie Mac into conservatorship, followed by its decision NOT to save Lehman Brothers and then to save AIG, greatly confused the market.

Conclusion Six: A Systemic Breakdown in Accountability & Ethics

Integrity of the financial markets and the public's trust in those markets are essential to the economic well-being of the United States. The soundness and the sustained prosperity of the financial system and our economy rely on the notions of fair dealing, responsibility, and transparency. There is an expectation that businesses and individuals pursue profits, as well as to produce products and services of quality and conduct themselves well.

Unfortunately, what we witnessed was the erosion of standards of responsibility and ethics, which exacerbated the financial crisis. Although not universal, the breaches did stretch from the ground level to the corporate suites. The financial consequences were significant, but the damage to the trust of investors, businesses, and the public in the financial system, is incalculable.

For example, the percentage of borrowers who defaulted on their mortgages within just a matter of months after taking a loan nearly doubled from the summer of 2006 to late 2007. This data indicates they likely took out mortgages that they never had the capacity or intention to pay. Mortgage brokers who were paid *"yield spread premiums"* by lenders to put borrowers into higher-cost loans so they would get bigger fees, often never disclosed it to borrowers.

The report details the rising incidence of mortgage fraud, which flourished in an environment of collapsing lending standards and lax regulation. There were a number of suspicious activity reports of possible financial crimes filed by depository banks and their affiliates related to mortgage fraud, which grew 20-fold between 1996 and 2005, and then more than doubled again between 2005 and 2009. One study places the losses resulting from fraud on mortgage loans made between 2005 and 2007 at $112 billion.

Lenders made loans that they knew borrowers could not afford and that could cause massive losses to investors in mortgage securities. Countrywide executives, for example, recognized that many of the loans they were originating could result in *"catastrophic consequences."* Less than a year later, they noted that certain high-risk loans they were making could result not only in foreclosures but also in "financial and reputational catastrophe" for the firm. But they did not stop.

The report shows that major financial institutions ineffectively sampled loans they were purchasing to package and sell to investors. They knew a significant percentage of the sampled loans did not meet their own underwriting standards or those of the originators. Nonetheless, they sold those securities to investors.

It would be easy to pin the crisis on flaws like greed and hubris, which would be too simplistic. It was the failure to account for human weakness that is relevant to this crisis. The crisis was a result of human mistakes, misjudgments, and misdeeds that resulted in systemic failures. However, the breadth of this crisis does not mean that "everyone is at fault"; many firms and individuals did not participate in the excesses that initiated this monumental ClusterPhuck.

Conclusion Seven: The Collapsing Mortgage-Lending Standards & Securitization

When housing prices fell and mortgage borrowers defaulted, Wall Street began to feel the collapse. Many mortgage lenders set the bar so low that lenders simply took eager borrowers' qualifications on faith, often with a willful disregard for a borrower's ability to pay.

Nearly one-quarter of all mortgages made in the first half of 2005 were interest only loans. During the same year, 68% of "option ARM" (adjustable-rate mortgage), loans originated by Countrywide and Washington Mutual had low, or no documentation requirements.

As irresponsible lending, including predatory and fraudulent practices, became more prevalent, the Federal Reserve and other regulators and authorities heard warnings but the Federal Reserve neglected its mission. The Office of the Comptroller of the Currency and the Office of Thrift Supervision, caught up in turf wars, preempted state regulators from reining in abuses.

Globally, investors were eager to put their cash into newly created mortgage-related securities. It appeared to financial institutions, investors, and regulators alike that the risk associated with these securities had been eliminated. Investors believed that they held highly rated securities they thought were sure to perform; the banks thought they had taken the riskiest loans off their books; and regulators saw firms making profits and borrowing costs reduced. But each step in the mortgage securitization pipeline depended on the next step to keep demand going.

One of the key things to remember is that everyone involved believed they could off-load their risks on a moment's notice to the next person in line. Obviously, they were wrong. When borrowers stopped making mortgage payments, the losses rushed through the pipeline. Unfortunately, these losses were concentrated in a set of systemically important financial institutions.

Conclusion Eight: Over-The-Counter Derivatives

The enactment of legislation in 2000 to ban the regulation by both the federal and state governments of over-the-counter (OTC) derivatives, was a key turning point in the march toward the financial crisis. The advantages of OTC derivatives over exchange-traded ones are mainly the lower fees and taxes, and greater freedom of negotiation and customization of a transaction, as it involves only a seller and a buyer and no standardization authority.

From financial firms to corporations, to farmers, and to investors, derivatives have been used to hedge against, or speculate on, changes in prices, rates, or indices or even on events such as the potential defaults on debts. Yet, without any oversight, OTC derivatives rapidly spiraled out of control and out of sight, growing to $673 trillion in notional amount.

These OTC derivatives contributed to the crisis in three significant ways:

1. **Credit Default Swaps** (CDS), which were fueling the mortgage securitization pipeline. CDS were sold to investors to protect against the default or decline in value of mortgage-related securities backed by risky loans. Companies sold protection to the tune of $79 billion.
2. CDS were essential to the creation of synthetic CDOs. These synthetic CDOs were merely bets on the performance of real mortgage-related securities. They amplified the losses from the collapse of the housing bubble by allowing multiple bets on the same securities and helped spread them throughout the financial system.

3. When the housing bubble burst and crisis followed, derivatives were in the center of the cluster. AIG, which had <u>NOT</u> been required to put aside capital reserves as a cushion for the protection it was selling, was bailed out when it could not meet its obligations. The government ultimately committed more than $180 billion because of concerns that AIG's collapse would trigger cascading losses throughout the global financial system. Further, the existence of millions of derivatives contracts of all types between systemically important financial institutions which were "unseen and unknown in this unregulated market", added to uncertainty and escalated panic.

Conclusion #9: Failure of Credit Rating Agencies

The three credit rating agencies were key enablers of the financial meltdown. The mortgage-related securities at the heart of the crisis could not have been marketed and sold without their seal of approval. Investors blindly relied on them. In some cases, they were obligated to use them, or regulatory capital standards were hinged on them. **This crisis could not have happened without the rating agencies.**

Try to grasp this...Moody's credit rating agency, rated nearly 45,000 mortgage-related securities as triple-A. This compares with six private-sector companies in the United States that carried this coveted rating in early 2010. In 2006 alone, Moody's put its triple-A stamp of approval on 30 mortgage-related securities every working day. The results were disastrous: **83% of the mortgage securities rated triple-A that year ultimately were downgraded.**

Moody's was under pressure from the financial firms that paid for their ratings, and their own drive to increase market share. Couple this with the lack of resources to do the job despite record profits, and the absence of meaningful public oversight, and you can see how they enabled this ClusterPhuck to grow out of control. Without the active participation of the rating agencies, the market for mortgage-related securities could not have been what it became.

For decades, government policy encouraged homeownership through a set of incentives, assistance programs, and mandates. These policies were put in place and promoted by several administrations and Congress. Both Presidents Bill Clinton and George W. Bush set aggressive goals to increase homeownership. The Community Reinvestment Act (CRA), was enacted in 1977 to combat "redlining" by banks, which is the practice of denying credit to individuals and businesses in certain neighborhoods without regard to their creditworthiness.

Although the Commission concluded the CRA was not a significant factor in subprime lending or the crisis, they did believe that the government failed to ensure that the philosophy of opportunity was being matched by the practical realities on the ground. What the Commission was trying to point out was that the Federal Reserve and other regulators failed to rein in irresponsible lending even when the financial disaster was well on its way to becoming a reality.

Of course, the Commission found that there were *"...dramatic breakdowns of corporate governance, profound lapses in regulatory oversight, and near fatal flaws in our financial system."* There were a series of choices and actions led to this catastrophe ClusterPhuck for which we were ill prepared to deal with.

The Commission report was published in 2011 after several months of collecting a tremendous amount of information. There were those out there that had competing views with the report, but some high-profile players are admitting they made mistakes, while others are paying a heavy price for their role in this **Multi-Faceted ClusterPhuck**.

Executive Bad Behavior & Consequences

According to the report "CEO Pay and the Great Recession", chief executive officers of the 50 firms that laid off the most workers since the start of the economic crisis earned nearly $12 million on average in 2009. By the way, that was 42 percent more than the average pay of CEOs at S&P 500 firms as a whole.

Fred Hassan of Schering-Plough was the highest paid layoff king, earning $50 million in 2009 while his firm merged with Merck and cut 16,000 workers. Interestingly, 72 percent of the firms that announced mass layoffs, also delivered positive earnings reports. Although massive layoffs cut costs and boost short-term profits, it is also bad for business over the long-term because it impacts worker morale, which can lead to lower productivity and even worse, an employee's motivation to create an internal ClusterPhuck through sabotage.

An employee of a telecommunications company, when asked to resign, responded by sabotaging company IT systems, shutting down their telecommunication system and blocking 911 services in four major cities. A disgruntled former employee, upset that he was not hired for a full-time position, remotely accessed the **Supervisory Control and Data Acquisition** or SCADA systems, for a sewage treatment plant and caused over 200,000 gallons of raw sewage to spill into nearby rivers and businesses.

Both of these cases show the devastating impact insider sabotage can have on an organization and society in general. A 2011 survey revealed that 43% of participating organizations had experienced at least one insider incident during the past year. A study also found that organizational and individual stressors also play a role in espionage and sabotage. Stressors, such as changes in management, pay cuts, and perceived variations in justice, has been linked to cases of sabotage.

By the way, perceived injustice, according to the study, is the most common cause of sabotage.

A recent joint study, which included the U.S. Secret Service, examined 49 cases of malicious insiders in critical infrastructure sectors within the United States. The research resulted in the discovery of some commonalities between cases including:

- Insider's actions were often preceded by a negative-workplace event, with revenge being the most frequently reported motive.
- A majority of insiders planned their activities in advance, and more than a quarter of the time others had information about their plans.
- A majority of insiders held technical positions.
- Most insiders acted out in a concerning manner in the workplace.
- Insider attacks often were carried out through compromised computer accounts, unauthorized back doors, or shared user accounts.
- A majority of insiders used remote access to carry out attacks, often outside of normal working hours.

The research also focused on modeling the insider's attack, including acquiring unknown access paths as part of attack setup and attack escalation as insider disgruntlement increases. A collaborative effort was formed to first develop a model of espionage and then compare it to the insider IT sabotage model. The analysis yielded the following findings:

- Most saboteurs and spies had common personal predispositions that contributed to their risk of committing malicious acts.
- In most cases, stressful events, including organizational sanctions, contributed to the likelihood of insider IT sabotage and espionage.
- Concerning behaviors were often observable before and during insider IT sabotage and espionage.
- Technical actions by many insiders could have alerted the organization to planned or ongoing malicious acts.
- In many cases, organizations ignored or failed to detect rule violations.
- Lack of physical and electronic access controls facilitated both IT sabotage and espionage.

As you can clearly see there are always warning signs, which again shows us that there is a need for Red Flag leaders. Unfortunately, there is really no dominant segment of the population that is more inclined to lead stupidly and cause a ClusterPhuck, which makes it hard to focus on a particular segment within our society.

An individual's occupation, color of your skin, gender, education, religion, and whether you are rich or poor, is irrelevant. Many of us grew up believing that policemen, politicians, firemen, doctors, lawyers, teachers, and scientists were above reproach. Nevertheless, there are ClusterPhuck creating individuals within the most respected occupations.

And don't for one minute think that the financial crisis that began in 2008 won't happen again. The fact is, we never learn out lesson when it comes to money and greed.

Here We Phucking Go Again

Margin Call is a 2011 movie that takes place over a 24-hour period at a large Wall Street investment bank during the initial stages of the financial crisis of 2007–08 you just read about. It focuses on the actions taken by the top leadership group during the ensuing financial collapse.

Through the night, they have meetings with division head Jared Cohen (Simon Baker), chief risk management officer Sarah Robertson (Demi Moore), and finally CEO John Tuld (Jeremy Irons). Cohen's plan is for the firm to quickly dump all of the toxic assets in a fire sale before the market learns of their worthlessness, thereby limiting the firm's exposure, a plan favored by CEO Tuld.

Sam Rogers (Kevin Spacey), is Head of Sales and Trading and protests that dumping the firm's toxic assets will spread the risk throughout the financial sector and destroy the firm's relationships with its counterparties. He also warns Cohen that their customers will quickly learn of the firm's plans once they realize that the firm is only selling the toxic securities, but is not buying any new ones.

The firm ends of selling the vast majority of their toxic assets. Rogers is feeling bad when he sits down with CEO Tuld in the executive dining room and states, "I just don't know how we fucked this up quite so much."

The response by the CEO is as follows:

"So you think we might have put a few people out of business today. That it's all for naught. You've been doing that every day for almost forty years, Sam. And if this is all for naught then so is everything out there. It's just money; it's made up. Pieces of paper with pictures on it so we don't have to kill each other just to get something to eat. It's not wrong. And it's

certainly no different today than its ever been. 1637, 1797, 1819, 37, 57, 84, 1901, 07, 29, 1937, 1974, 1987 - Jesus, didn't that fucker fuck me up good - 92, 97, 2000 and whatever we want to call this. It's all just the same thing over and over; we can't help ourselves. And you and I can't control it or stop it, or even slow it, or even ever-so-slightly alter it. We just react. And we make a lot of money if we get it right. And we get left by the side of the road if we get it wrong. And there have always been and there always will be the same percentage of winners and losers, happy fuckers and sad suckers, fat cats and starving dogs in this world. Yeah, there may be more of us today than there's ever been. But the percentages-they stay exactly the same."

You may want to read that paragraph from CEO Tuld a few times. When he says that "we can't help ourselves", he is referring to the fact that we will continue to step into the same stupid trap over and over again. How do I know this? It is happening right now under our noses.

And away we go!

In March of 2018, The Senate passed extensive changes to several of the rules adopted in the wake of the 2008 financial crisis. The proposal is designed to provide relief to thousands of community banks and dozens of regional lenders. It will loosen regulations for mortgage lenders, expand access to free credit freezes for Americans and change rules for student loan defaults.

Sen. Sherrod Brown, the top Democrat on the banking panel stated:

"This legislation threatens to undo important rules protecting us from risk...This legislation again puts taxpayers on the hook for bailouts."

The measure would also shield more than two dozen banks from some Fed oversight under the 2010 Dodd-Frank regulatory law. Those banks would no longer be required to have plans to be safely dismantled if they fail. And they would have to take the Fed's bank health test only periodically, not once a year.

Some new consumer protections were also added to the bill including offering Americans free credit freezes and barring lenders from declaring a student loan in default when a co-signer dies or declares bankruptcy.

The nonpartisan Congressional Budget Office (CBO), weighed in with its take prior to the initial vote, and came to the conclusion that the bill, if passed, would increase the chances of **another 2008-style collapse**. The CBO stated, *"CBO's estimate of the bill's budgetary effect is subject to considerable uncertainty, in part because it depends on the probability in any year that a systemically* *important financial institution (SIFI) will fail or that there will be a financial crisis,"* before adding *"CBO estimates that the probability is small under current law and would be slightly greater under the legislation."*

*****

At its core this book is about leadership and decision making. However, some people hold non-leader positions within an organization that can cause massive ClusterPhucks, exposing the organization to great financial and reputational risks.

A **Whistleblower** *"...is a person who exposes misconduct, alleged dishonest or illegal activity occurring in an organization. The alleged misconduct may be classified in many ways; for example, a violation of a law, rule, regulation and/or a direct threat to public interest, such as fraud, health and safety violations, and corruption. Whistleblowers may make their allegations internally or externally."*

Ideas about whistleblowing vary widely. Whistleblowers are sometimes seen as selfless martyrs for public interest and organizational accountability; others view them as traitors or defectors, solely pursuing personal glory and fame. It kind of reminds me of the controversy surrounding the definition of terrorism.

The difficulty in defining terrorism is in agreeing on a basis for determining when the use of violence (directed at whom, by whom, for what ends) is legitimate; therefore, the modern definition of terrorism is inherently controversial, like who is or isn't a true whistleblower.

Perhaps you remember former tobacco company executive Jeffrey Wigard who on the news show *"60 Minutes"* claimed, rightfully, that cigarette companies were packing their products with addictive levels of nicotine. Hundreds of thousands of people die each year due to tobacco related products. Wigard, at great personal and professional risk, did indeed raise the Red Flag. Interesting how tobacco products are still on the market though.

For every Wigard, there is also a Linda Tripp. The former White House staff member was a key figure in the Monica Lewinsky scandal that led to an attempt to remove President Bill Clinton from office during his second term. Tripp taped twenty-two hours of phone conversations between her and friend and colleague, Monica Lewinsky, and was about to write a behind the scenes book about the White House. She portrayed herself as trying to be honest, even though she reportedly lied on a security clearance form for the Pentagon.

A poll taken by the Wall Street Journal/NBC News during that time showed that 75% believed Tripp was wrong to tape conversations with Monica Lewinsky, while 70% called her motives either political or mercenary. It would be difficult for me to classify her as a legitimate whistleblower, but a small majority do categorize her as being exactly that. Regardless as to whether you believe Tripp was right or wrong, former banker Bradley C. Birkenfeld could make you rethink the rules governing whistleblowers.

Birkenfeld, served two and a half years in prison for conspiring with a wealthy California developer to evade income taxes. However, the information he provided was so helpful he received a $104 million whistleblower award for revealing the secrets of the Swiss banking system. By divulging the schemes that UBS used to encourage American citizens to dodge their taxes, Mr. Birkenfeld's help led to an investigation that has greatly diminished Switzerland's status as a secret haven for American tax swindlers, and allowed the Treasury to recover billions in unpaid taxes.

During the investigation, Mr. Birkenfeld was charged with fraud for withholding crucial information from federal investigators, which led to his prison sentence. Some federal officials have urged the I.R.S. to invoke a rule that allows them to deny an award to informants who withhold information or engage in illegal activity.

Some officials, however, felt that such a move might scare off potential whistleblowers if Birkenfeld ended up empty-handed, with nothing more to show for his efforts than a criminal record. Empty handed? The stupidity of giving a criminal $104 million is outrages. Who negotiated this deal anyway? I am willing to bet, given the circumstances, he would have settled for $10 million…or less.

In May of 2013, Edward Snowden created one of the biggest ClusterPhucks in American history when he disclosed classified details of several top-secret United States and British government mass surveillance programs to the press. As a computer specialist, and former Central Intelligence Agency (CIA) employee and National Security Agency (NSA) contractor, Snowden had access to material that some have deemed the most significant leak in US history.

As Snowden remains in asylum in Russia, defense contractors and government officials have been taking steps to ensure that an incident of this magnitude does not happen again. Did leadership officials miss warning signs that could have prevented the leaks?

When Snowden was preparing to leave Geneva, and a job as a CIA technician in 2009, his supervisor wrote a derogatory report in his personnel file, noting a distinct change in the young man's behavior and work habits. The CIA suspected that Mr. Snowden was trying to break into classified computer files to which he was not authorized to have access, and decided to send him home. The supervisor's concerns and the NSA's suspicions apparently were not forwarded to the NSA or its contractors, and surfaced only after federal investigators began investigating Mr. Snowden.

Although many believe Mr. Snowden should receive "whistleblower" status for his role in uncovering the NSAs spying program, it is not that simple. Snowden deliberately tried to break into classified files. What if Snowden worked for a major defense contractor that was bidding on a multi-billion dollar contract, but he was upset with some of the weapons systems that were deployed around the world and stole his corporations bidding numbers and passed them along to one of their competitors...would you grant him whistleblower status? An employee's fate is largely tied to how many contracts the company has in the "que". Losing a multi-billion dollar contract could mean a substantial amount of layoffs.

In May of 2014, Snowden, in an NBC news interview, claimed that he was "...trained as a spy in sort of the traditional sense of the word -- in that I lived and worked undercover, overseas, pretending to work in a job that I'm not -- and even being assigned a name that was not mine."

Whether you believe a person is a legitimate whistleblower or someone that needlessly or selfishly initiated a ClusterPhuck is probably a decision that you would make on a case-by-case basis. For example, the **Editorial Board of the New York Times** came out in support of Mr. Snowden's actions, and considers him a legitimate whistleblower. They point out that two federal judges have accused the NSA of violating the Constitution, along with a panel appointed by President Obama, which called for a major overhaul of its operations.

The Board's position is that the abuses Snowden exposed was a *"great service"* to the United States and that he should face *"...reduced punishment in light of his role as a whistle-blower, and have the hope of a life advocating for greater privacy and far stronger oversight of the runaway intelligence community."*

The Board goes on to state that *"Mr. Snowden was clearly justified in believing that the only way to blow the whistle on this kind of intelligence-gathering was to expose it to the public and let the resulting furor do the work his superiors would not."*

The Board also listed *"...just a few of the violations he revealed or the legal actions he provoked"*, which were:

- The NSA broke federal privacy laws, or exceeded its authority, thousands of times per year, according to the agency's own internal auditor.

- The agency broke into the communications links of major data centers around the world, allowing it to spy on hundreds of millions of user accounts and infuriating the Internet companies that own the centers. Many of those companies are now scrambling to install systems that the NSA cannot yet penetrate.

- The NSA systematically undermined the basic encryption systems of the Internet, making it impossible to know if sensitive banking or medical data is truly private, damaging businesses that depended on this trust.

- His leaks revealed that James Clapper Jr., the director of national intelligence, lied to Congress when testifying in March that the NSA was not collecting data on millions of Americans. (There has been no discussion of punishment for that lie.)

- The Foreign Intelligence Surveillance Court rebuked the NSA for repeatedly providing misleading information about its surveillance practices, according to a ruling made public because of the Snowden documents. One of the practices violated the Constitution, according to the chief judge of the court.

- A federal district judge ruled earlier this month that the phone-records-collection program probably violates the Fourth Amendment of the Constitution. He called the program "almost Orwellian" and said there was no evidence that it stopped any imminent act of terror.

Former US Attorney General Eric Holder stated that Snowden performed a "public service" by initiating a debate over surveillance techniques, but he still must pay for illegally leaking classified intelligence documents. What if Snowden's actions resulted in the death of an undercover agent? Perhaps it's my background in intelligence, anti-terrorism, risk management, and even military recruiting, that won't allow me to quite get my head around as to why Snowden chose Russia…the country that attacked our 2016 Presidential Elections, as his place to hide from prosecution.

Some of you may argue that Snowden landed in Moscow in June in 2013, and knew little, if anything, about Russia's coordinated attack on the Presidential Elections. That being said, Snowden's stay in Russia was supposed to be temporary. However, in January of 2017, Snowden applied for, as was granted, an extension to remain in Russia until 2020. Can we be absolutely sure that he wasn't influenced by some Russian operative?

By the way, these are the countries that currently have no extradition treaty with the United States:

Afghanistan, Algeria, Andorra, Angola, Armenia, Bahrain, Bangladesh, Belarus, Bosnia and Herzegovina, Brunei, Burkina Faso, Burma, Burundi, Cambodia, Cameroon, Cape Verde, the Central African Republic, Chad, Mainland China, Comoros, Congo (Kinshasa), Congo (Brazzaville), Djibouti, Equatorial Guinea, Eritrea, Ethiopia, Gabon, Guinea, Guinea-Bissau, Indonesia, Ivory Coast, Kazakhstan, Kosovo, Kuwait, Laos, Lebanon, Libya, Macedonia, Madagascar, Maldives, Mali, Marshall Islands, Mauritania, Micronesia, Moldova, Mongolia, Montenegro, Morocco, Mozambique, Namibia, Nepal, Niger, Oman, Qatar, Russia, Rwanda, Samoa, São Tomé & Príncipe, Saudi Arabia, Senegal, Serbia, Somalia, Sudan, Syria, Togo, Tunisia, Uganda, Ukraine, United Arab Emirates, Uzbekistan, Vanuatu, Vatican, Vietnam and Yemen.

Snowden chose **Russia**...AND, by the way...who is paying his bills in Russia?

To Blow or Not to Blow the Whistle

Many people do not consider blowing the whistle not just because of fear of retaliation, but also because of fear of losing their relationships at work and outside work. It can be even more difficult to come forward when you are a high-ranking executive that may find it challenging to find another high paying position in the future. Sherron Watkins, for example, was Vice President of Corporate Development at a corporation called **Enron**.

Enron was an American energy, commodities, and services company based in Houston, Texas. Before its bankruptcy in 2001, Enron employed approximately 20,000 people and was one of the world's major electricity, natural gas, communications, pulp and paper companies, that claimed revenues of nearly $101 billion during 2000. They were named "America's Most Innovative Company" for six consecutive years by Fortune Magazine.

By 2001, it was revealed that their reported financial condition was sustained substantially by a *"...institutionalized, systematic, and creatively planned accounting fraud."* The scandal also brought into question the accounting practices and activities of many corporations in the United States and was a factor in the creation of the Sarbanes–Oxley Act of 2002, which was enacted as a reaction to a number of major corporate and accounting scandals.

In August 2001, Watkins did alert then Enron CEO Kenneth Lay of accounting irregularities in financial reports. However, she was criticized for not reporting the fraud to government authorities and not speaking up publicly sooner about her concerns, as her memo did not reach the public until five months after it was written.

Whether you are an employee in academia, business or government, internal policies might pose threats of retaliation to those who report fraud. Private company employees in particular might be at risk of being fired, demoted, denied raises, and so on for bringing risks to the attention of appropriate authorities.

Government employees could be at a similar risk for bringing threats to health or the environment to the public's attention. Given the pressure associated with coming forward, is it really all that surprising that Ms. Watkins waited?

Cynthia Cooper served as the Vice President of Internal Audit at WorldCom. In 2002, Cooper and her team of auditors worked together in secret to investigate and unearth $3.8 billion in fraud at WorldCom. At the time, this was the largest incident of accounting fraud in U.S. history. Their discoveries sent WorldCom into bankruptcy, left thousands of their colleagues without jobs, and shook the stock market. As she pursued the trail of fraud, Ms. Cooper was obstructed by fellow employees, some of whom disapproved of WorldCom's accounting methods but were unwilling to contradict their bosses or impede the company's goals.

It was clear to Ms. Cooper's team that their findings would be devastating for WorldCom. They were also very concerned that they would be fired if their superiors found out what they were up to prior to going before the board with their evidence. There was a concern about whether their findings would result in layoffs and they obsessed about whether they were jumping to unwarranted conclusions and that they would somehow end up being blamed for this ClusterPhuck.

Although whistleblowers are often protected under law from employer retaliation, there have been many cases where punishment for whistleblowing has occurred, such as termination, suspension, demotion, wage garnishment, and harsh mistreatment by other employees, which are of course a very legitimate concern.

In the United States, most whistleblower protection laws provide for limited *"make whole"* remedies or damages for employment losses if whistleblower retaliation is proven, which really does not guarantee that the harassment will end. Meaning, not all whistleblowers are seen as heroes.

***

Chapter 4

Presidential Leadership & The Oval Office

In the book, The Presidents Club, authors Nancy Gibbs and Michael Duffy write:

"Every president enters office determined to turn the page. Kennedy couldn't wait to toss out Eisenhower's military management style for a more supple and activist approach. Ford practiced radical normalcy, in order to send the clearest possible signal that the dark age of Nixon was over. Clinton wanted to prove that he was not the second coming of Jimmy Carter; George W. Bush was all about not being Clinton; Barack Obama was about not being either of them."

They go on to write:

A senior advisor to three presidents recalls watching the revelation unfold, as talented, confident men realize what they've gotten themselves into. "When you get in, you discover nothing is what you expect, or believed, or have been told, or have campaigned on....it's much more complicated. Your first reaction is: I've been set up. Second is: I have to think differently. Third is: Maybe they all had it right. And it isn't long before they ask, who am I going to talk to about this?"

I will go out on a limb here and say that most people in the United States believe that the President of the United States of America has the toughest job in the country, if not the world. At any given time there is the distinct possibility that 60 million people, and that's just in the United States, could hate you for a decision you made for what you thought, at the time, was for the greater good of the country.

Perhaps you heard that the President is the most powerful man in the world. I always wondered what that was based on. Apparently, having the world's best economy and the most powerful military in the world under your control gives you the right to that title.

That being said, as President, the chances of you NOT creating, or at the very least, being part of a ClusterPhuck is ZERO...regardless of the leadership actions you take, or fail to take. That is why the President, like a corporate CEO, must employ a 3D leadership mentality.

The 3D Chess Leadership Mentality

Three-Dimensional Chess (or 3D chess) refers to any of various chess variants that use multiple boards at different levels, allowing the chess pieces to move in three physical dimensions. Three-dimensional variants have existed since the late

19th century, one of the oldest being Raumschach, which was invented in 1907 by Dr. Ferdinand Maack and is considered the classic 3D game.

Those of you that are fans of the old TV series **Star Trek,** or currently **The Big Bang Theory**, may have an idea of what the game is about. The inventor of the game believed that for chess to be more like modern warfare, attack should be possible not only from a two-dimensional plane but also from above (air), and below (underwater).

As President, you will be attacked by members of the opposite political party(s), and at times even from members of your own party. The media will report every word you say about every conceivable topic...every single day. Even if you don't say a word or tweet for an entire day, you will be talked about by **pundits** that support you or think you are way off target. Some will attack your patriotism, competence, citizenship, and of course your leadership style, which includes your decision making process and the actions you take. That being said, it is not that hard to initially run for the office for President.

The Low Cost To Enter The Fray

The barriers to entry to become a presidential candidate are low in the preliminary stage because all you need is money, which isn't so hard to find given Internet fundraising and the endless stream of rich patrons who funnel their wealth through "super" Political Action Committee's (PACs.) The more money that your campaign accumulates, the more media attention you receive, usually resulting in more money heading your way.

Perhaps you've wondered in the past why so many people, who have absolutely no chance of winning the presidency, run for the office anyway. There are those, of course, that believe they can be the next underdog to win like Jimmy Carter or Ronald Reagan. However, there are those who can find future opportunities that include lucrative jobs, retainers, paid speeches or book advances. There are others that may realize that their chances of winning are slim, but run to bring attention to a particular issue or ideology.

Former Arkansas Governor Mike Huckabee who had an unsuccessful bid for the Republican nomination, has parlayed that into his own show on the Fox network. There are a huge list of others that seem to show up as contributors or on panels frequently on CNN, MSNBC, Fox, and other networks.

Former Speaker of the House Newt Gingrich, who did run for president in 2012, cashed in on Donald Trump's popularity. His speaking agency, Worldwide Speakers Group, sent out a notice with the subject line "Newt Gingrich Fee Increase." The email went on to say, "Few people in the world have as much insight into President-elect Trump's philosophies, principles and objectives as Newt Gingrich.

As the senior voice in the Republican Party and advisor to the new Administration, Gingrich has been at the forefront of the Republican strategy for the last two years." If you wanted Gingrich's services during the 2016 campaign season, it would have cost you $25,000 plus ground transportation. For speeches east of Chicago, he was charging $60,000 plus first class travel for two. For speeches west of Chicago, he was reportedly asking $75,000 plus first class travel for two.

There is nothing wrong with Mr. Gingrich or any former presidential candidate positioning themselves for personal economic gain if it is legal. However, if you do end up winning, your life does not belong to you anymore.

A Demanding Life & Pace

The president's official day begins with the **President's Daily Brief**, which is a highly classified document prepared by the Director of National Intelligence (DNI). It provides the president with sensitive intelligence on international matters and events. The material is available to other very senior officials on a strictly need-to-know basis. It varies on how each President is briefed. President Obama, for example, was usually presented with 20 to 30 pages.

Typically, the president then moves into a series of meetings or events. This part of his day includes a briefing by one of his Cabinet officers or White House staff. He may also have meetings with White House staff and congressional leaders concerning the president's legislative strategy.

Most days also involve delivering remarks to one or more groups of citizens, which includes everything from a roundtable of educators on raising high school performance, to business people on American competitiveness, to thanking volunteers who responded to a natural disaster.

There are various press events in the schedule and prime time presidential press conferences. President Trump utilizes *Twitter* to deliver a quick message to the public on an individual issue or respond quickly to some positive or negative press story. Although many people thought that Trump would reduce his use of Twitter when he entered the oval office, they have been proven wrong.

The President also holds important events that includes meetings with foreign leaders, which may include hosting a state dinner.

The president's out-of-town schedule is usually demanding as well. It runs the gamut from official visits to important allied countries, to participation in international meetings such as the United Nations General Assembly each fall, to political events in key states.

Imagine a day in which the president must deal with an intelligence report of a planned terrorist attack, a crisis in the Middle East, dire financial news from Europe, a domestic hot-button issue like healthcare legislation, looming budget and national debt issues, and his own personal scandals that reach the news media.

A President is therefore expected to lead pretty much the entire day. President Obama revealed that at times he made "hundreds" of decisions a day. When a reporter asked him why he has to make so many decisions when he has people leading departments, his answer was that the decisions he makes are the ones ONLY the president can make. It stands to reason that the more decisions you make the higher the probability that some will lead to a ClusterPhuck or two.

Persian Gulf War: Multiple Leadership Styles in Play

Years before being forcibly removed from office, Iraqi leader Saddam Hussein ordered the invasion and occupation of neighboring Kuwait in early August in 1990. Arab powers such as Saudi Arabia and Egypt called on the United States and other Western nations to intervene. At this point in time President H.W. Bush had to convince the American people that he would have to send their sons, daughters, husbands and wives to war. Additionally, Bush turned to Congress for congressional authorization even though some in the administration argued that it was unnecessary.

Charismatic Leadership is required, or at least is more appropriate, in situations that require a combination of highly involved active leadership plus an emotional commitment and extraordinary effort by both leader and followers in pursuit of ideological goals. This was one of those situations, and President Bush utilized it effectively. However, that wasn't the only leadership style Bush used prior to, during, and after the war.

The Arab countries that called for help from the Western nations initially misread Hussein's intentions. The Bush administration was concerned at the prospect of Iraq controlling Kuwait's oil resources and immediately began to assemble a coalition to oppose Iraq. President Bush utilized the Shared/Distributed, Strategic, and Pragmatic Leadership styles during this phase of the planning.

The **Shared/Distributed leadership** is mostly relevant for teams, like the 35 country coalition, where individual members exercise leadership influence based on their expertise to meet shared goals and objectives, which in this case was two-fold. The Arab countries wanted the Iraqi forces out of Kuwait, but at the same time they wanted to send a message that if Hussein attempted an invasion of other Arab countries he would be met with the same kind of resistance.

President Bush also utilized the **Pragmatic Leadership** style, which requires a "deep knowledge of the social fabric of the relevant parties" who have a stake in the problems (Arab countries), and the economic (oil production), and technical issues (command and control), associated with problems and their solutions.

This style of leadership problem-solving approach is believed to require a greater degree of intelligence, critical thinking, judgment, wisdom and expertise. It can be argued that President Bush's background played a vital role in his decision making process and professional experiences, which includes:

- U.S. Congressman
- Ambassador to the United Nations
- Ambassador to the People's Republic of China
- Chairman of the Republican National Committee
- Director of Central Intelligence.
- Vice President of the United States

President Bush also had to employ his **Strategic and Operational Leadership** traits as well for several reasons. The coalition leaders intended for the war to be fought on a limited basis, and at minimum cost. If the objectives and goals failed, the fallout would fall squarely on the shoulders of President Bush. A Gulf War analysis revealed that Bush's decision to execute the plan was daring, considering the sheer size of the force to be deployed.

Strategic Leadership is concerned with defining the overall vision and mission, which was getting the Iraqi forces out of Kuwait. In order to achieve the mission strategies, systems, and structures must be developed. From an **Operational Leadership** perspective, leaders must ensure that that organizational processes are effectively carried out on a day-to-day basis, performance is monitored, constraints are addressed, and that all stakeholders understand what is to be done and are provided with the necessary resources.

President Bush and his military commanders understood that the United States had a number of exposed deficiencies. The success of the plan once put into action emphasized the value of detailed, deliberate planning. Nearly all situations encountered throughout Operation DESERT SHIELD were addressed during the deliberate planning process and gaming of the plan. As a result, options for solving those deficiencies were well thought through.

President Bush decided to suspend offensive operations as the first step to a negotiated cease-fire and resolution of the crisis. The basis for the decision to suspend offensive operations was the coalition leaders' desire to limit friendly casualties and conduct the operations guided by the principle of "proportional use of force".

Throughout the operation the political goals of the coalition remained paramount. As the national, coalition, and theater strategies shifted, the campaign plan adapted to insure that military action could properly support those political goals.

Although that decision would have lasting effects for years to come, both in the Persian Gulf region and around the world, there were good reasons not to advance.

Catastrophic ClusterPhuck Avoidance

Cost Avoidance is defined as "Action taken to reduce future costs, such as replacing parts before they fail and cause damage to other parts. Cost avoidance may incur higher (or additional) costs in the short run but the final or life cycle cost would be lower." When at all possible, it is best to avoid a ClusterPhuck because of the enormous costs involved. President Bush and the coalition was criticized in the years to come because they did not take Hussein out of power when it was perceived that they had the opportunity.

However, some experts, including those in the Bush Administration, argued that if U.S. forces moved north toward Baghdad, they would have had to trudge through more than 200 miles of heavily populated agricultural and urban lands. They would also have been faced with bitter, house-to-house fighting in a country larger than South Vietnam. It was also thought that those Iraqis who may have had the stomach to fight to maintain their country's conquest of Kuwait would have been far more willing to sacrifice themselves to resist a foreign invader.

Further, the UN Security Council had authorized member states to use military power to enforce its resolutions demanding an Iraqi withdrawal from occupied Kuwait. There **was no authorization** to invade Iraq. The U.S., by basic tenets of international law, and in the eyes of the international community, would have become the aggressor.

The broad coalition of nations so diligently put together by President George Bush would have fallen apart. Foreign ministers and other government officials of the Arab Gulf monarchies following the war indicated absolutely **no support** for carrying the war any further. There was already a strong sense that the U.S. had inflicted unnecessary damage on Iraq's civilian infrastructure with serious humanitarian consequences, going well beyond what was necessary to rid Iraqi forces from Kuwait.

The Iraq War & Flawed Decision Making

In 2002, President George W. Bush sponsored a new U.N. resolution calling for the return of weapons inspectors to Iraq; U.N. inspectors reentered Iraq that November. Amid differences between Security Council member states over how well Iraq had complied with those inspections, the United States and Britain began amassing forces on Iraq's border. Bush, without U.N. approval, issued an ultimatum demanding that Saddam Hussein step down from power and leave Iraq within 48 hours. Hussein refused, and the second Persian Gulf War, more generally known as the Iraq War, began three days later.

From the very beginning, Vice President Cheney felt that Saddam Hussein was involved in the 9/11 attacks. Secretary of Defense Rumsfeld and his principal deputy, Paul D. Wolfowitz, a "hard right" ideologue and Bush appointee, had argued for military action against Iraq. In the early meetings, Rumsfeld put the question: "Why shouldn't we go against Iraq, not just Al Qaeda?"

Before the attacks, the Pentagon had been working for months on developing a military option for Iraq. Everyone at the table believed Saddam Hussein was dangerous, and bent on acquiring and possibly using weapons of mass destruction. Any serious full-scale war against terrorism, they believed, would have to make Iraq a target, if not now, eventually. Rumsfeld was raising the possibility that they could take advantage of the opportunity offered by the terrorist attacks to go after Saddam immediately.

Hindsight

Hindsight has been defined as the *"recognition of the realities, possibilities, or requirements of a situation, event, decision etc., after its occurrence."*

114

The Bush Administration wanted a regime change in Iraq, presumably to create a state that would be stable and legitimate, yet also friendly to the United States. Many argue, however, that the particular way the Bush administration went about regime change, increased the chances of failure.

The administration had to legitimize war on a state that did not threaten the US. The issue of WMDs (Weapons of Mass Destruction), was hit upon as a way to turn the 'war on terrorism' against Iraq; to do so, Bush had to claim that Saddam Hussein was linked to al-Qaida and was actively developing weapons of mass destruction which he might turn over to terrorists or use on their behalf, and hence that Iraq represented an imminent threat to the US.

Gulf security experts strongly believed that the US made "multiple strategic mistakes". For example, they only planned to fight-against a **debilitated** Iraq army, not against a prolonged insurgency. They expected a quick painless war, and went in "undermanned and under-resourced", expecting to eliminate the top layer of leadership, take control of a functioning state, install imported pro-Western exiles, and be out by six weeks.

Additionally, Secretary of Defense Donald Rumsfeld brushed aside the recommendations of his generals that 400,000 troops would be needed for the occupation and forced them to accept a fraction of that. He stated, "You go to war with the Army you have. They're not the Army you might want or wish to have at a later time."

US proconsul Paul Bremer, according to experts, worsened the situation through his dissolution of the Iraqi army, creating tens of thousands of experienced and armed fighters that would join the resistance. Baghdad has a population of 7.6 million people. New York City has a population of 8.5 million people. There are 40,000 police officers in New York City alone. Imagine if there was an invasion of New York City and the entire police force was fired. Do you really think that those former highly-skilled officers would sit on the sidelines while the city was being invaded?

Former General and Secretary of State Colin Powell stated, "My own personal belief was, after taking Baghdad, we made terrible strategic mistakes", and, pointing in particular to the disbanding of the Iraqi army, stated, "I think the execution of the operation was flawed, badly flawed."

Backlash against the war increased after it was revealed that the decision to invade was based on faulty intelligence on the existence of weapons of mass destruction in Iraq. Powell also stated, ***"If we had known the intelligence was wrong, we would not have gone into Iraq. But the intelligence community, all 16 agencies, assured us that it was right."***

Powell also noted that, at the time, public and political opinion was unified in support of the invasion, and that nearly every member of Congress voted in support of invading. That may be true, but wasn't that support based on faulty intelligence? Furthermore, the George H.W. Bush Administration put together a strong coalition and successfully completed their mission of removing Iraqi forces out of Kuwait. George W. Bush and his team acted as if they never researched the reasons why it was unwise to invade Baghdad. How did so many bad leadership decisions occur?

Flawed Decisions Lead to Massive ClusterPhucks

There are two factors at play in a flawed decision. The individual or group who "made an error of judgment" and a "decision process that fails to correct the error." A bad decision also starts with at least one influential person making an error of judgment.

But, normally, the decision process will save the day. How? Facts will be brought to the table that challenge the flawed thinking, or people with different views will influence the outcome. So the second factor that contributes is the way the decision is managed. So, for whatever reason, as the decision is being discussed, the initial erroneous views are not exposed and corrected.

The brain can also be tricked into false judgments. There are four conditions under which flawed thinking is most likely to happen, which have been referred to as **"red flag conditions"**, because they provide a warning that, when these conditions exist, even an experienced decision maker may get it wrong. These conditions are:

1. **Misleading Experiences**: These are memories that seem similar to the situation we are facing, but are not. They are most likely to disrupt our thinking as we assess the situation, either because we misrecognize the pattern or because the emotion tagged to the pattern gives us an unsuitable action orientation.

2. **Misleading Pre-Judgments**: are previous decisions or judgments that mislead current judgments. They are most likely to create distortions when we evaluate outcomes. They cause us to get committed to the wrong plans. In addition, they can cause us to fixate on a particular plan

of action, often something that has worked in the past.

3. **Inappropriate Self-Interests**: are personal interests that conflict with the responsibilities we have for other stakeholders.

4. **Inappropriate Attachments**: are strong emotional feelings we have towards a group, place or possession that are inappropriate given the decision we are trying to make.

The "misleading experiences" with regards to the Iraq War, that it could very well be the relatively quick victory that occurred in the Gulf War, was wrong. The "Misleading Pre-Judgments", that the United States would be seen as liberators instead of invaders, was wrong. The US was warned by Middle East leaders and area experts that the war would have unpredictable, disastrous consequences for the Middle East.

Also, keep in mind that Rumsfeld, despite warnings from experienced Generals, believed that the war could be won with a smaller force than was actually needed to accomplish the mission. Additionally, as studies have demonstrated, the single most compelling generator of "terrorism" is foreign occupation. The key decision makers prejudged, wrongly, both strength requirements and the sustained resistance after the invasion.

One could argue that the invasion showed "inappropriate self-interests" in that the Bush Administration managed to alienate the publics of allied states, like Turkey, Jordan, Egypt and Saudi Arabia, in which America had invested over decades. If there is one underlying explanation for why US policy has produced results the opposite of what Washington intended, it is that military force, when lacking in legitimacy, stimulates resistance rather than compliance.

Lastly, "inappropriate attachments" can also lead to flawed decision making. The "emotional feelings" President Bush, and many others for that matter, was in part due to some of the atrocities Hussein was responsible for. In March of 1988, Iraqi jets dropped poison gas has on a town and an estimated 5,000 people, mostly women and children.

Additionally, in his speech in 2002 to the United Nations on Iraq, Bush mentioned the alleged plot to kill a former U.S. president but did not mention that it was his father. The alleged assassination attempt came when former President Bush visited Kuwait during the Clinton administration.

The Bush doctrine and the 2002 National Security Strategy was formulated in response to the 9/11 attacks on the United States. The strategy was geared towards a "preventive war" posture, rather than the traditional US foreign policy based on the containment of threats. It wasn't the only reason however. Reshaping the Middle East (Transformational Leadership), in order to protect oil reserves concentrated in the Persian Gulf, was also part of the strategy. Oil, of course, is a strategic commodity that everybody needs and is crucial to military power while assuring its flow to the world economy makes US power globally indispensable, but at what cost?

More than 4,486 American soldiers have died in the Iraq War, which like all wars, is expected. In the book "***The Three Trillion Dollar War: The True Cost of the Iraq Conflict***", the authors Bilmes and Stiglitz write:

*"**Combining past and future required expenditures, health and disability costs for veterans, and the expenditures hidden in the Defense Department budget, we estimate total expenditures for Iraq alone to be from $1.3 to $2 trillion-not counting interest payments. When we add the present discounted value of interest through 2017 alone, the total comes to $1.75 trillion for the best case scenario and $2.65 trillion for the more realistic one..."*

However...9/11

I awoke on the 11th of September, 2001 at the Tobyhanna Army Depot, about 20 or so minutes from Scranton, Pa. The only thing I had on my mind was heading to the Battalion Headquarters in Harrisburg, process out, and head straight to my next assignment in Brunswick, Maine. A few weeks earlier I dropped my family off in Michigan, at my in-laws, until I found housing at the new assignment.

As I entered the main office on the first floor of the building, there were soldiers staring at the television. Apparently, a plane had hit the World Trade Center in New York City. It had to be an accident, I thought. As it was driving towards my old office to tell the soldiers goodbye, a second plane hit. The radio announcer was saying that there was a plane headed, they believed, to the White House, Capital, or the Pentagon.

We didn't know how many planes, or guided missiles, were still in the air. A friend of mine who worked at the Pentagon was on the opposite side of the building, and revealed to me that he got knocked out of his seat when the plane hit. Several of the 125 people killed that day were friends of his. He told me he knew for a fact that a female soldier friend of his had to see the plane coming since her desk faced towards the window where the plane hit. My then Battalion Commander revealed that he had just gotten off the phone with a General at the Pentagon who agreed to be our guest speaker at our annual conference. The General was dead five minutes after he hung up with the Battalion Commander.

There was much confusion, disbelief, and anger as the next 24 hours unfolded. But what was President Bush thinking in the first few hours after the attack?

According to author Bob Woodward, as soon as Bush heard about the attack on the World Trade Towers, he stated, "I made up my mind at that moment we were going to war." The day after the attacks, Bush met with the press and stated, "The deliberate and deadly attacks which were carried out yesterday against our country were more than acts of terror. They were acts of war.... This will be a monumental struggle between good and evil. But good will prevail."

Crisis Leadership & ClusterPhuck Speed

The term *Crisis* has been described as "A low-probability, *high-impact* event that threatens the viability of the organization and is characterized by ambiguity of cause, effect, and means of resolution, as well as by a belief that decisions must be made swiftly."

Crisis Leadership can best be described as the "*actions taken by a leader* to bring about immediate change. The leader provides stability, reassurance, confidence, and a sense of control throughout the crisis."

Presidential Crisis Leadership

Whether you are the CEO of a major corporation or President of the United States, there are five core tasks that are expected of a leader from the outset of a crisis, which are:

1. Becoming centrally involved in figuring out what is going on.

2. Setting the direction about what to do.

3. Giving significance to what is happening.

4.　　　Declaring that the crisis along with its extraordinary dynamics is over, and an accounting begins.

5.　　　Trying to learn from what has happened so that the organization will adapt and respond better in the future.

The President of the United States will most likely be faced with a major crisis or two at some point during his or her time in office. Their goal is to stop or minimize the impact of the crisis before it truly becomes a major expanding ClusterPhuck. Public perception plays a vital role as to how the President's leadership is being perceived during the crisis. If the President fails to embrace the five core tasks above, it can tarnish his or her reputation long after they have left the oval office.

Hurricane Katrina

Hurricane Katrina hit the Gulf Coast on the morning of Monday, Aug. 29, 2005. It spread across 400 miles with sustained winds that reached as high as 125 mph. A storm surge rolled across levees and drainage canals, and led to widespread flooding and the displacement of hundreds of thousands of people from their homes in Louisiana, Mississippi and Alabama. The death toll was more than 1,000 people, and the damage was estimated at $100 billion.

The American people were shocked by the television images of Katrina's immediate aftermath. There were people standing on rooftops waving their arms and pleading for help as the flood waters inundated their communities. There were also people pleading for help in the football stadium (Superdome).

However, President Bush decided not to visit the devastated area right away, because, according to White House aides, he didn't want to cause disruptions in rescue and recovery efforts by diverting security and communications to himself. Bush allies did privately concede later that the President could have quickly visited somewhere along the Gulf Coast with minimal disruption, to show solidarity with victims of the hurricane and the first responders.

The optics couldn't have been worse for the President. At the time, 67 percent of New Orleans was African American and 30 percent of the residents were poor, creating the impression that the government was insensitive and neglectful of minorities and the less fortunate.

Bush decided to instead fly over the area in Air Force One. Regarding that decision, he would later write in his book Decision Points:

"That photo of me hovering over the damage suggested I was detached from the suffering on the ground. That was not how I felt. But once that impression was formed, I couldn't change it."

The polls were not kind to President Bush because of the way in which he handled the crisis. A Washington Post-ABC News survey found that his response to Katrina dragged down Bush's job approval rating in mid-September 2005 to 42 percent, which was the lowest of his presidency until that point, while 57 percent disapproved of his performance. Only 49 percent felt that Bush could be trusted in a crisis. Contrast that from a year earlier when 60 percent trusted him to effectively handle a crisis.

While all this was going on, the President continued a vacation at his 1,600-acre ranch in Crawford, Texas. When Katrina made landfall, Bush had been on vacation at his ranch for 27 days, which gave off the impression that he was not fully involved of what was happening.

At the time of the crisis, several countries around the world were offering their help with the crisis, but Bush declined. According to the 2004 National Response Plan:

"The Secretary of State is responsible for coordinating international prevention, preparedness, response, and recovery activities relating to domestic incidents, and for the protection of U.S. citizens and U.S. interests overseas."

At the time, Condoleezza Rice was the Secretary of State, who, like Bush, was also on vacation during the crisis.

She would later write in her book, **No Higher Honor**, *"I didn't think much about the dire warnings of an approaching hurricane called Katrina."* And, *"[I] sat there kicking myself for having been so tone-deaf...I wasn't just the secretary of State with responsibility for foreign affairs; I was the highest-ranking black in the administration and a key advisor to the president. What had I been thinking?"*

Her absence was significant because there were several countries offering to bring in resources to help support rescue efforts.

Some critics, for good reason, contend that President Bush and Secretary Rice displayed **Passive**, **Reactive**, and even **Callous** Leadership styles during the crisis. At the very least, they both lacked a great deal of situational awareness.

Bush supporters would later acknowledge that his slow reaction and the weak federal, state and local response to the hurricane, undermined his reputation for being an effective crisis manager and a decisive leader. His reputation never improved even though he later made repeated visits to the hurricane zone and steered billions of federal dollars into recovery programs.

Both Democrats and Republicans have been blasted over the past several years due to a lack of preparedness and adequate response with regards to Katrina. In 2006, The White House released a 228 page report titled, **The Federal Response to Hurricane Katrina Lessons Learned.** The report stated, among other things, that:

> *"An effective National Preparedness System requires that management and response personnel, especially those in the field, are well versed in their missions. At all levels of government, we must build a leadership corps that is fully educated, trained, and exercised in our plans and doctrine. Training is not nearly as costly as the mistakes made in a crisis. Equally important, this corps must be populated by leaders who are prepared to exhibit innovation and take the initiative during extremely trying circumstances."*

One has to wonder about this quote, especially the part stating how all levels of government *"…must build a leadership corps that is fully educated, trained, and exercised in our plans and doctrine."*

Apparently, leadership, education, and training was nonexistent at all levels within the US government prior to Katrina, and provides us with a pretty good explanation as to why this massive ClusterPhuck emerged.

Yes, the leadership surrounding the Hurricane Katrina had its challenges, but, as you will see, once you sit in that oval office chair, it is inevitable that you will face a crisis that will affect your reputation and legacy that will be examined, criticized, and studied for eternity.

The Near Miss Nuclear Confrontation

Beginning in 2017, the rhetoric between the United States and North Korea had ramped up to a fever pitch that some felt was on the path to a nuclear confrontation. However, the 13-day Cuban Missile Crisis was arguable far more serious. The pilot of an American U-2 spy plane making a high-altitude pass over Cuba on October 14, 1962, photographed a Soviet SS-4 medium-range ballistic missile being assembled for installation.

The missiles were capable of quickly reaching targets in the eastern U.S. If allowed to become operational, the missiles would fundamentally alter the complexion of the nuclear rivalry between the U.S. and the Soviet Union, which was led by Nikita Khrushchev. This was akin to the United States having a gun pointed an inch or two from their head. How much reaction time would you have to move away safely if the gunman decided to use the weapon? But why would Khrushchev take such an aggressive approach?

The Soviets, for good reason, were concerned about the number of nuclear weapons that were targeted at them from sites in Western Europe and Turkey. They viewed the deployment of missiles in Cuba as a way to level the playing field. Another key factor was the hostile relationship between the U.S. and Cuba. The Kennedy administration had already launched one failed attack on Cuba, known as the Bay of Pigs invasion, which was arguable the catalyst behind Khrushchev's move to place missiles in Cuba.

Bay of Pigs: When a Strategy Fails Miserably

On January 1, 1959, a young Cuban nationalist, Fidel Castro, drove his guerilla army into Havana and overthrew General Fulgencio Batista, the nation's American-backed president. For the next two years, officials at the U.S. State Department and the Central Intelligence Agency (CIA) attempted to remove Castro from power.

In April 1961, the CIA launched a full-scale invasion of Cuba by 1,400 American-trained Cubans who had fled their homes when Castro took over. However, the invasion failed, because they were badly outnumbered by Castro's troops. The CIA backed army surrendered after less than 24 hours of fighting. Why was Castro seen as such a threat to the United States?

Almost as soon as he came to power, Castro took steps to reduce American influence in Cuba. He nationalized American-dominated industries such as sugar and mining, introduced land reform schemes and called on other Latin American governments to act with more autonomy. In response to these moves by Castro, it was President Eisenhower who authorized the CIA to recruit an army and begin training them to overthrow Castro.

In May 1960, Castro established diplomatic relations with the Soviet Union. The U.S. government severed diplomatic relations with Cuba and stepped up its preparations for an invasion. When Kennedy took office, he believed that Castro posed no real threat to America, but orchestrating Castro's removal would show Russia, China and skeptical Americans that he was serious about winning the Cold War.

Even after the invasion failed, According to many historians, the CIA and the Cuban exile brigade believed that President Kennedy would eventually allow the American military to intervene in Cuba on their behalf. However, Kennedy was determined not start a fight that might end in World War III. Despite the pressure Kennedy was feeling from Cuban Americans, the CIA and others within his administration, he nevertheless showed strong leadership. Yes, his Proactive Leadership approach to taking out Castro failed, but starting World War III would have been far worse for the United States and the world.

So now you know the history leading up to the Cuban Missile Crisis. If the crisis wasn't resolved, Kennedy knew that there was a distinct possibility of a nuclear war.

President Kennedy's public address to the nation about the presence of the missiles, explained his decision to enact a naval blockade around Cuba and made it clear the U.S. was prepared to use military force if necessary to neutralize this perceived threat to national security. Following the news, many people feared the world was on the brink of nuclear war.

On the 12th day of the crisis, a Soviet missile shot a U-2 reconnaissance plane out of the sky and killed of U.S. Air Force Major Rudolf Anderson Jr. This action was the "tipping point" of the crisis. Up until that point there were no casualties. As then Attorney General Robert F. Kennedy would later write in his memoir titled **Thirteen Days**, "There was the feeling that the noose was tightening on all of us, on Americans, on mankind, and that the bridges to escape were crumbling."

After the downing of the plane, Kennedy's military leaders overwhelmingly urged Kennedy to launch airstrikes against Cuba's air defenses the following morning. Kennedy, however, correctly suspected that Soviet leader Nikita Khrushchev had not authorized the downing of unarmed reconnaissance planes, and wasn't prepared to abandon diplomacy just yet.

Kennedy learned a great deal from the Bay of Pigs failure. He developed, at that time, an inherent distrust of the military leadership. He believed they were hawkish, confrontation-seeking, and overly reliant on military solutions that did not work. He stated, "The first advice I'm going to give my successor is to watch the generals and to avoid feeling that because they were military men their opinions on military mattes were worth a damn....These brass hats have one great advantage in their favor....If we...do what they want us to do, none of us will be alive later to tell them the they were wrong."

Historian Arthur Schlesinger Jr., an advisor and supporter to President Kennedy, described Kennedy's thinking process was to keep strong, keep cool, and have unlimited patience. More importantly, he believed that you should never corner an opponent and always assist them in saving face, see things through their eyes, and avoid self-righteousness.

Cooler Heads Prevail

Have you ever been in a fight? Personally, I have been in perhaps a handful, at best, awkward ones as a kid. There was one near fight that sticks out the most that occurred when I was a Platoon Sergeant in the Army. One of my former First Sergeants kicked open my office door and made threatening moves. No, this was not normal Army leadership behavior. The tension was high between the both of us and it had come to a head. So after he hung up the phone, and threw it against the wall according to his secretary, he traveled the 15 minute drive and kicked open my door.

The one thing that I learned very early in the military is that you NEVER put your hands on an individual…first. So as I stood up from my office desk I was prepared to do whatever it took to defend myself. I was waiting on him to come around my desk and physically attack me. However, there were two other Platoon Sergeants, both of which I knew very well, were accompanying him. They would later tell me that as the First Sergeant stormed in the building, as they were about to leave the building, he ordered them to follow him and that they were going to be witnesses.

Getting into a fight with anyone that has a higher rank than you typically does not end well…for either you. That being said, the person that throws the first punch is the one that will likely be arrested, so I was willing to absorb the first punch. Well, the first punch never came. One of the two Platoon Sergeants was a colleague and, and he looked at me and said "just leave", which was good advice.

Ask anyone that has been in the Army for a few of years and they will tell you that people argue back and forth frequently, especially among Noncommissioned Officers. The Operations Master Sergeant, who was with the Sergeants Major heading to a unit when he heard of the incident, revealed to me later that if I had struck the First Sergeant, nothing would have happened to me because kicking open my door represented an aggressive act.

In the end, the Sergeants Major laid down the law about kicking in doors, along with what steps he would take if it were to occur again. I bring up this particular incident because those of you who have ever felt the adrenalin build as you are anticipating a confrontation understand how difficult it is to pull back when the other person is the aggressor. There are a lot things going through your mind, like being seriously injured or perhaps even hurting or killing the person. We've all seen that movie where a person is confronted and they push or punch the aggressor, and their head hits the coffee table and they die by some fluke accident. Your life is upended over something that could have been deescalated if you would have perhaps played it smarter.

When the U.S. pilot was shot down and killed by the Soviet Union, which was not ordered by Khrushchev both leaders came to the realization that the crisis was rapidly spiraling out of their control. Khrushchev's son Sergei would later write, *"It was at that very moment—not before or after—that father felt the situation was slipping out of his control."*

President Kennedy worried that retaliatory airstrikes would inevitably result in all-out war. He told his advisors, *"It isn't the first step that concerns me, but both sides escalating to the fourth or fifth step and we don't go to the sixth because there is no one around to do so."*

Despite the enormous tension, Kennedy and Khrushchev found a way out of the impasse. Each leader offered each other a way out of what would have been a colossal ClusterPhuck. Khrushchev removed missiles from Cuba and the U.S. removed their missile installations in Turkey.

President Kennedy's leadership during the crisis has been held up as a model of both decision-making restraint and success in international crisis situations. He was actively involved in all phases of the decision-making process; had a basic plan of action as to how to proceed in assessing and resolving the dispute; held a commitment to moderation and the avoidance of war; utilized fully the resources of the national governments and the expertise available in the private sector; and had the intelligence, patience, and judgment to find a way out of an unwelcome and unexpected confrontation with the world's other superpower.

From a **Crisis Leadership** perspective, President Kennedy did utilize the five core tasks that are expected from a leader. It was an impressive policymaking exercise in the most limited of time frames. However, sometimes the 4th task, "declaring that the crisis is over", may not come soon enough, or at all, as President Carter discovered.

President Carter and the Iran Hostage Crisis

On November 4, 1979, a group of Iranian students stormed the U.S. Embassy in Tehran, taking more than 60 American hostages. The immediate cause of this action was President Jimmy Carter's decision to allow Iran's deposed Shah, a pro-Western autocrat who had been expelled from his country some months before, to come to the United States for cancer treatment.

However, the hostage-taking was about more than the Shah's medical care; it was a dramatic way for the student revolutionaries to declare an end to American interference in its affairs. It was also a way to raise the profile of the revolution's leader, the anti-American cleric Ayatollah Ruhollah Khomeini.

After five months of planning, organizing, training, and a complicated series of tentative mission rehearsals, the capability to rescue people being held hostage was now a reality. President Carter approved the plan for Operation Eagle Claw, and a target date of late April. However, the plan failed miserably. There were helicopter crashes, casualties, and of course an abundance of second guessing critics.

Like all presidential decisions of this magnitude, the hostage rescue attempt has been dissected numerous times over the years. Just like Kennedys Cuban Missile Crisis or the Bay of Pigs failure, there is seemingly some back story warning that a confrontation was evitable. When President Carter made the decision to allow the Shah to receive medical attention in the United States, he was influenced by prominent conservatives, some within his administration, to stand by the Shah.

Carter gave in to the pressure and authorized the Shah's immediate entry into the United States. He also disregarded warnings that he would no longer be able to guarantee the safety of the U.S. Embassy in Tehran. He took no steps to bolster security at the facility or to evacuate all U.S. personnel before admitting the Shah.

The hostages were freed on January 21, 1981, 444 days after the crisis began and just hours after President Ronald Reagan delivered his inaugural address. The U.S. had to unfreeze $8 billion in order for the hostages to be released however.

Proactive leadership, with regards to removing American personnel from the embassy in Iran would have likely prevented the hostage crisis. President Carter utilized a more **Reactive Leadership** approach, meaning that he failed to stop and think about the bigger problem when faced with an issue of allowing the Shah into the United States. Carter would later somewhat defend his decision acknowledging that he had acted on inaccurate or incomplete information, and passively submitted (**Passive Leadership**) to powerful lobbyists.

A few months after the hostages were released in early 1981, Carter explained the logic behind his decision to admit the Shah. Carter stated:

"I was told that the Shah was desperately ill, at the point of death. I was told that New York was the only medical facility that was capable of possibly saving his life and reminded that the Iranian officials had promised to protect our people in Iran. When all the circumstances were

described to me, I agreed."

In 2015, Carter stated:

"I wish I had sent one more helicopter to get the hostages, and we would've rescued them, and I would've been reelected."

It is feasible for Carter to believe that if he had rescued the hostages, he would be reelected. However, his assessment of how sending in one more helicopter would have changed the outcome, is wrong.

The choice of helicopters was crucial to the failure of the mission. The **RH-53 Sea Stallion** was never meant to undertake long flights over land. It is not a combat assault helicopter, because it " lacks power, armor, and armament." It also did not help that the RH-53s used in the event itself had been poorly maintained. Of the 110 flight hours needed to keep the RH-53s fully operational between January and April, only 25 had been flown.

The Shah did not have to come to the U.S. to receive quality health care. One alternative was to send him to Mexico and set up a treatment center for him there. Additionally, Carter declined a suggestion from the Deputy Prime Minister that he allow Iranian physicians to examine the Shah, which could have mitigated the popular suspicion that the Shah's arrival signaled an American conspiracy to return him to power.

Although the failed rescue attempt affected his reelection campaign, it wasn't the only reason why he wasn't given a second term. Throughout his presidency, Carter struggled to stimulate the nation's economy. There was high unemployment, rising inflation and the effects of an energy crisis that began in the early 1970s.

Though he claimed an increase of 8 million jobs and a reduction in the budget deficit by the end of his term, many business leaders as well as the public blamed Carter for the nation's continuing struggles. Although he was considered by many to be an **Ethical leader**, he failed as a **Strategic or Proactive leader**, with regards to the economy, because he didn't have a coherent or effective policy to address the economic issues effectively.

President Clinton: Self-Inflicted ClusterPhuck

Speaking of self-inflicted wounds, Gary Hart was the front-runner for the 1988 Democratic presidential nomination until he dropped out over allegations of an extramarital affair with Donna Rice. According to the Gallup polling organization, Hart had a double-digit lead over the rest of the potential Democratic field among Democrats and Democratic-leaning Independents.

In a preview of the general election against the presumed Republican nominee, Vice President George H. W. Bush, Hart was polling over 50 percent among registered voters and beating Bush by 13 points, with only 11 percent saying they were undecided. He would have been very hard to stop.

Hart was described as a brilliant and serious man, and by many, the most visionary political mind of his generation. Hart was a Kennedy-like figure on a fast track to the presidency but his affair with a woman half his age and the picture of her sitting on his lap cozying up would live forever in the mind of voters.

People would ask, how could such a smart guy have been that *stupid?* Franklin Roosevelt, John Kennedy and Lyndon Johnson were adulterers, before and during their presidencies, and we can safely assume they had plenty of company. It is of course one thing for people to hear rumors about you having extramarital affairs, but pictures seem to erase all doubt.

In November 1995, President Clinton began an affair with 21-year old intern Monica Lewinsky. Lewinsky was transferred to the Pentagon in 1996. That summer, she first confided in Pentagon co-worker Linda Tripp about her sexual relationship with Clinton. Tripp began secretly recording conversations with Lewinsky, in which Lewinsky gave Tripp details about the affair.

Former U.S. Solicitor General Kenneth Starr, a Republican, had already been appointed to the Office of Independent Counsel in August 1994 to investigate President Clinton's involvement with the Whitewater Development Corporation, a failed real estate venture. Clinton was never prosecuted after three separate inquiries found insufficient evidence linking him with the criminal conduct, but his affair with Lewinsky was pulled into the investigation.

When the Starr Report was released, it identified 11 possible examples of grounds for impeachment, including the several times the p

President lied under oath about his relationship with Lewinsky. As a result, the House of Representatives initiated President Clinton's impeachment process on December 19, 1998. The first charges to be presented included perjury, intentionally lying under oath, and obstruction of justice, which failed to pass the Senate. Though lawmakers called for his impeachment, and the House of Representatives voted to do so, President Clinton was not removed from office, after the trial went to the Senate, which voted to acquit him despite his **Bad** and

Unethical Leadership actions.

Unethical Leadership are "behaviors conducted and decisions made by organizational leaders that are illegal and/or violate moral standards, and those that impose processes and structures that promote unethical conduct by followers." After breaking seven months of near silence, President Clinton stated:

"Indeed I did have a relationship with Ms. Lewinsky that was not appropriate. In fact, it was wrong. It constituted a critical lapse in judgment and a personal failure on my part for which I am solely and completely responsible."

This ethical lapse was one of allegedly many sex related lapses that Clinton was involved in dating back to his days as the Governor of Arkansas. That being said, Clinton had a very high approval rating when he left office despite the scandal that dogged his presidency. It is reasonable to expect a President to utilize a variety of (good and bad) leadership styles during their time in office. Clinton's use of multiple leadership styles can provide us with a clear insight as to why his approval ratings remained high.

It's The Economy Stupid!

Clinton campaign strategist James Carville is credited with coining the phrase "it's the economy, stupid." At that time, Carville was attempting to emphasize the importance of the struggling economy in then-candidate Bill Clinton's 1992 presidential campaign. Although originally intended for an internal audience of campaign workers, the phrase became an actual slogan for the entire campaign.

According to the National Bureau of Economic Research (NBER), the economy has four distinct economic stages:

- Expansion
- Peak
- Contraction
- Trough

An **expansion** is characterized by increasing employment, economic growth, and upward pressure on prices. A **peak** is the highest point of the business cycle, when the economy is producing at maximum allowable output, employment is at or above full employment, and inflationary pressures on prices are evident.

The economy usually enters into a "correction", which is characterized by a **contraction** where growth slows, employment declines, unemployment increases, and pricing pressures lessen. The slowing ceases at the **trough** and at this point the economy has hit a bottom from which the next stage of expansion and contraction will emerge.

The importance of this short economic lesson is based on the opinion of many experts who determined that the economy was the main factor for Bush's defeat to Bill Clinton. On Election Day, 7 in 10 voters said the economy was either "not so good" or "poor". On the eve of the election, the unemployment rate was at 7.8%, which was the highest in about eight years. Add that to Bush's dismal 37% approval rating, and you can see why the "It's the economy stupid" slogan was right on the money.

If the economic cycle was right, the stage the U.S. economy was in was a **trough**. That meant an **expansion** was right around the corner, and Bill Clinton would be walking into office just at the right time. But just how good was the economy during Clinton's eight years in office?

Under Clinton, the U.S. had strong economic growth rate of about 4% annually, and record job creation number of 22.7 million. He employed a combination of **Proactive & Transformational Leadership** styles to stimulate the economy by raising taxes on higher income taxpayers during his first term and cutting defense spending. This contributed to a rise in revenue and decline in spending relative to the size of the economy.

These factors helped bring the federal budget into surplus from fiscal years 1998-2001, the only surplus years after 1969. Besides the record-high surpluses and the record-low poverty rates, the economy could boast the longest economic expansion in history; the lowest unemployment since the early 1970s; and the lowest poverty rates for single mothers, black Americans, and the aged.

Clinton signed the North American Free Trade Agreement (NAFTA) into law along with many other free trade agreements. He also enacted significant welfare reform.

Additionally, Clinton appointed a number of women and minorities to top government posts, including Janet Reno, the first female U.S. Attorney General, and Madeleine Albright, the first female U.S. Secretary of State. So, even with the backdrop of the impeachment and Lewinsky, Clinton did get a lot of things right. That being said, even when a President attempts to do the right thing, bad things tend to happen.

Military Action: Good & Bad

While in office a president can expect to take some type of military action to either prevent something from happening or retaliation for something that has already happened. President Clinton took the following actions:

- **Iraq (1993):** Launched cruise missiles into Baghdad, hitting Iraqi intelligence headquarters, in retaliation for assassination plot against President George H.W. Bush.
- **Somalia (1993):** Increased troop deployment for security and stability mission with 35 other nations under U.N. Security Council resolution.
- **Haiti (1994):** Deployed troops for peacekeeping and nation-building mission as authorized by U.N. Security Council resolution.
- **Bosnia (1994-96):** Launched airstrikes with NATO allies over 18 months, culminating with bombings, artillery attacks and cruise missile strikes against Bosnia Serbs, by request of U.N. Secretary General Boutrous Boutrous-Ghali and to enforce no-fly zones as authorized by at least three U.N. Security Council resolutions. Deployed troops in year-long NATO peacekeeping mission.
- **Iraq (1996):** Launched cruise missiles at targets in southern Iraq in retaliation against attacks on U.S. jets enforcing no-fly zones to protect Iraqi minorities as authorized by U.N. Security Council resolution.
- **Sudan, Afghanistan (1998):** Launched cruise missiles at terrorist training camps in Sudan and Afghanistan in retaliation against U.S. Embassy bombings in Kenya and Tanzania that killed more than 220 people, including 12 Americans.
- **Iraq (1998):** Launched cruise missiles and airstrikes on a number of Baghdad targets to punish Saddam Hussein for not complying with U.N. chemical weapons inspections as required under U.N. Security Council resolutions.
- **Kosovo: (1999):** Launched airstrikes and cruise missiles over more than three months at Yugoslavian military targets, power stations, bridges and other facilities as part of NATO mission.

The toughest leadership action for a President to take is ordering a military strike that will end innocent civilian lives. However, what are the potential repercussions of not taking military actions?

The day prior to the terrorist attacks on the United States on the 11th of September, 2001, Former President Clinton reportedly made this statement:

"I nearly got him. And I could have killed him, but I would have to destroy a little town called Kandahar in Afghanistan and kill 300 innocent women and children, and then I would have been no better than him."

According to the 2004 **9/11 Report** by the National Commission on Terrorist Attacks upon the United States, intelligence indicated, in December 1998, that Bin Laden was staying at the governor's residence in Kandahar. U.S. officials again considered a missile strike against Bin Laden in May 1999, but decided not to act because the intelligence seemed unclear.

At the time, according to the commission, an accidental bombing of the Chinese embassy in Belgrade during the NATO war against Serbia complicated the decision. If you haven't figured it out by now, presidential leadership is H-A-R-D.

The Oklahoma City Bombing

Shortly after 9:00 a.m. on April 19, 1995, a Ryder rental truck exploded with terrifying force in front of the nine-story Alfred P. Murrah Federal Building in downtown Oklahoma City. The powerful explosion blew off the building's entire north wall, and emergency crews from around the country quickly moved in to provide support for the city. President Clinton made the following public address to the nation:

"The bombing in Oklahoma City was an attack on innocent children and defenseless citizens. It was an act of cowardice, and it was evil. The United States will not tolerate it. And I will not allow the people of this country to be intimidated by evil cowards.

I have met with our team, which we assembled to deal with this bombing. And I have determined to take the following steps to assure the strongest response to this situation:

First, I have deployed a crisis management team under the leadership of the FBI, working with the Department of Justice, the Bureau of Alcohol, Tobacco and Firearms, military and local authorities. We are sending the world's finest investigators to solve these murders.

Second, I have declared an emergency in Oklahoma City. And at my direction, James Lee Witt, the Director of the Federal Emergency Management Agency, is now on his way there to make sure we do everything we can to help the people of Oklahoma deal with the tragedy.

Third, we are taking every precaution to reassure and to protect people who work in or live near other Federal facilities.

Let there be no room for doubt: We will find the people who did this. When

133

we do, justice will be swift, certain, and severe. These people are killers, and they must be treated like killers.

Finally, let me say that I ask all Americans tonight to pray—to pray for the people who have lost their lives, to pray for the families and the friends of the dead and the wounded, to pray for the people of Oklahoma City. May God's grace be with them.

Meanwhile, we will be about our work.

Thank you."

Clinton's address to the nation, and to the world, did exactly what it was supposed to do, show strong **Forceful Leadership** in the face of a devastating crisis.

Taking Charge of a Bad Situation

President Clinton left no doubt that he was thoroughly involved (**Crisis Leadership**) and in charge of the crisis. During the crisis he demonstrated **Crisis, Strategic**, and **Proactive** leadership traits. A **Strategic leader** is concerned with "defining the overall vision and mission", which Clinton accomplished in his address to the nation. He immediately deployed a crisis management team that encompassed many law enforcement agencies that had a clear mission to find the individuals responsible.

He also took a **Proactive** leadership approach by protecting people in or near federal buildings around the country. At the time I was assigned as Senior Trainor, in the federal building, in Syracuse, New York. However, I was at Fort Jackson attending a two-week course at the time of the bombing. Prior to me leaving for the course the path to my office on the top floor was simple. By the time I returned, there were scanners and enough security that rivaled what we now see at airports today.

When the crisis was over the deceased included 19 young children who were in the building's day care center at the time of the blast. More than 650 other people were injured in the bombing, which damaged or destroyed over 300 buildings in the immediate area.

Timothy McVeigh, the driver of the truck bomb, was already in jail, having been stopped a little more than an hour after the bombing for a traffic violation and then arrested for unlawfully carrying a handgun. Shortly before he was scheduled to be released from jail, he was identified as a prime suspect in the bombing and charged.

That same day, Terry Nichols, an associate of McVeigh's, surrendered in Herington, Kansas. Both men were found to be members of a radical right-wing survivalist group based in Michigan.

This was a wakeup call for the country. President Clinton issued a directive that clarified the FBI's status as the lead agency in investigating terrorist attacks against Americans. This directive aimed to cut down on conflict and duplication and to indicate how cooperation in such cases should be handled.

The **Anti-Terrorism and Effective Death Penalty Act** followed, increasing protections afforded to federal workers and the facilities they work in, as well as expanding the FBI's authority to investigate terrorist attacks against U.S. persons overseas.

More presidential directives were issued, which addressed the detection, prevention and response to terrorist attacks at home and endorsed the FBI's Joint Terrorism Task Force approach to these matters. The FBI created a counterterrorism division, bringing together responsibility for foreign and domestic terrorist investigations for the first time since the 1970s.

The bureau also upgraded its crisis response center, opening a new Strategic Information and Operations Center at FBI headquarters in Washington DC. Simply put, President Clinton was displaying a combination of leadership skills in an effort to ensure that Americans had a fighting chance against terrorism both domestically and abroad.

What if there never was a Monica Lewinsky or impeachment of President Clinton? How would Clinton rank against his presidential peers?

President Obama and the Perfect Storm

A **Perfect Storm** is *"an event in which a rare combination of circumstances drastically aggravates the event. The term is used by analogy to an unusually severe storm that results from a rare combination of meteorological phenomena."*

Republican John McCain inherited and contributed to the perfect storm that cost him the election to Obama. McCain could not overcome a hostile economic environment, distance himself from an unpopular president or convince voters he could lead them out of the crisis. While Obama looked healthy, vibrant, and confident, McCain often looked tired and appeared confused and out of touch at times.

135

As the blame game began, analysts also said McCain's choice of inexperienced Alaska Gov. Sarah Palin as his vice presidential running mate raised doubts about his judgment. It ultimately may have alienated more voters than it attracted. His lack of a coherent economic message loomed large as the issue trumped the Iraq War in voters' minds.

Be careful what you wish for

Remember the economic cycle and the four stages? I recall telling people that whoever wins the election is going to get their butt kicked during the first term, but they will see an economic surge at some point in their second term. That is, if they made it that far.

President Obama inherited what proved to be the worst U.S. recession since the 1930s. The economy contracted by more than 8%. Unemployment doubled, from 5% to 10%, a net loss of some 8 million jobs. Average housing prices dropped by 30%. The cumulative wealth of Americans fell by nearly a quarter: a loss on paper of some $15 trillion.

As the **Great Recession** echoed around the world, Europe's economy went into reverse. Nations from Greece to Iceland flirted with default on their sovereign debts, while emerging markets from Rio to New Delhi and Moscow to Beijing began to sputter and stall.

However, it wasn't just the economy Obama had to fix, he was also going to have to contend with a two front war that was costing lives and billions of dollars. Little did anyone know, outside of a handful of individuals, that President Obama's number one priority, with regards to fighting terrorism, was to capture or kill one particular individual that was on more than one presidents radar…Osama Bin Laden.

In 2007, the presidential candidate Obama stated, with regards to going after bin Laden in Pakistan:

"What I have said is we're going to encourage democracy in Pakistan, expand our non-military aid to Pakistan so that they have more of a stake in working with us, but insisting that they go after these militants. And if we have Osama bin Laden in our sights and the Pakistani government is unable or unwilling to take them out, then I think that we have to act, and we will take them out."

Obama went on to state:

"Now, I understand that President Musharraf has his own challenges. But let me make this clear... There are terrorists holed up in those mountains who murdered 3,000 Americans. They are plotting to strike again. It was a terrible mistake to fail to act when we had a chance to take out an al-Qaida leadership meeting in 2005. If we have actionable intelligence about high-value terrorist targets and President Musharraf will not act, we will."

Bin Laden: Priority Number One

Once in the oval office, now President Obama went to the CIA and said, *"I want to put a priority on finding Osama bin Laden.... this is my number-one priority in terms of fighting Al-Qaeda. Put whatever resources you need into it."*

Once a month intelligence officials briefed Obama and his Chief of Staff on Osama bin Laden even if they came in to say they had nothing to report. This approach created a "culture of accountability" that guaranteed the assignment would never fade into the background. Those of you that aspire to be President or a CEO, remember this lesson. Meaning, you can't just give lip service to something you feel is your top priority as a leader. Bring the team you assigned to report to you weekly if you must. They WILL get the message that you are serious.

In the course of a year or so, intelligence officials were able to track down a courier they thought would lead them to bin Laden. In early February of 2011, the CIA had identified a large compound in Abbottabad, which was near the capital city of Islamabad. Intelligence officials estimated that there was a 40 to 80 percent chance of bin Laden being in the compound.

Admiral Bill McRaven, the architect of the raid to take down Osama bin Laden, stated that Obama would bring in all the people he thought could provide him with some different options for how they might go after bin Laden, if he was in the compound.

McRaven also revealed that until the final decision to conduct the mission, there was never intelligence verifying bin Laden was in the target. There were some who were very confident and there were some who were absolutely convinced that it was not bin Laden.

However, the bin Laden raid would have not been the first time Obama would have to give the go-ahead on a high risk raid. In September 2009, **Obama** signed off on a raid in Somalia that took out a top al-Qaida leader. After much deliberation, he bypassed a plan to launch offshore missiles and selected a riskier strategy instead. Special Operations forces swooped in with helicopters, demolished the terrorist's car, and briefly landed to collect DNA. It was perfect example of the President's approach and a preview of what was to come in the bin Laden raid.

In early 2011, military commanders presented President Obama with three possible options for attacking the compound at Abbottabad:

Option One: Use a massive bombing raid to level the compound. Among the concerns about utilizing this particular strategy what that if you did a massive bombing raid, you were invariably going to kill women and children. As you may recall, this is why President Clinton did not take action when he had a chance to kill bin Laden. As McRaven would later state concerning Obama's decision not to use this option, *"I don't think it was an intellectual call on his part. I think it was absolutely a moral call and a personal call. He knew we couldn't do that because that's not what great societies and great people do."*

Option Two: Target the individual referred to as Pacer when he is out in the open with a single bomb. Intelligence officials indicated that a very tall person would come outside in a courtyard area now and then that resembled bin laden, but they couldn't be sure it was him. This option was problematic because there was no guarantee that the bomb would only take out its intended target.

Option Three: The Special Forces raid option with U.S. Navy Seals. Helicopters would fly the 162 miles in, fast rope onto or near the compound, and surround the compound. They would then breach the compound walls, make their way to wherever bin Laden was, and either capture or kill him, get back on the helicopters and come home.

As time went on, it became more and more apparent that the third option, a Scal Team raid, would give the President an opportunity to verify that in fact bin Laden was killed or captured. As McRaven put it, "This is straightforward for us. We do compound raids every night, many times a night in Afghanistan. It's a larger compound but the approach is still the same."

Even though McRaven was confident he also knew that if this went wrong Obama would be a one-term president, like Jimmy Carter. McRaven also pointed out that nobody would've criticized Obama for saying no to the raid because the intelligence wasn't there to give them a definitive answer. But instead Obama said, "Yes, let's go do the raid," knowing all along that if it went south, he would shoulder the burden.

Like Kennedy, Carter, both Bush's, and all other Presidents that faced similar situations, there are always downside risks. In this particular case there was a fire fight, a helicopter crash, a complete crisis in US-Pakistan relations, without even knowing that bin Laden was there.

If the intelligence was completely wrong and U.S. forces had gone into Pakistan and inadvertently killed innocent Pakistanis, he would have taken a considerable hit both domestically and internationally. However, the mission was a success and on May 1st, 201,1 at 11:35 PM EST, President Obama gave the following speech to the nation:

"Good evening. Tonight, I can report to the American people and to the world that the United States has conducted an operation that killed Osama bin Laden, the leader of al Qaeda, and a terrorist who's responsible for the murder of thousands of innocent men, women, and children.

It was nearly 10 years ago that a bright September day was darkened by the worst attack on the American people in our history. The images of 9/11 are seared into our national memory -- hijacked planes cutting through a cloudless September sky; the Twin Towers collapsing to the ground; black smoke billowing up from the Pentagon; the wreckage of Flight 93 in Shanksville, Pennsylvania, where the actions of heroic citizens saved even more heartbreak and destruction.

And yet we know that the worst images are those that were unseen to the world. The empty seat at the dinner table. Children who were forced to grow up without their mother or their father. Parents who would never know the feeling of their child's embrace. Nearly 3,000 citizens taken from us, leaving a gaping hole in our hearts.

On September 11, 2001, in our time of grief, the American people came together. We offered our neighbors a hand, and we offered the wounded our blood. We reaffirmed our ties to each other, and our love of community and country. On that day, no matter where we came from, what God we prayed to, or what race or ethnicity we were, we were united as one American family.

We were also united in our resolve to protect our nation and to bring those who committed this vicious attack to justice. We quickly learned that the 9/11 attacks were carried out by al Qaeda -- an organization headed by Osama bin Laden, which had openly declared war on the United States and was committed to killing innocents in our country and around the globe. And so we went to war against al Qaeda to protect our citizens, our friends, and our allies.

Over the last 10 years, thanks to the tireless and heroic work of our military and our counterterrorism professionals, we've made great strides in that effort. We've disrupted terrorist attacks and strengthened our homeland defense. In Afghanistan, we removed the Taliban government, which had given bin Laden and al Qaeda safe haven and support. And around the globe, we worked with our friends and allies to capture or kill scores of al Qaeda terrorists, including several who were a part of the 9/11 plot.

Yet Osama bin Laden avoided capture and escaped across the Afghan border into Pakistan. Meanwhile, al Qaeda continued to operate from along that border and operate through its affiliates across the world.

And so shortly after taking office, I directed Leon Panetta, the director of the CIA, to make the killing or capture of bin Laden the top priority of our war against al Qaeda, even as we continued our broader efforts to disrupt, dismantle, and defeat his network.

Then, last August, after years of painstaking work by our intelligence community, I was briefed on a possible lead to bin Laden. It was far from certain, and it took many months to run this thread to ground. I met repeatedly with my national security team as we developed more information about the possibility that we had located bin Laden hiding within a compound deep inside of Pakistan. And finally, last week, I determined that we had enough intelligence to take action, and authorized an operation to get Osama bin Laden and bring him to justice.

Today, at my direction, the United States launched a targeted operation against that compound in Abbottabad, Pakistan. A small team of Americans carried out the operation with extraordinary courage and capability. No Americans were harmed. They took care to avoid civilian casualties. After a firefight, they killed Osama bin Laden and took custody of his body.

For over two decades, bin Laden has been al Qaeda's leader and symbol, and has continued to plot attacks against our country and our friends and allies. The death of bin Laden marks the most significant achievement to date in our nation's effort to defeat al Qaeda.

Yet his death does not mark the end of our effort. There's no doubt that al Qaeda will continue to pursue attacks against us. We must — and we will -- remain vigilant at home and abroad.

As we do, we must also reaffirm that the United States is not — and never will be — at war with Islam. I've made clear, just as President Bush did shortly after 9/11, that our war is not against Islam. Bin Laden was not a Muslim leader; he was a mass murderer of Muslims. Indeed, al Qaeda has slaughtered scores of Muslims in many countries, including our own. So his demise should be welcomed by all who believe in peace and human dignity.

Over the years, I've repeatedly made clear that we would take action within Pakistan if we knew where bin Laden was. That is what we've done. But it's important to note that our counterterrorism cooperation with Pakistan helped lead us to bin Laden and the compound where he was hiding. Indeed, bin Laden had declared war against Pakistan as well, and ordered attacks against the Pakistani people.

Tonight, I called President Zardari, and my team has also spoken with their Pakistani counterparts. They agree that this is a good and historic day for both of our nations. And going forward, it is essential that Pakistan continue to join us in the fight against al Qaeda and its affiliates.

The American people did not choose this fight. It came to our shores, and started with the senseless slaughter of our citizens. After nearly 10 years of service, struggle, and sacrifice, we know well the costs of war. These efforts weigh on me every time I, as Commander-in-Chief, have to sign a letter to a family that has lost a loved one, or look into the eyes of a service member who's been gravely wounded.

So Americans understand the costs of war. Yet as a country, we will never tolerate our security being threatened, nor stand idly by when our people have been killed. We will be relentless in defense of our citizens and our friends and allies. We will be true to the values that make us who we are. And on nights like this one, we can say to those families who have lost loved ones to al Qaeda's terror: Justice has been done.

Tonight, we give thanks to the countless intelligence and counterterrorism professionals who've worked tirelessly to achieve this outcome. The American people do not see their work, nor know their names. But tonight, they feel the satisfaction of their work and the result of their pursuit of justice.

We give thanks for the men who carried out this operation, for they exemplify the professionalism, patriotism, and unparalleled courage of those who serve our country. And they are part of a generation that has borne the heaviest share of the burden since that September day.

Finally, let me say to the families who lost loved ones on 9/11 that we have never forgotten your loss, nor wavered in our commitment to see that we do whatever it takes to prevent another attack on our shores.

And tonight, let us think back to the sense of unity that prevailed on 9/11. I know that it has, at times, frayed. Yet today's achievement is a testament to the greatness of our country and the determination of the American people.

The cause of securing our country is not complete. But tonight, we are once again reminded that America can do whatever we set our mind to. That is the story of our history, whether it's the pursuit of prosperity for our people, or the struggle for equality for all our citizens; our commitment to stand up for our values abroad, and our sacrifices to make the world a safer place.

Let us remember that we can do these things not just because of wealth or power, but because of who we are: one nation, under God, indivisible, with liberty and justice for all.

Thank you. May God bless you. And may God bless the United States of America."

President Obama's address to the nation did exactly what it was supposed to do, which was to remind the country how devastating the attack on the United States was with regards to the loss of life, and to thank the men and women who worked tirelessly over the years to make the raid successful. Perhaps even more importantly, Obama stated, "*We will be relentless in defense of our citizens and our friends and allies.*"

That particular sentence was meant for the world to hear. Osama bin Laden's legend was near a mythical status to his followers. To many he seemed untouchable. If President Obama would have taken the option to blow up the compound, there would have been no solid proof that bin Laden was dead.

***

As stated earlier, regardless of their best intentions, there are decisions, whether they are made by the President or someone in their administration, that will have

142

unintended consequences.

The Fast & Furious Scandal

In 2012, after what ABC news called "hundreds of thefts by TSA officers of passenger belongings", purposely left behind 10 iPads at TSA checkpoints at major airports with a history of theft by government screeners. Two weeks later, ABC News, which had a tracking device on the iPad, confronted a TSA officer, at his home. He first denied having the missing iPad, but ultimately turned it over after blaming his wife for taking it from the airport.

According to the TSA, between 2003 and 2012, 381 TSA officers have been fired for theft. ABC News successfully highlighted the criminal activity of the TSA in the most embarrassing way possible, and they were forced take accountability of its officers. However, the point I trying to make is the way in which ABC News planted the iPad that ultimately led them to the perpetrators home. Unfortunately, it didn't work out so well for the so-called Operation Fast and Furious.

Similar to the iPads, U.S. agents in Arizona purposely let slip into Mexico as many as 2,000 guns bought by low-level suspects. The agents begin to track what are known as "straw buyers", which are gun purchasers who are suspected of buying for others, which is illegal. The ATF agents decide not to pursue low-level buyers aggressively, but were instead trying to build a larger case against a gun-smuggling ring.

However, in 2010, U.S. Border Patrol Agent Brian Terry was shot dead in a remote area of Arizona after a group of Mexican men who had crossed the border hoping to rob drug traffickers come across his unit. The attackers leave behind two semi-automatic rifles with serial numbers that match two in the Fast and Furious database.

On September 19th, 2012, and less than a month from the Presidential Elections, The Justice Department's inspector general released a report faulting 14 department employees for systematic failures that led the operation to go awry. Of course, politics played a role in keeping the controversial methods in the news as much as possible leading up to the election.

Like I stated in the beginning of this chapter, it is virtually impossible for any President to not get caught up in a ClusterPhuck. Luckily for President Obama it didn't derail his reelection bid, like the Iran Hostage crisis did to President Carter's campaign.

***

As Harvard Professor John Kotter commented: *'Conducting business as usual is very difficult if the building seems to be on fire. But in an increasingly fast-moving world, waiting for the fire to breakout is a dubious strategy."*

UnPhucking the Financial Cluster

President Obama knew what he was getting into…for the most part. But does any president truly know what they are getting into once they take the oval office seat? Charismatic leaders, like President Obama, are masters at influencing and inspiring audiences. They display an image of confidence, competence, and trustworthiness. To their skilful use of rhetoric, the charismatic leader is able to captivate listeners to work towards team and organizational goals. As Time Magazine stated in their commemorative edition of "Barack Obama: Eight Years":

"Barack Obama entered the White House as something new in American history. He wasn't chosen on the basis of experience, nor for his role as leader of a party or a movement. He had not been a governor or a general or a veteran legislator. He did not become president by the accident of his predecessor's death in office.

Obama was elected purely for himself—his message, his persona and what he symbolized. In 48 brief months, he rose from the obscurity of a state legislature to become the first Democrat in more than three decades to win more than half of the popular vote. Messenger and message were inseparable; he offered himself as Exhibit A in the case for hope and change. Obama was a mirror in which millions of people saw their cherished ideals reflected: tolerance, cooperation, equality, justice."

Transformative Leadership begins with a drastic rethinking of who, what, where, when, and how of leadership. As the Great Recession worsened people were looking for strong leadership to get them out this gigantic mess. Obama immediately got to work on the largest economic-stimulus bill, about $800 billion, ever enacted by Congress. Most of the money went to tax relief, unemployment insurance and other direct infusions of cash into the pockets of Americans who would, in turn, the administration hoped, would spend or invest it.

He also saw this as the opportunity to pump billions into priorities that would normally struggle to receive much smaller sums. The stimulus bill was packed with record spending on renewable energy, a modern electrical grid, computerization of health-care records, high-speed rail, and new bridges and roads. He also directed billions to basic scientific research, hoping that it would yield the next wave of American innovation.

The auto industry was crashing as well. At the onset of the meltdown, sales of cars and light trucks had been humming at about 16 million per year. But over the end stretch of the Bush administration, that production plummeted. President Obama, with only a few days into the job, saw that number was down to 9 million, a year-over-year drop of more than 40%. General Motors and Chrysler were on the brink of bankruptcy, with Ford at risk close behind. The entire auto supply chain, with millions of workers at countless companies across the country, was at risk.

"Nothing in the world is more dangerous than sincere ignorance and conscientious stupidity."

Martin Luther King, Jr.

In the midst of the financial meltdown, Detroit's Big Three automakers, General Motors, Ford and Chrysler, pleaded with Congress for a $25 billion lifeline to save their companies from collapse.

Former General Motors CEO Rick Wagoner told the Senate Banking Committee that he blamed the industry's predicament not on failures by its leadership, but on the deepening global financial crisis. Let's not forget that the Big Three have been retooling their firms since the mid-80s, when they started facing real competition, and had wasted about $500 billion in recent years attempting a turnaround. Yet, here they were asking for billions of dollars of taxpayers money.

In the spirit of leading stupidly, the CEOs of all three automakers flew to the nation's capital in private jets to make their case. Wagoner's private jet trip to Washington cost his company an estimated $20,000 roundtrip. Ford CEO Mulally's corporate jet was a perk included for both he and his wife as part of his employment contract along with a $28 million salary.

There is nothing wrong with negotiating the best financial package possible. However, showing up in private jets begging for government assistance shows a serious lack of situational awareness, which you will see, often leads to ClusterPhucks.

Mulally made his case before the committee saying he had cut expenses, laid-off workers and closed 17 plants. Mulally stated, "We have also reduced our work force by 51,000 employees in the past three years."

145

Obama felt that he had to move forcefully and fast because he could see all the jobs at stake, and he pictured the families and communities behind those jobs. But rather than just hand out tax dollars, Obama utilized a **Transactional Leadership** approach, which required automakers to adhere to some reforms.

One of the key elements of the transactional style of leadership is for the leader to get involved and "apply corrective measures" only when the ClusterPhuck is already in play, which is exactly what Obama did.

Of course there were critics who were concerned that the federal government was far too involved in the free market by dictating terms and conditions, even though they were begging for the government to bail them out. The initial estimates of the bailout price tag exceeded $80 billion, but as the bank industry recovered, taxpayers recovered all of the money Obama pumped into it and almost all of what went to Detroit. By 2015, American car and truck makers were banking record profits on booming sales at little cost to taxpayers.

As unpopular as the bailout of the banking industry was, that began under President Bush, by most measures, it worked. Instead of a slew of bank failures, Americans ended up with a stronger financial system, and the public got its money back. All the tax dollars devoted to the bank rescue wound up being repaid.

Healthcare and Leadership Stupidity

While the economy was crashing around him, Obama still wanted to deliver on a promise that Democrats have made for generations, medical insurance for all. Obama pushed through Congress, without a single Republican vote, the Affordable Care Act. But like any major complex undertaking, implementing what was now called Obamacare, was fraught with the same problems that the rollout of Medicare and Medicaid initially experienced.

Republicans spent years criticizing Obamacare for high premiums, high deductibles, high copays, and daunting complexity. How could something that virtually everyone wants for themselves and their families, go so wrong?

The Obama administration wanted to make health insurance more accessible to those who had traditionally struggled to get covered, such as the people who were sicker, older, poorer, and did not have access to employer-sponsored coverage. Democrats didn't just want to get millions covered. They had specific demographics in mind they wanted to benefit. They had to make very clear trade-offs to advantage this older, sicker population.

For example, the law limits the premiums that insurers could charge their oldest consumers to just three times whatever they billed the youngest enrollees. The Affordable Care Act mandated that insurers must cover 10 "essential health benefit" categories. These changes were great for those who were older and required significant medical care. But bringing unhealthy people into the market is difficult, because it requires the healthy people, who had pretty good deals in the past, to pay higher rates.

In 2012, the Obama administration wanted one-third of the marketplace enrollees to be between the ages of 18 and 34, however they never met that goal. One of President Obama's key health care advisers believed that they tilted the playing field too far in favor of the sick and elderly, making it difficult for young people to sign up. In hindsight, according to an advisor, the administration should have let insurers charge older people more, perhaps four times as much as the youngest consumers.

This is not the legacy Obama wanted. When President Obama, now out of office, reflected back on how they started the pursuit of universal healthcare, stated:

"We said, 'What's a system out there that seems to be providing coverage for everybody that politically we could get through a Congress, which we can get Republican support?...And lo and behold, there had been a plan in Massachusetts that had been designed on a bipartisan basis, including by a Republican governor who ultimately became the nominee for the Republican Party, that came close to providing universal coverage. I would have thought — since this was an idea that had previously gotten a lot of Republican support — it would continue to get a lot of Republican support. And yet magically, the minute we said, 'This is a great idea, and it's working,' the Republicans said, 'this is terrible, and we don't want to do this.'"

Integrative Public Leadership refers to the work of *"...integrating people, resources, and organizations across various boundaries to tackle complex public problems and achieve the common good."* President Obama met repeatedly with congressional Republicans to find common ground, and so did Congressional Democrats, to no avail. It didn't matter what the cost would be, how the law would be designed, or how it would work. They simply refused to work together to design a bill that would please both parties.

But why wouldn't you, as a person that is getting paid by tax payers to look out for my best interests, work with the other party to come up with a bipartisan solution to healthcare? Republican Senate Leader Mitch McConnell explained his strategy, when he stated:

"We worked very hard to keep our fingerprints off of these proposals...Because we thought — correctly, I think — that the only way the American people would know that a great debate was going on was if the measures were not bipartisan. When you hang the 'bipartisan' tag on something, the perception is that differences have been worked out, and there's a broad agreement that that's the way forward."

Apparently, there is evidence to suggest that McConnell is right. Voter's judge bipartisanship based on votes rather than ideas, so keeping Republicans united against Obama's major proposals was an effective strategy against a President who had promised a more civil and collaborative culture.

McConnell's biggest fear was having a handful of Senate Republicans voting for the Affordable Care Act and then praising Obama's commitment to bipartisan ideas and governance. The campaign ads would have been powerful and Obama's approval ratings would have soared. Remember how Republicans turned on Chris Christie when he praised Obama's leadership during the storm? Is this what we have grown to believe is good leadership?

So McConnell admits to not participating in the healthcare proposals for political reasons. However, in 2013, Alan K. Simpson, a former U.S. Senator from Wyoming, squarely blamed the Democrats and stated the following:

"The spectacularly-botched Affordable Care Act is messed up precisely because the President and the Democrats exploited any and all congressional procedures to ram it through over the strong opposition of the minority, using special budget reconciliation procedures that prevented the minority from amending the legislation. Now, three years later, the public is sadly finding out that the valid concerns of the minority were absolutely right all along -- that many people would really lose their previous health coverage under the law, and that the financing mechanisms underlying the law would swiftly unravel, which they have already begun to do. Had there been some honest effort to incorporate the views of those across the aisle, the ACA might not have been so badly screwed up. Instead we now have a law that is a complete mess, with one side determined to kill it, and the other side determined to implement it without alteration despite all evidence of its massive problems.

It's because of this arrogance and hubris of ignoring the minority that we now have a law with no bipartisan investment in even trying to fix the damn thing and making it work. To prevent similar outcomes in the future, we need more bipartisan cooperation, not more partisan bullying."

So, you have McConnell admitting that they purposely kept their *"fingerprints off"* of the healthcare proposals, and former Senator Simpson totally contradicting McConnell by saying it was the Democrats that wouldn't accept "views of those" across the aisle.

This is why the American people are fed up with politics and politicians. They were looking for transformative leaders to solve their healthcare needs, but instead got pseudo-transformational leaders, that is, giving importance to their own interests while neglecting the well-being of their constituents.

Are We Missing Something?

According to a recent 2017 opinion poll, 83 percent of the American public thinks laws are more effective when parties compromise and arrive at a bipartisan solution. Only 17 percent think laws are more effective when one party has complete control.

Regarding healthcare, 87% of Democrats and 73% of Republicans want **collaboration** on healthcare. Couple that with a recent Gallop poll that revealed that 54% percent of Americans want political leaders in Washington to compromise to get things done. This far outpaces the 18% who would prefer that leaders stick to their beliefs even if little gets done, while the views of 28% fall somewhere in between.

There is not only a clear communications gap between political parties and the public, but also a glaring failure of leadership. The vast majority of the American people were screaming for both parties to work together to fix problems that affect them directly. This leadership failure can be attributed to a lack of **Situation Awareness**.

Situational awareness involves being aware of what is happening in the vicinity, in order to understand how information, events, and one's own actions will impact goals and objectives, both immediately and in the near future. An individual with an adept sense of situation awareness generally has a high degree of knowledge with respect to inputs and outputs of a system, along with an innate feel for situations, people, and events.

***

Presidential Leadership Rankings

In 2017, C-SPAN released the results its third historian's survey of presidential leadership. Historians Survey of Presidential Leadership, in which a cross-section of 91 presidential historians ranked the 43 former occupants of the White House on the following ten **Individual Leadership Characteristics:**

- **Crisis Leadership**
- **Economic Management**
- **Moral Authority**
- **International Relations**
- **Administrative Skills**
- **Relations with Congress**
- **Vision / Setting an Agenda**
- **Pursued Equal Justice For All**
- **Performance Within Context of Times**
- **Public Persuasion**

C-SPAN's academic advisors "devised a survey in which participants used a one ("not effective") to ten ("very effective") scale to rate each president on ten qualities of presidential leadership. Surveys were distributed to historians and other professional observers of the presidency, drawn from a database of C-SPAN's programming, augmented by suggestions from the academic advisors. Ninety-one agreed to participate. Participants were guaranteed that individual survey results remain confidential. Survey responses were tabulated by averaging all responses in a given category for each President. Each of the ten categories was given equal weighting in arriving at a president's total score."

The top five presidents on the list, when you consider the above attributes, ranks Abraham Lincoln, George Washington, Franklin D. Roosevelt, Theodore Roosevelt, and Dwight D. Eisenhower as the best.

When you focus just on modern day presidents, you have Ronald Reagan at #9, Barack Obama at #12, Bill Clinton at #15, George H.W. Bush at #20, and George W. Bush at #33.

In March of 2018, a survey of 170 presidential historians released their Presidents & Executive Politics Presidential Greatness survey. President Abraham Lincoln topped the list with George Washington, Franklin Delano Roosevelt, Teddy Roosevelt and Thomas Jefferson rounding out the top five. The only change in the top five was Thomas Jefferson edging out Dwight D. Eisenhower. The modern day presidential rankings had Obama at #8, Reagan at #9, Clinton at #13, George H.W. Bush at #17, and George W. Bush at #30.

Presidential surveys go back to the 1940s conducted by American academics, historians and political scientists. First in the field was Arthur M. Schlesinger Sr. with his polls in 1948 and 1962, grading all the presidents since George Washington in these categories: Great, Near Great, Average, Below Average and Failure.

Arthur M. Schlesinger Jr, updated the survey on the same basis to poll 32 experts on the presidents from Washington to Clinton. Over the years, many other studies have appeared, criticizing the whole idea of ranking presidents as meaningless; alleging that such an exercise has a built-in bias towards so-called 'activist' presidents or that the respondents' political orientations skew the results.

John F. Kennedy's response to a 1962 Schlesinger poll, stated, 'How the hell can you tell?' He argued that only the president himself could know what his real pressures and real alternatives were, and suggested that the difference a president really made and the quality of presidential performance could in the end only be judged by someone who had held the office.

Situational factors, such as wars, international crises, economic problems, the difficulty of the issues and the overall situation facing the president, was acknowledged by some studies, and though these factors were difficult to measure, quantify or compare them.

It is argued that this means that the rankings reveal more about the views and values of the academic respondents than about actual presidential performance.

Whatever the precise methodology, the results of the different US presidential studies have generally turned out to be remarkably similar, rating Lincoln, Washington and Franklin D. Roosevelt at the top and Grant and Harding at the bottom. However, it appears that Harding may finally get out of the bottom slot.

The survey of the 170 presidential historians that was released in March of 2018, rank Donald J. Trump as the worst president in history. The survey also found that Trump was considered the "most polarizing" president. He also ranked in the bottom five among all categories of respondents including **Republican, Democrats, Independents, Liberals, Conservatives and Moderates**. Is this a fair assessment of President Trump? Shouldn't he have more time to show that he is among the best presidents in history, or has he truly, in the eyes of presidential historians, the worst president the United States has ever elected? Let's look at the evidence.

Chapter 5

Dr. Gregory L. Cotton

The Trump Presidency

Some of you may be wondering why I didn't include President Trump in the Presidential Leadership chapter with the other presidents. The truth is, Trump needed his own chapter because he is by far the most unique president that the United States has ever elected to office. When I use the term "unique", I am referring to the way in which he campaigned, crushed his Republican rivals, beat Hillary Clinton, as well as the many legal clouds he had on his way to becoming President.

But how did we get here? As you will see, there were plenty of warning signs of what a Trump presidency would look like...but here we are.

On September 14, 2012, on the 225th anniversary of the Constitution, former Supreme Court Justice David Souter discussed the meaning of the Constitution, and the importance of educating young people on how their government works. Judge Souter stated:

"I don't worry about our losing Republican government in the United States because I'm afraid of a foreign invasion. I don't worry about it because I think there is going to be a coup by the military as has happened in some of other places. What I worry about is that when problems are not addressed, people will not know who is responsible. And when the problems get bad enough, as they might do, for example, with another serious terrorist attack, as they might do with another financial meltdown, some one person will come forward and say, 'Give me total power and I will solve this problem.'

"That is how the Roman republic fell. Augustus became emperor, not because he arrested the Roman Senate. He became emperor because he promised that he would solve problems that were not being solved.

"If we know who is responsible, I have enough faith in the American people to demand performance from those responsible. If we don't know, we will stay away from the polls. We will not demand it. And the day will come when somebody will come forward and we and the government will in effect say, 'Take the ball and run with it. Do what you have to do.'

"That is the way democracy dies. And if something is not done to improve the level of civic knowledge, that is what you should worry about at night."

***

You may want to go back and read what Judge Souter said, 2 or 3 times to really let it sink in.

Judge Souter predicted that a candidate like Donald Trump would come to power and promise to solve all of the problems that people had been hoping the Republican or Democratic parties would solve.

Over and over during his campaign Trump would tell followers that only he could keep Americans safe and only he could fix the political system, and that only he could "make possible every dream you've ever dreamed." It didn't matter to people that he wouldn't release his tax returns or bankrupted several businesses. It didn't matter about the hundreds of lawsuits or the women that accused him of sexual harassment. It also didn't matter that he encouraged violence during his campaign speeches, or that he attacked the ethnicity of a federal judge and called for the imprisonment of his opponent.

It also didn't matter that for years he lied about President Obama, saying that he was NOT born in the United States, or publicly stating that Senator John McCain wasn't a war hero because he was shot down. This coming from a man that never served in the military, due to five deferments, because he had bone spurs. For good measure, he also mocked a disabled reporter. When I say "mocked", I mean he literally stood at the podium in front of his supporters and made fun of a disabled person.

In a 2016 poll conducted by Bloomberg News, people were asked what bothered them most about Donald Trump out of all of his controversies. The "likely voters" selected one action above all others, and that was when then candidate Trump mocked a reporter with a disability. I would venture a guess that most Americans haven't seen the video of Trump mocking a disabled reporter or had the time to delve deeply into all of his controversies prior to the election. However, there are people that did take a deep dive into Trumps background, and tried their very best to warn the voting public.

Pseudo-Transformational Leadership is defined by *"...self-serving, yet highly inspirational leadership behaviors, unwillingness to encourage independent thought in subordinates, and little caring for one's subordinates more generally."*

Anticipating Trump's Leadership Style

Prior to Trump taking office, Aubrey Immelman conducted a personality-based analysis of what Mr. Trumps likely leadership style as president would be like. According Immelman, Trump's psychological profile predicted the following generalized expectancies regarding his leadership style as president:

Leadership Motivation. As an extraordinarily confident individual with an unshakable belief in his own talents, leadership ability, and potential for success, a quest for power will be the prime motivator for Trump's leadership behavior, punctuated by a need to control situations and dominate adversaries. Furthermore, Trump's outgoing nature suggests concern with popular approval and a striving for self-validation to affirm his inflated self-esteem. In addition, he will likely be more pragmatic than ideological in pursuing his political objectives.

Leadership Orientation. Given his supreme self-confidence and high dominance, Trump will likely be more goal directed than relationship oriented. As a task-oriented leader, Trump will not permit the maintenance of good relations to stand in the way of goal achievement. This orientation will be offset to some extent by Trump's outgoing tendencies which, in addition, will also prime him to place a high premium on loyalty among his advisers and members of his administration.

Job Performance. Big egos have a strong drive to prove themselves. Thus, Trump can be expected to be tireless (committed and energetic) in the amount of effort invested in carrying out the duties of his office. This tendency will be reinforced by strong power motivation stemming from high dominance and dynamic energy derived from his extraverted, outgoing personality.

Managerial Style. In organizing and managing the decision-making process, Trump will be heavy on self-promotion and persuasion, making him more of an advocate for his policy agenda than a consensus builder or an arbitrator.

Executive Style. In dealing with Congress, members of his Cabinet, and senior government officials, Trump will likely be highly involved, acting in ways that could variously be described as attention seeking, demanding, domineering, antagonistic, competitive, controlling, combative, manipulative, and exploitative—though he certainly is capable of behaving in a collegial, cooperative, harmonious fashion if he believes it will serve his own self-interest.

Media Relations. In his dealings with the press, Trump will maintain a measure of harmony, to the extent he feels he can dictate or manipulate the media. However, the likelihood of a highly critical press, in conjunction with Trump's sensitivity to personal slights, portends a relatively closed (inaccessible, uninformative, unfriendly) relationship with the media characterized by a lack of cooperation that could quickly escalate into outright hostility.

Public Relations. In relating to the public, outgoing, confident leaders such as Trump typically are active (preferring direct engagement), articulating and defending their policies in person rather than relying on surrogates and proxies. This tendency will be reinforced by Trump's dominant, strong-willed, outspoken personality and fueled by his extraversion, which will feed his preference for direct engagement with the public.

Ms. Immelman concluded that you could expect a President Trump to have an "…an inclination to act impulsively without fully appreciating the implications of his decisions or the long-term consequences of his policy initiatives…" She went on to say that you can also expect President Trump to "…favor personal connections and loyalty over competence in his staffing decisions and appointments—all of which could render a Trump administration relatively vulnerable to errors of judgment and political scandal."

There were of course others that strongly believed that a Trump Presidency would be mired in a series of ClusterPhucks.

Peter Wehner, who served in the Reagan and both Bush administrations, stated, *"Mr. Trump's virulent combination of ignorance, emotional instability, demagogy, solipsism and vindictiveness would do more than result in a failed presidency; it could very well lead to a national catastrophe. The prospect of Donald Trump as commander in chief should send a chill down the spine of every American.…If Mr. Trump heads the Republican Party, it will no longer be a conservative party, it will be an angry, bigoted, populist one."*

Can't Blame Romney For Trying

Marty Linsky, a lecturer at Harvard's Kennedy School and former Republican state legislator, stated, "I think there's really a Romney One and a Romney Two. Romney One really worked very hard to try to do what he thought was in the best interests of the commonwealth; Romney Two worked very hard to position himself to run for President of the United States." Could Romney three be the individual that tried to stop Trump from ruining the Republican Party?

Take a good look at Romney's remarks warning the country about Donald Trump:

"Let me put it plainly, if we Republicans choose Donald Trump as our nominee, the prospects for a safe and prosperous future are greatly diminished. Let me explain why.

First, the economy: If Donald Trump's plans were ever implemented, the country would sink into a prolonged recession.

A few examples: His proposed 35% tariff-like penalties would instigate a trade war that would raise prices for consumers, kill export jobs, and lead entrepreneurs and businesses to flee America. His tax plan, in combination with his refusal to reform entitlements and to honestly address spending would balloon the deficit and the national debt. So even as Donald Trump has offered very few specific economic plans, what little he has said is enough to know that he would be very bad for American workers and for American families.

But wait, you say, isn't he a huge business success that knows what he's talking about? No he isn't. His bankruptcies have crushed small businesses and the men and women who worked for them. He inherited his business, he didn't create it. And what ever happened to Trump Airlines? How about Trump University? And then there's Trump Magazine and Trump Vodka and Trump Steaks, and Trump Mortgage? A business genius he is not.

Now not every policy Donald Trump has floated is bad. He wants to repeal and replace Obamacare. He wants to bring jobs home from China and Japan. But his prescriptions to do these things are flimsy at best. At the last debate, all he could remember about his healthcare plan was to remove insurance boundaries between states. Successfully bringing jobs home requires serious policy and reforms that make America the place businesses want to plant and grow. You can't punish business into doing the things you want. Frankly, the only serious policy proposals that deal with the broad range of national challenges we confront, come today from Ted Cruz, Marco Rubio, and John Kasich. One of these men should be our nominee.

I know that some people want the race to be over. They look at history and say a trend like Mr. Trump's isn't going to be stopped.

Perhaps. But the rules of political history have pretty much all been shredded during this campaign. If the other candidates can find common ground, I believe we can nominate a person who can win the general election and who will represent the values and policies of conservatism.

Given the current delegate selection process, this means that I would vote for Marco Rubio in Florida, for John Kasich in Ohio, and for Ted Cruz or whichever one of the other two contenders has the best chance of beating Mr. Trump in a given state.

Let me turn to national security and the safety of our homes and loved ones. Trump's bombast is already alarming our allies and fueling the enmity of our enemies. Insulting all Muslims will keep many of them from fully engaging with us in the urgent fight against ISIS. And for what purpose? Muslim terrorists would only have to lie about their religion to enter the country.

What he said on "60 Minutes" about Syria and ISIS has to go down as the most ridiculous and dangerous idea of the campaign season: Let ISIS take out Assad, he said, and then we can pick up the remnants. Think about that: Let the most dangerous terror organization the world has ever known take over a country? This is recklessness in the extreme.

Donald Trump tells us that he is very, very smart. I'm afraid that when it comes to foreign policy he is very, very not smart.

I am far from the first to conclude that Donald Trump lacks the temperament of be president. After all, this is an individual who mocked a disabled reporter, who attributed a reporter's questions to her menstrual cycle, who mocked a brilliant rival who happened to be a woman due to her appearance, who bragged about his marital affairs, and who laces his public speeches with vulgarity.

Donald Trump says he admires Vladimir Putin, while has called George W. Bush a liar. That is a twisted example of evil trumping good.

There is dark irony in his boasts of his sexual exploits during the Vietnam War while John McCain, whom he has mocked, was imprisoned and tortured.

Dishonesty is Trump's hallmark: He claimed that he had spoken clearly and boldly against going into Iraq. Wrong, he spoke in favor of invading Iraq. He said he saw thousands of Muslims in New Jersey celebrating 9/11. Wrong, he saw no such thing. He imagined it. His is not the temperament of a stable, thoughtful leader. His imagination must not be married to real power.

The President of the United States has long been the leader of the free world. The president and yes the nominees of the country's great parties help define America to billions of people. All of them bear the responsibility of being an example for our children and grandchildren.

Think of Donald Trump's personal qualities, the bullying, the greed, the showing off, the misogyny, the absurd third grade theatrics. We have long referred to him as "The Donald." He is the only person in America to whom we have added an article before his name. It wasn't because he had attributes we admired.

Now imagine your children and your grandchildren acting the way he does. Will you welcome that? Haven't we seen before what happens when people in prominent positions fail the basic responsibility of honorable conduct? We have, and it always injures our families and our country.

Watch how he responds to my speech today. Will he talk about our policy differences or will he attack me with every imaginable low road insult? This may tell you what you need to know about his temperament, his stability, and his suitability to be president."

Of course, this didn't go over very well with Trump. He did however interview Romney for the position of Secretary of State, which some believe was only an opportunity for Trump to see him "grovel" and apologize. After the dinner/interview, Romney stated that Trump, "…did something I tried to do and was unsuccessful in," and that the president-elect could be "the very man who can lead us to that better future." That was a pretty quick turnaround given the speech you just read from Romney. Was Romney being hypocritical or trying to put himself in a position to head off a series of Trump ClusterPhucks? Or, could it be that Romney actually dodged a bullet?

The Resistance From Within

On the 5th of September, 2018, the New York Times newspaper published on anonymous essay from a "senior official in the Trump administration whose identity is known to us and whose job would be jeopardized by its disclosure."

The anonymous official stated:

"To be clear, ours is not the popular "resistance" of the left. We want the administration to succeed and think that many of its policies have already made America safer and more prosperous. But we believe our first duty is to this country, and the president continues to act in a manner that is

detrimental to the health of our republic."

The anonymous official went on to also state:

"That is why many Trump appointees have vowed to do what we can to preserve our Democratic institutions while thwarting Mr. Trump's more misguided impulses until he is out of office. The root of the problem is the president's amorality. Anyone who works with him knows he is not moored to any discernible first principles that guide his decision making. Although he was elected as a Republican, the president shows little affinity for ideals long espoused by conservatives: free minds, free markets and free people. At best, he has invoked these ideals in scripted settings. At worst, he has attacked them outright."

Remember what several people said about what a Trump presidency would look like if he were elected? So now we have officials inside the White House trying to protect the United States from some of Trumps worst impulses. Some of you may look at this as being a case of **Proactive Leadership** on the part of the anonymous officials inside the White House, while others may be looking at this as the officials being disloyal to the President. So, is it disloyal to try and prevent massive ClusterPhucks…by saving the President Trump from himself?

The Mueller Report & Trump Obstruction

As parents, keeping our kids healthy, happy, and nurturing them in a way that ensures that they will be good citizens, is our main objective. They have all developed a keen sense of understanding right from wrong and I couldn't be more proud of how they have conducted themselves over the years.

That being said, like most parents, you do what you can to prevent your children from making life changing mistakes that could end them up in jail or worse. In other words, we try and prevent our children from creating or being involved in ClusterPhucks.

The Mueller Report, which was released on April 18, 2019, is the official report documenting the findings and conclusions of Special Counsel Robert Mueller's investigation into Russian efforts to interfere in the 2016 presidential elections. Mueller was specifically investigating whether the Trump campaign conspired or coordinated with Russia, as well as if Trump obstructed justice during the investigation.

Although there is a lot to dissect in this 448 page report, I would first like to focus in on the section of the report dealing with obstruction of justice as it relates to

President Trump. But what is obstruction of justice? According to the Merriam-Webster dictionary it is:

"The crime or act of willfully interfering with the process of justice and law especially by influencing, threatening, harming, or impeding a witness, potential witness, juror, or judicial or legal officer or by furnishing false information in or otherwise impeding an investigation or legal process."

So the argument that President Trump obstructed justice is based on the following:

- Asking the F.B.I director, James Comey to lay off of his then National Security Advisor, Michael Flynn
- His firing of F.B.I. director James Comey
- His attempt to get rid of Attorney General Jeff Sessions because he recused himself from the Russia investigation.
- His order to White House counsel Don McGahn to fire Special Counsel Mueller.
- His attempt to have his former campaign manager, Corey Lewandowski, to tell the Attorney General to unrecuse himself.
- Told Lewandowski to ask Sessions to issue a public statement saying that Trump hadn't done anything wrong and there shouldn't even be a special-counsel investigation.

In summarizing President Trumps behavior, according to the report, the following paragraph is pretty much all you need to read. It states:

"Our investigation found multiple acts by the President that were capable of exerting undue influence over law enforcement investigations, including the Russian-interference and obstruction investigations. The incidents were often carried out through one-on-one meetings in which the President sought to use his official power outside of usual channels. These actions ranged from efforts to remove the Special Counsel and to reverse the effect of the Attorney General's recusal; to the attempted use of official power to limit the scope of the investigation; to direct and indirect contacts with witnesses with the potential to influence their testimony. Viewing the acts collectively can help to illuminate their significance. For example, the President's direction to McGahn to have the Special Counsel removed was followed almost immediately by his direction to Lewandowski to tell the Attorney General to limit the scope of the Russia investigation to prospective election-interference only—a temporal connection that suggests that both acts were taken with a related purpose with respect to the investigation."

The most perplexing thing about Trumps leadership behavior during the Mueller investigative period is that he took actions to obstruct as if he was guilty, even though the Mueller Report concluded that the Trump campaign didn't criminally conspire with Russia during the 2016 elections. However, the report did conclude that his campaign did expect it would benefit *"…electorally from information stolen and released through Russian efforts."*

Additionally, several Russians, directed by the highest levels of the Kremlin, repeatedly contacted at least 17 Trump campaign officials, advisors, and associates. The report shows not only Russia's ambitious effort to influence the Trump campaign, but also how Trump aides' were eager to accept Russia's help whenever it was offered. Further, Trump officials were willing to meet with Russians in the U.S., London or Moscow and even arrange a face-to-face meeting with Putin, according to the report.

This is clearly **Unethical Leadership**, but apparently not criminal, according to the report. Although Attorney General William Barr attempted to clear Trump of obstruction of justice, Mueller did not. As a matter of fact, he was creating a path for Congress to make the decision if Trump obstructed justice, and if his actions were impeachable offenses. But why didn't Mueller make the decision?

Office of legal Counsel Policy

In 1973, the Justice Department's Office of Legal Counsel concluded:

"…the indictment or criminal prosecution of a sitting President would impermissibly undermine the capacity of the executive branch to perform its constitutionally assigned functions. It goes on to state, "Where the President is concerned, only the House of Representatives has the authority to bring charges of criminal misconduct through the constitutionally sanctioned process of impeachment."

So Mueller knew, given the policy, he could NOT indict President Trump. That being said, should he be indicted for obstruction? In May of 2019, more than 900 former federal prosecutors signed onto a letter saying President Trump would have been charged with obstruction of justice if he were anyone other than the president. The letter stated:

We are former federal prosecutors. We served under both Republican and Democratic administrations at different levels of the federal system: as line attorneys, supervisors, special prosecutors, United States Attorneys, and senior officials at the Department of Justice. The offices in which we served were small, medium, and large; urban, suburban, and rural; and located in all parts of our country.

Each of us believes that the conduct of President Trump described in Special Counsel Robert Mueller's report would, in the case of any other person not covered by the Office of Legal Counsel policy against indicting a sitting President, result in multiple felony charges for obstruction of justice.

The Mueller report describes several acts that satisfy all of the elements for an obstruction charge: conduct that obstructed or attempted to obstruct the truth-finding process, as to which the evidence of corrupt intent and connection to pending proceedings is overwhelming. These include:

· The President's efforts to fire Mueller and to falsify evidence about that effort;

· The President's efforts to limit the scope of Mueller's investigation to exclude his conduct; and

· The President's efforts to prevent witnesses from cooperating with investigators probing him and his campaign.

Attempts to fire Mueller and then create false evidence

Despite being advised by then-White House Counsel Don McGahn that he could face legal jeopardy for doing so, Trump directed McGahn on multiple occasions to fire Mueller or to gin up false conflicts of interest as a pretext for getting rid of the Special Counsel. When these acts began to come into public view, Trump made "repeated efforts to have McGahn deny the story"—going so far as to tell McGahn to write a letter "for our files" falsely denying that Trump had directed Mueller's termination.

Firing Mueller would have seriously impeded the investigation of the President and his associates—obstruction in its most literal sense. Directing the creation of false government records in order to prevent or discredit truthful testimony is similarly unlawful. The Special Counsel's report states: "Substantial evidence indicates that in repeatedly urging McGahn to dispute that he was ordered to have the Special Counsel terminated, the President acted for the purpose of influencing McGahn's account in order to deflect or prevent scrutiny of the President's conduct toward the investigation."

Attempts to limit the Mueller investigation

The report describes multiple efforts by the president to curtail the scope of the Special Counsel's investigation.

First, the President repeatedly pressured then-Attorney General Jeff Sessions to reverse his legally-mandated decision to recuse himself from the investigation. The President's stated reason was that he wanted an attorney general who would "protect" him, including from the Special Counsel investigation. He also directed then-White House Chief of Staff Reince Priebus to fire Sessions and Priebus refused.

Second, after McGahn told the President that he could not contact Sessions himself to discuss the investigation, Trump went outside the White House, instructing his former campaign manager, Corey Lewandowski, to carry a demand to Sessions to direct Mueller to confine his investigation to future elections. Lewandowski tried and failed to contact Sessions in private. After a second meeting with Trump, Lewandowski passed Trump's message to senior White House official Rick Dearborn, who Lewandowski thought would be a better messenger because of his prior relationship with Sessions. Dearborn did not pass along Trump's message.

As the report explains, "[s]ubstantial evidence indicates that the President's effort to have Sessions limit the scope of the Special Counsel's investigation to future election interference was intended to prevent further investigative scrutiny of the President's and his campaign's conduct"—in other words, the President employed a private citizen to try to get the Attorney General to limit the scope of an ongoing investigation into the President and his associates.

All of this conduct—trying to control and impede the investigation against the President by leveraging his authority over others—is similar to conduct we have seen charged against other public officials and people in powerful positions.

Witness tampering and intimidation

The Special Counsel's report establishes that the President tried to influence the decisions of both Michael Cohen and Paul Manafort with regard to cooperating with investigators. Some of this tampering and intimidation, including the dangling of pardons, was done in plain sight via tweets and public statements; other such behavior was done via private messages through private attorneys, such as Trump counsel Rudy

Giuliani's message to Cohen's lawyer that Cohen should "[s]leep well tonight[], you have friends in high places."

Of course, these aren't the only acts of potential obstruction detailed by the Special Counsel. It would be well within the purview of normal prosecutorial judgment also to charge other acts detailed in the report.

We emphasize that these are not matters of close professional judgment. Of course, there are potential defenses or arguments that could be raised in response to an indictment of the nature we describe here. In our system, every accused person is presumed innocent and it is always the government's burden to prove its case beyond a reasonable doubt. But, to look at these facts and say that a prosecutor could not probably sustain a conviction for obstruction of justice—the standard set out in Principles of Federal Prosecution—runs counter to logic and our experience.

As former federal prosecutors, we recognize that prosecuting obstruction of justice cases is critical because unchecked obstruction—which allows intentional interference with criminal investigations to go unpunished— puts our whole system of justice at risk. We believe strongly that, but for the OLC memo, the overwhelming weight of professional judgment would come down in favor of prosecution for the conduct outlined in the Mueller Report.

***

What would possess hundreds of former Republican and Democratic federal prosecutors to feel they needed to publicly speak out about President Trumps obstruction of justice? One could argue that this ClusterPhuck was cultivated by Attorney General William Barr, who has perhaps lost his credibility faster than any attorney general in history, by writing a four page summary that cleared Trump and his campaign of wrongdoing. His summary clearly "misled" the public on the findings, which prompted Special Counsel Robert Mueller to send Barr a letter, which in part stated:

"The summary letter the Department sent to Congress and released to the public late in the afternoon of March 24 did not fully capture the context, nature, and substance of this Office's work and conclusions,"...There is now public confusion about critical aspects of the results of our investigation. This threatens to undermine a central purpose for which the Department appointed the Special Counsel: to assure full public confidence in the outcome of the investigations."

Barr's leadership as attorney general is now in serious question, and will be examined in the next chapter, as we delve into institutional leadership and those that enable bad behavior. But for now we continue on with President Trumps leadership actions.

As you have read, there were plenty clouds of doubts forming as to candidate Trumps competence, fitness, and temperament to hold the most powerful executive position in world. You have to ask yourself, did he really expect or want to be president?

The Accidental President?

In his book Fire & Fury, Michael Wolff wrote that Trump's longtime friend and former head of Fox News Roger Ailes, used to say ***"if you want a career in television, first run for president."*** His assertion was that Trump's plan was to start a news network and become "the most famous man in the world." Wolff went on to say that Trump wanted the fame that goes along with running a successful campaign, but that he wasn't quite as happy claiming the job of president. Trump and his campaign never planned to win and were unprepared when he entered office.

Wolff wasn't the only one who felt that Trump wasn't serious about winning the presidency. The former communications director of the Make America Great Again PAC, Stephanie Cegielski, wrote that Donald Trump never really wanted to be president. She went on to state, ***"I'll say it again: Trump never intended to be the candidate. But his pride is too out of control to stop him now."***

She goes on to say that Trump "doesn't want" the White House, but he "…wants to be able to say that he could have run the White House." Cegielski revealed that she was "…part of the silent majority that led to Trump's rise…" that wanted Trump to "be real", but that "…Trump only cares about Trump."

If all of this is true about Trumps real motivation behind running for president, would it worry you as to how he would lead the country? Even more importantly, how has President Trump faired in the eyes of the world with regards to his leadership actions and personal behaviors since taking office?

A Culture of Lies and Misleading Statements

We all have told lies, or made misleading statements. We do it to protect ourselves, our loved ones, to get out of trouble, or lie for the company we work for. Since 1976, Gallup has been polling Americans to rank various professions from least to most ethical.

Nurses are nearly always perceived to be the most honest, while politicians are consistently ranked on the opposite end. People polled believe that members of Congress are more unethical than car salesmen and telemarketers, and this was before Trump became a politician.

Presidents throughout history have lied or misled as well. President Lyndon B. Johnson disseminated a myriad of falsehoods and cover-ups surrounding Vietnam. John F. Kennedy was one of the most dishonest presidents to have ever lived, given his affairs with allegedly three White House secretaries (one was his wife Jackie's press secretary), and a 19-year-old college sophomore, and White House intern.

There were also reportedly numerous Hollywood stars and starlets and call girls who were paid by Dave Powers. Kennedy's worst lie to the public concerned the Bay of Pigs, when he promised that there would be "no military intervention in Cuba." Just five days later, on April 17, 1961, Kennedy approved a covert invasion by the CIA.

President Franklin D. Roosevelt went to great lengths to hide the extent of his health problems from voters during his New York gubernatorial and presidential campaigns. When he was trying to win a third White House term, he stated, "I have said this before, but I shall say it again and again and again…your boys are not going to be sent into any foreign wars."

Roosevelt, even as he made these assurances, knew war with Germany and Japan was likely inevitable, as he and Winston Churchill were secretly planning for that eventuality. Also, according to his biographer, Roosevelt had an affair with his wife's secretary, and it was she, not his wife, who was the face he saw before he died.

President Obama lied and earned Polititact's "Lie of the Year" with his repeated claim that "if you like your health care plan, you can keep it." Nixon tried to cover up his role in the Watergate scandal, Clinton was impeached by the House of Representatives for lying under oath, and of course, there is President George W. Bush proclaiming that there was "no doubt" Iraq had weapons of mass destruction.

Like I stated in the last chapter, all presidents create ClusterPhucks, some with a lie, whether intentionally or not, and some with controversial leadership actions they take….there is simply no way around it. That being said, President Trump has told more lies and has created more ClusterPhucks, than any other president in history.

On April 26, 2019, according to The Washington Post, which established a Fact Checker database, President Trump crossed the 10,000 "false or misleading claims mark" since he has taken over the Oval Office.

He continuously lies about immigration, such as stating that "open borders bring tremendous crime", although there is no documented link between illegal immigration and crime. He claimed he passed the biggest tax cut in history, and had cut the estate tax to "zero", which are lies.

He lied about being one vote away from repealing Obamacare, as well as falsely claiming that the United States paid for "almost 100 percent" of NATO, and that Saudi Arabia signed $450 billion in deals with the Trump administration, and even that the United States subsidizes the Saudi military, which really amounts to about $10,000 a year. He exaggerated the size of trade deficits with Japan, China and the European Union and falsely claimed the United States loses money from such deficits.

According to the economists at **Deutsche Bank**, The U.S. has a surplus of $20 billion with China and $1.4 trillion with the rest of the world. They point out that while trade and corporate data aren't usually combined, if you add up all trade data, sales by U.S. companies in foreign countries and foreign firms in the U.S., the *"U.S. companies have sold more to the rest of the world than other countries have sold to the U.S. in the past ten years"*

Years before becoming President, Trump continuously fostered the *"birther"* lie that President Obama was a Muslim and not born in the United States. This led to many voters doubting Obama's documented place of birth and thus the legitimacy of his presidency. In September 2016 Trump finally did admit that Obama was born in the United States, but falsely accused Hillary Clinton of starting the birther lie.

There were more outlandish lies like claiming that he saw Muslims celebrating in New Jersey on 9/11, or saying that he would have won the popular vote in 2016 if millions of illegal aliens had not voted for Hillary Clinton. He claimed that the U.S. unemployment rate was 42 percent, when it was actually around five percent.

He claimed that the United States had the highest taxes in the world, and also claimed that President Obama had tapped the phones of his transition operation. In 2017, he declared that the U.S. murder rate was the highest in 47 years when the national murder rate had been steadily falling since the 1990s.

This type **Intemperate and Callas Leadership** is dangerous in many ways. First, the President is the most powerful person in the world, when you consider the United States' economic and military power. If Trumps lies become "normalized", which is arguably the case in some circles, we risk succumbing to a lie that could start another unwanted drawn-out war. Furthermore, employees and executive staff typically take their cues from their leader. Meaning, if the leader lies, it basically empowers others to lie as well.

The Mueller Report documented at least 77 specific instances where President Donald Trump's campaign staff, administration officials and family members, Republican backers and his associates, lied or made false assertions (sometimes unintentionally) to the public, Congress, or authorities. The report also revealed that a number of lies came from Trump himself, and most of them took place while he was President.

The public was warned early on that telling falsehoods, misstatements, or outright lies, would perhaps be the norm in the Trump administration. In 2017, President Trump directed then press secretary Sean Spicer to go to the White House briefing room to talk about the inauguration crowd size, in which he stated that Trump had attracted *"the largest audience ever to witness an inauguration in person and in the world...period."*

Of course, this was a lie that could easily be debunked simply by comparing Obama's 2009 inauguration aerial photos against Trumps.

Nevertheless, Senior White House Advisor Kellyanne Conway, defended Spicer by stating, *"our press secretary -- gave alternative facts."* Alternative facts are simply lies. Spicer and Conway lost all credibility in the eyes of the public. By the way, after resigning his position as press secretary, Spicer was asked if he regretted making the statements concerning the inauguration, in which his response was, "Of course I do, absolutely."

Spicer wouldn't be the last press secretary to lie to the public. Current press secretary Sarah Sanders told the public that "countless members of the FBI" had contacted her to say they had lost confidence in FBI Director James Comey. However, the Mueller Report shows that she lied about FBI members calling her. She called it a "slip of the tongue" even though she was reading it from a prepared statement. She has since been on television attempting to rationalize her lie...only making things worse. There have been calls for her to step down, but when you have a boss that is considered by many to be a pathological liar, why wouldn't she?

Bad Hiring Practices = ClusterPhucktual Organization

In computer science, **garbage in, garbage out** (**GIGO**), describes the concept that *flawed, or nonsense input data produces nonsense output or "garbage"*.

Having spent several years in Army recruiting, I was privy to many, many antidotes from commanding generals. One in particular talked about the concept of "garbage in, garbage out". In recruiting, what he was trying to convey, was that if you filled your daily appointments with people who are unqualified, or have questionable backgrounds (garbage in), the result (garbage out), will be that very few will actually be able to join the Army. In other words, he was telling us to stay in the "quality" market.

As a candidate, Trump stated that he would "surround myself only with the best and most serious people" if he was elected. In just the first year and a half of his presidency, 57% of Trump's "A Team" staffers had left the White House, which is at a much higher rate than his predecessors. There were seven Cabinet officials included in the numbers.

Additionally, Trump has hired people that are corrupt, incompetent, and completely unqualified to serve in the most important building in the world...The White House. You've already read the laundry list of corrupt actions by Pruitt in an earlier chapter.

By July 2018, Pruitt was under at least 15 separate federal investigations by the Government Accountability Office, the EPA inspector general, the White House Office of Management and Budget, and the U.S. Office of Special Counsel. He demonstrated multiple times that he has an **Unethical Leadership** style, bordering on **Callas Leadership**, given that he does not care for the environment and the people affected by it.

Pruitt was appointed to lead the Environmental Protection Agency, whose mission is "to protect human and environmental health." Prior to his EPA position, Pruitt was Oklahoma's Attorney General...who sued the Environmental Protection Agency at least 14 times regarding the agency's actions. To make matters worse, Pruitt rejected the scientific consensus that human-caused carbon dioxide emissions are a primary contributor to climate change.

This would be like placing a person to lead the Pentagon, whose work experience is limited to having a background as a grounds keeper, with no military training, who is a pacifist, feels that the military is a useless organization, and believes we should go back to fighting with World War II era weapons. By the way, he also has a financial interest in World War II weapons. Is it a surprise to anyone that Pruitt is the most corrupt administrator in the history of the EPA? He is not the only "best and serious" people Trump brought to the White House, of course.

Dr. Ben Carson, who was a candidate for President, ranks in the same category as Pruitt as it pertains to **Incompetent Leadership**. The retired neurosurgeon was confirmed as Housing and Urban Development Secretary, despite the fact that he had no prior government experience and had a staunchly conservative view of public assistance.

To make matters worse, Carson had put out word that he wasn't qualified to run a federal agency…but somehow he felt that he was qualified to be President of the United States? His **Incompetent Leadership** style has been on full display since he took over the agency.

Under Carson's tenure, HUD has steadily devolved into a do-nothing department, which, by the way, is directly responsible for the housing needs of millions of low-income Americans. HUD has gradually slowed or ceased many existing initiatives, especially if those initiatives pertained to protecting the rights of LGBTQ people. Additionally, virtually all the top political jobs below Carson remained vacant.

He awarded large salaries to staffers with little experience and few academic credentials:

The raises, documented in a Washington Post analysis of HUD political hires, resulted in annual salaries between $98,000 and $155,000 for the five appointees, all of whom had worked on Donald Trump's or Ben Carson's presidential campaigns. Three of them did not list bachelor's degrees on their résumés.

Carson has also shown other **Corrupt** and **Unethical Leadership** tendencies as well. According to the GAO's general counsel, HUD broke the law when it obligated over $31,000 for the purchase of a dining set and nearly $9,000 for the purchase and installation of a new dishwasher and water treatment system. Under law, federal employees are "prohibited from spending in excess of an appropriation and an agency is restricted under law from spending more than $5,000 to furnish or redecorate an office without notifying Congress."

Carson has shown to be totally incompetent, unprofessional, and an utter embarrassment, due to his lack of basic knowledge of what his job responsibilities are. There are others, of course. Kelly Sadler, a former White House communications aide, mocked Senator John McCain and his battle against brain cancer. McCain was opposed to CIA nominee Gina Haspel. Sadler stated, "It doesn't matter, he's dying anyway."

Retired General Michael Flynn, who President Obama told Trump not to hire, had the shortest stint in history as national security adviser. By the way, Flynn was under FBI investigation when he denied that he and Russian Ambassador

Kislyak discussed Russia's reaction to new U.S. sanctions over election interference. However, a transcript of the conversation, based on a secret wiretap, showed that they had. Flynn pleaded guilty to lying to the FBI in a Jan. 24, 2017 interview.

Omarosa Onee Manigault Newman, best known as a contestant on the first season of NBC's reality television series **The Apprentice**, was hired as an assistant to the president and director of communications for the Office of Public Liaison.

Always controversial, when she got married in 2017, Omarosa took her bridal party to do a photo shoot in the White House, without permission, and was also unable to post her photos because of concerns over ethics and security. Eventually, enough was enough, and she was fired, but not before recording many of her conversations within the White House. She wrote a "tell-all" book about how bad Trump was and that he was a "racist". As expected, Trump responded by calling her a "dog". By the way, there is zero sympathy for her in the African-American community.

The deep hostility that African-Americans harbor for Newman stems largely from her defense of Trump and her public silence as he repeatedly attacked the American citizenship of former President Barack Obama; insulted various minority groups and described some African nations as "shithole" countries.

She was the highest-profile African-American on the White House staff, and pushed back on accusations that Trump was racist. She once told PBS' "Frontline" that *"Every critic, every detractor will have to bow down under President Trump."* Yes, her 15 minutes of fame are coming to an end.

To be fair, she is not the only staffer who has defended Trumps bad behavior. Yes, no doubt, she was unqualified to be anywhere near the White House. However, there are three types of staffers working for Trump:

1. They defend Trump, regardless of what comes out of his mouth, when a microphone is thrust in front of their faces.
2. They keep low profiles, do their jobs, and stay away from the media.
3. They smile and nod in the background, or presents a stoic demeanor as Trump lies or misleads the public.
4. They feel that they have a duty to serve the country, and stomach what goes on…BUT, will leave when working for Trump has become unbearable.

So, given the chaos, unethical behaviors, and the overall toxic environment created both internally and externally within Trumps White House, how would you view your employment opportunities once you left?

According to "current and former administration officials, top recruiters, and lobbyists", people who worked in the Trump White House are "toxic" and that companies are worried about legal drama. All companies welcome the positive publicity behind hiring someone that came from the White House…if, of course, they are not subject to some kind of subpoena later down the road. Why take the reputational risk? Especially when the potential employee was allowed a security clearance for which they were horribly unqualified to receive.

When Security Doesn't Matter

A **Security Clearance** is basically *"a license issued by an agency, the head of a department, or a branch of the federal government. Federal employees and most employees operating in the private sector are required to obtain security clearance. These employees require clearance because their position grants them access to classified information and documents. Any employee working in an organization that is developing, receiving, or sending information that the federal government considers significant to National Security will require a level of security clearance"*.

Currently, there are three levels of security clearance, which are:

Confidential: This level often refers to clearance of materials and documents. If these materials and documents are not properly concealed, they may cause considerable damage to national security. For the most part, all military personnel are granted this entry level of clearance.

Secret: The Secret level of clearance pertains to information and the disclosure of information. This level is considerably more important because any release of this type of information can cause severe damage to national security.

Top Secret: Employees at this level have access to materials, documents, and information that if released can cause unusually severe damage to national security.

The only requirement for obtaining a higher security clearance is enduring a more extensive background check. In addition, Secret and Top Secret clearance levels will almost certainly have some type of military involvement in the clearance process.

Tricia Newbold was a veteran manager in the White House office that processes security clearances, and had worked there since 2000. Carl Kline was the director of the White House Presidential Personnel Office. Multiple sources stated in January 2019, that in at least 30 cases, professional security experts expressed concerns about granting top-secret clearances to specific Trump officials, including his son-in-law, Jared Kushner. Kline took it upon himself and overruled their concerns, and allowed people who were "rejected", to obtain security clearances.

How would you feel as a parent, if you found out that the person babysitting your child, was not allowed to be near children because of several incidents of child neglect…but was cleared anyway by a local child care service manager? Would you feel betrayed? Pissed off? Basically, Carl Kline has singlehandedly sold out his country to please his boss. Again, another display of **Unethical Leadership** in the Trump White House.

Remember, entire corporations have been destroyed by the decisions made by 2 or 3 individuals. Kline is responsible for planting 30 sleeper, high-potential ClusterPhuckers, in the White House. This is how organizations are destroyed from within.

A Mob Boss Mentality & Corrupt Intent

Have you ever heard of the saying, "Deny, deny, deny, and file counter charges." It is used as a defensive measure for when someone accuses you of wrongdoing. In 2018, President Donald Trump and congressional Republicans were urging the Justice Department to look into corruption allegations involving the Clinton foundation.

However, it was the Trump Foundation that proved to be corrupt. The New York state's attorney general's office found *"a shocking pattern of illegality involving the Trump Foundation — including unlawful coordination with the Trump presidential campaign, repeated and willful self-dealing, and much more."*

The organization has undergone widespread scrutiny with allegations that Trump used the charity as a wing of his 2016 presidential campaign. President Trump finally agreed to shut down the charity and disperse the remaining funds in its account. There remains an ongoing lawsuit that is seeking $2.8 million in restitution and penalties.

The lawsuit is also seeking to bar Trump and his three eldest children from serving on the boards of other New York charities. The attorney general went on to say that the foundation has been functioning *"as little more than a checkbook to serve Mr. Trump's business and political interests.* "

Remember Trump University? When the so-called "school" was established in 2005, the New York State Education Department warned that it was in violation of state law for operating without a NYSED license. Trump ignored these warnings. Students were "scammed" into paying as much as $60,000 to the "fake" school.

How could this happen? The New York State suit suggests the following:

"The free seminars were the first step in a bait and switch to induce prospective students to enroll in increasingly expensive seminars starting with the three-day $1495 seminar and ultimately one of respondents' advanced seminars such as the "Gold Elite" program costing $35,000."

The suit goes on to say:

"At the "free" 90-minute introductory seminars to which Trump University advertisements and solicitations invited prospective students, Trump University instructors engaged in a methodical, systematic series of misrepresentations designed to convince students to sign up for the Trump University three-day seminar at a cost of $1495."

The Atlantic, which obtained a 41-page "Private & Confidential" playbook from Trump University, wrote:

"The playbook says almost nothing about the guest speaker presentations, the ostensible reason why people showed up to the seminar in the first place. Instead, the playbook focuses on the seminars' real purpose: to browbeat attendees into purchasing expensive Trump University course packages."

When all was said and done, the two class action lawsuits against Trump were settled for $25 million, and the "school" was closed down.

Some of you may feel a little duped concerning Trumps business acumen. After all, he did get on television and tell the world that he was worth "$10 billion". Perhaps you recall back in 2016 when Trump showed off a table piled high with Trump-branded products. There was a Trump magazine that went out of circulation in 2009, along with steaks that were not actually a Trump brand, but appeared to be from a company named "Bush Brothers."

Also on the table were several bottles of Trump Wine, in which he declared, "I own it 100 percent, no mortgage, no debt." This too was a lie. According to the winery's website, which states:

"Trump Winery is a registered trade name of Eric Trump Wine Manufacturing LLC, which is not owned, managed or affiliated with Donald J. Trump, The Trump Organization or any of their affiliates."

Then there was the Trump Airline, which was purchased from "troubled" Eastern Air Lines shuttle service for $365 million. Trump, of course, put his name on the planes and waited for the business to take off. It didn't. It instead took on too much debt, and eventually defaulted. It was sold to USAir.

So, the "show" he put on was basically how to start a business and fail…or perhaps, lie about your successes and hope no one looks too closely. By the way, there was no mention or display on the table of Trumps six businesses that he bankrupted due to his leadership.

The Racketeer Influenced and Corrupt Organizations Act (RICO)

Under the RICO Act, when an organization is found to have ***"…committed at least two acts of racketeering activity within the last ten years, then prosecutors can seek to charge the organization as a criminal enterprise and pursue everyone involved in the organization as part of an organized conspiracy."***

A person who has committed at least two acts of racketeering activity within a 10-year period can be charged with racketeering if a person's acts relate in one of four ways to the enterprise:

- the person invested the proceeds of the pattern of racketeering activity in the enterprise; or
- the person acquired or maintained an interest in, or control of, the enterprise through the pattern of racketeering activity; or
- the person conducted or participated in the affairs of the enterprise "through" the pattern of racketeering activity; or
- the person conspired to do one of the above.

Those found guilty of racketeering can be sentenced up to 20 years in prison for each racketeering count. In addition, the racketeer "must forfeit all ill-gotten gains and interest in any business obtained through a pattern of racketeering activity."

Some of you may recall that the RICO Act was used to prosecute the Mafia as well as others who were actively engaged in organized crime. Several top leaders of crime families received life sentences, and by the year 2000, virtually all of the top leaders of the New York Mafia had been sent to prison.

Now, If some of the crimes that Trumps "fixer" Michael Cohen testified to are proven, then there is a risk that the Trump Organization could be charged as a racketeering enterprise.

Given the number of investigations into the Trump organization, the Trump Organization appears to be vulnerable is to a RICO prosecution.

Indicting the Trump Organization as a "criminal enterprise" would enable prosecutors to sidestep the question of whether a sitting President can be indicted in office. How?

Prosecutors could lay out a whole pattern of criminal activity, indicting numerous players while leaving the President as a named unindicted coconspirator. Investigators would be allowed to make public all the known activity for Congress and the public to consider as part of impeachment hearings or reelection.

It would also activate the forfeiture tools for prosecutors to seize the Trump organization's assets and cut off its income streams. Think about that… if the Trump organization were to be convicted as a criminal enterprise under the RICO Act, there might be no business for Trump to go back to if he loses in 2020.

Former FBI Director James Comey released a book titles **"A Higher Loyalty,"** in which he compares Trump to a mafia don and calling his leadership of the country "ego driven and about personal loyalty."

Well, Comey does have a valid point…especially considering some of Trumps mob-like language and criticisms of common law enforcement techniques. For example, Trump has criticized the practice of criminals making deals with prosecutors. "It's called flipping and it almost ought to be illegal," Trump has said.

Clearly, Trump is siding with the interests of the criminal's collaborators ahead of the State. Do you recall Trumps tweet that "Cohen's father-in-law would suffer" if Cohen gave testimony to Congress? Be honest…does this not have a mobster vibe to it?

When Cohen did testify in front of Congress, he described a culture of lying at the heart of the Trump organization, stating:

"Everybody's job at the Trump Organization is to protect Mr. Trump. Every day, most of us knew we were coming and we were going to lie for him about something. That became the norm. Mr. Trump did not directly tell me to lie to Congress. That's not how he operates. Mr. Trump doesn't give orders. He speaks in code. And I understand that code."

The public knew all about Trumps issues before casting their votes. Many people thought that he would become "presidential" once he was in office and rationalized it that way, while others used the excuse that they only vote Republican and could never vote for a Democrat.

Immigration Lies, Falsehoods, and Child Abuse

Trump, and other right wing supporters, have told many lies about the people who immigrate to the United States to have better lives. Immigration has been a major source of population growth and cultural change throughout much of the U.S. history. Because the United States is a "settler colonial society", all Americans, with the exception of the small percentage of Native Americans, can trace their ancestry to immigrants from other nations around the world.

The backlash against immigrants does not add up. In March of 2019, the United States Labor Department, posted nearly 7.6 million open jobs in January. There are now actually about 1 million more open jobs than unemployed workers. But you won't hear that from President Trump. As a matter of fact, agriculture needs anywhere from 1.5 -2 million hired workers.

At least 50-70 percent of farm laborers in the United States today are unauthorized. Why? Because few U.S. workers are willing to fill available farm labor jobs. Yet, people complain about the immigration "problem", and how "they" are taking "our" jobs. Do you mean the jobs that you won't do?

Trump has built much of his presidency, and his 2020 reelection campaign, around a simple message that illegal immigration is a national crisis. Trump says that undocumented "immigrants threaten national security", and they also "hurt American workers by taking jobs and lowering overall wages".

For years, including into his presidency, the Trumps golf clubs employed undocumented workers as waiters, groundskeepers and housekeepers, according to the accounts of more than 40 former workers and supervisors. Trump acquired the financial benefits of using undocumented employees, and payed them lower wages, fewer benefits, as he continued to attack their existence. Yes, this is **Unethical, Corrupt, and Callas Leadership** all rolled into one.

You shouldn't be surprised about this. He rails against China, for good reason by the way, but at the same time since 2005, Trump has filed for 126 trademarks in China for his business empire, and as recently as June 2016, his lawyers applied for three new trademarks in clothing and footwear. Trump already has 77 trademarks in effect in China, and in 2018, China approved 16 more for Ivanka Trump. Since there is no limit to this hypocrisy, Ivanka is also scheduled to receive 5 more trademarks in 2019. Apparently, doing business with China is bad for the rest of the country…but NOT for Trump.

One more thing about the hypocrisy surrounding immigrants. Immigrants make up about 13% of the US population, which is about 42 million people. In 2016, 17.2% of immigrants ages 25 and older had a bachelor's degree and another 12.8% had attained a postgraduate degree, according to a Pew Research Center analysis of U.S. Census Bureau data.

By the year 2000, 23% of scientists with a PhD in the U.S. were immigrants, including 40% of those in engineering and computers. Roughly a third of the United States' college and universities graduate students in STEM fields (science, technology, engineering, and mathematics) are foreign nationals, and in some states it is well over half of their graduate students.

In 2016, current school enrollment figures show that although immigrants lag behind native-born populations in attending pre-school and K-12 education, they proportionally outpace native-born populations in attending colleges or universities.

So, given the fact that the United States needs more workers to keep the economy moving, and that the vast majority of immigrants want to excel and become productive members of society, why the resistance? Actually, the "resistance" is coming from Trump, and less than 20 percent of the population.

According to a February 2019 Gallop poll, at least 81 percent of Americans would like to see immigrants provided with a path to citizenship. Despite this, the Trump administration has implemented a "zero-tolerance" immigration policy that calls for the prosecution of all individuals who illegally enter the United States.

Former Secretary of Homeland Security, Kirstjen Nielsen, left the role she held for two years, but will be remembered as one of the key officials in creating and implementing the set of policies that led the administration to separate more than 2,700 children from their parents. However, it was the Trump administration and then Homeland Security Secretary, John Kelly, that put forth the goal of separating children from their parents to deter immigration.

This multi-faceted ClusterPhuck, as of 23 May, 2019, has resulted in the deaths of 6 migrant children. The large, unprecedented number of child deaths in the care of border protection agents is partially because more children are being held by U.S. Customs and Border Protection and HHS, and for longer periods of time.

There are literally thousands of children without their parents. Some of the parents were deported without their children, and it is estimated that it could take up to two years before all families are reunited!

The inspector general for the Department of Health and Human Services estimates that thousands of children were separated prior to zero tolerance, but the government argued that reuniting those children is too difficult.

Judge Dana Sabraw of the Southern District of California, ordered the Trump administration to begin identifying and reuniting those children anyway. Notice the speed associated with this stupidity displayed by members of the Trump administration.

Absolutely NO PLANNING went into the policy as it related to reuniting families after the children were taken from their parents. **Incompetence**, as well as **Evil** and **Callas Leadership** styles were displayed by Trump and Jeff Sessions, who also wanted to curb LEGAL immigration.

Where did the Trump administration get the research study showing them that taking children from their parents would "deter" people from fleeing their country to come to the United States? My guess is that there was no research done at all, thus making the situation even worse than it started. By the way, there was a time when some officials thought that the death penalty would have a **"deterrent effect"** on the murder rate.

A study contained in the ***Journal of Criminal Law and Criminology,*** revealed that "most experts do not believe that the death penalty or the carrying out of executions serve as deterrents to murder, nor do they believe that existing empirical research supports the deterrence theory." In fact, an overwhelming 88.2% of the experts feel that way.

Now, imagine if the Trump administration actually conducted research before making a snap ClusterPhuctual decision…or better yet, created a path to citizenship…like the vast majority of the people in the United States wants from their leaders.

A Love for Authoritarian Leaders

Authoritarian Leadership, is defined as a leadership style characterized by *"…individual control over all decisions and little input from group members. They typically make choices based on their ideas and judgments and rarely accept advice from followers."*

Well before he was President, Donald Trump had high praise for Russian President Vladimir Putin. He praised Putin's "strong leadership" in a country where Putin's political opponents are harassed, jailed, or simply disappear. Now that Trump is President, his defense of Putin has advanced to a level that has confused and thoroughly disgusted Republicans, Democrats, Independents, and leaders around the world.

On June 13, 2018, Special Counsel Robert Mueller charged 12 officers of the GRU, the Russian intelligence agency, with committing "large-scale cyber operations to interfere with the 2016 U.S. presidential election." Three days later, President Donald Trump met with Russian President Vladimir Putin in Helsinki, Finland. Speaking at a press conference beside Putin, Trump absolved Russia of any hacking, stating:

"He just said it's not Russia. I will say this: I don't see any reason why it would be."

He went on to state:

"So I have great confidence in my intelligence people, but I will tell you that President Putin was extremely strong and powerful in his denial today. And what he did is an incredible offer. He offered to have the people working on the case come and work with their investigators, with respect to the 12 people. I think that's an incredible offer."

So Putin, a former Russian KGB intelligence spy, offered to have his people work with our intelligence people to get to the bottom of the attack on the 2016 presidential elections that was perpetrated by the Russians in the first place! That would be like the **Apple** corporation inviting members of the **Samsung** corporation to come in and see and take notes on all of their pending inventions, or the New England Patriots football team not just providing its Super Bowl opponent their playbook, but tell them what plays they will run and when.

This is **Incompetent Leadership** at its very worst. Are you really surprised that Trump would think that this would be a good thing? Keep in mind that in 2016, Trump asked a foreign policy expert, that was advising him at the time, why the United States can't use nuclear weapons. He asked three times by the way.

Just so you know, a 1 megaton nuclear bomb "creates a firestorm that can cover 100 square miles…and a 20 megaton blast's firestorm can cover nearly 2500 square miles." The bombs that were dropped on Hiroshima and Nagasaki Japan are now considered "small bombs" by today's standards.

Trumps Helsinki remarks to Putin hurt his approval ratings and those Republicans who'd been reluctant to criticize Trump were shocked to see him taking the Kremlin's word over that of his own aides and the U.S. intelligence community. Incidentally, Putin, when asked if he wanted Trump to win the 2016 presidential elections, stated, *"'Yes, I did. Yes, I did. Because he talked about bringing the U.S.-Russia relationship back to normal."*

Now, fast forward to May of 2019. Two weeks after Mueller's report laid out a detailed account about the dimensions of Russian interference in the election, Trump again failed to condemn Putin or complain about the attack on the 2016 presidential elections. As a matter of fact, he didn't even bring it up.

There are plenty of theories as to why Trump continues to defend Putin. Some believe that Putin has some type of damaging information on Trump, while others believe that he wants to get "Trump Tower Moscow" built, and wants to keep Putin happy. Trump stated, "I have nothing to do with Russia."

However, in November 2018, Michael Cohen, then Trumps lawyer and "fixer", pleaded guilty to lying to Congress about the Trump Tower Moscow in a prosecution brought by the office of the special counsel. In May of 2019, Cohen started his three year prison term. Still, others believe that Trump is simply a terrible negotiator, and is bad at one-on-one discussions.

Trump has displayed **Callas Leadership** as it pertains to authoritarian leaders. Meaning, he tends to believe and defend them even though there is overwhelming evidence of barbaric their acts. On the 2nd of October, 2018, Jamal Khashoggi, a well-known journalist and critic of the Saudi government, walked into the country's consulate in Istanbul, and was murdered.

For more than two weeks Saudi Arabia first denied the killing, and consistently denied any knowledge and of Khashoggi's fate. The Crown Prince Mohammed stated that Khashoggi had left the consulate "after a few minutes or one hour" and added "We have nothing to hide."

This has proven to be a lie because Turkish officials furnished evidence, including audio recordings, that the journalist was killed by a team of Saudi agents on orders that came from the highest levels.

U.S. intelligence intercepts show that Mohammed was desperate to lure Khashoggi back to Saudi Arabia and detain him, which indicates, for many around the world, that this assassination was ordered by Mohammed himself.

When Saudi Arabia discovered that there was evidence of the killing, their public prosecutor publically stated that Khashoggi was killed inside the building on the orders of a "rogue" intelligence officer. President Trump soon adopted the "rogue killers" excuse, and backed the Saudi Prince frequently in public.

President Trump stated, "I just spoke with the King of Saudi Arabia, and he denies any knowledge of what took place with regards to, as he said, to Saudi Arabia's citizen." Several times Trump referred to Khashoggi as a "Saudi Arabia citizen", despite the fact that he lived in the United States and was a reporter for the Washington Post.

This type of response may seem familiar to some of you because it is reminiscent of Trump's consistent denials that the Russian government interfered with the 2016 elections, including that it illegally accessed the computer network of the Democratic Party. Back then he stated, that the hacking could be by a "…guy sitting on their bed who weighs 400 pounds." The point is that Trump has a history of deflecting blame when it has to do with authoritarian leaders…regardless of the degree of ClusterPhuck they may have created.

Although the body of Mr. Khashoggi has never been found, since he was reportedly dismembered with a bone saw, the Trump administration did pass targeted sanctions on 17 Saudis accused of involvement in the murder, but NOT on MBS.

The Senate did vote to end U.S. involvement in the war in Yemen, marked the first time that lawmakers have formally terminated a U.S. military engagement since ending the U.S. war in Vietnam. It was meant to signal strongly that Congress will no longer tolerate business as usual with Saudi Arabia, but President Trump vetoed it.

By the way, the trial for the men accused of murdering Khashoggi has begun, with prosecutors confirming they will seek the death penalty for at least five of 11 people charged in the assassination. Typically, the alleged mastermind would have been on trial as well, but it appears that Trumps relationship with MBS is more important than the assassination of a Washington Post reporter, living in the United States, who has four children, and was visiting the embassy to get a marriage certificate…while his fiancée was in the car waiting…unbeknownst that her soon to be husband was being dismembered by a bone saw.

Philippine President Rodrigo Duterte, has boasted about killing suspected drug dealers when he was a local mayor. Extrajudicial killings of drugs suspects have risen since Duterte became President in June 2016. He has bragged about killing those "suspected" of being drug dealers. The U.S. State Department noted last year that "police and unknown vigilantes have killed more than 6,000 suspected drug dealers and users as the government pursued a policy aimed at eliminating illegal drug activity in the country by the end of the year."

Evil leadership, which is defined as a leader that *"... commits atrocities, uses pain as an instrument of power. The harm done to men, women, and children is severe rather than slight. The harm can be physical, psychological, or both."* Duterte is an evil leader. How many of those suspected drug dealers or drug users that have been killed by his forces, were set up? Imagine if in the United States a person could point at you and declare that you are a drug user or dealer, without due process.

How safe would you feel...especially if you did not see eye to eye with the President? How should a U.S. President respond to this leader? Donald Trump response was: "I just wanted to congratulate you because I am hearing of the unbelievable job on the drug problem." This is a display of **Callas Leadership**... on the part of President Trump.

However, this is not surprising when you consider what he said during a speech to law enforcement on the 28th of July, in 2017. In his speech, Trump maintained that his team was "rough" and encouraged police officers not to be concerned about preventing physical harm to people being taken into custody.

"Please don't be too nice" to SUSPECTS was the message, because according to the President of the United States, the laws were "stacked against" the police, and brutality was fine...regardless of the tensions between the police and its citizens over the past few years. This was truly another example of leading stupidly by the President. His **Divisive Leadership** style was on full display with police officers standing behind him applauding. I will say this...a few officers did NOT applaud and did NOT seem at all amused by the President's speech.

The reaction to Trumps performance from law enforcement agencies from Boston to Los Angles was swift. The Suffolk County Police Department released a statement letting the public know that it "...has strict rules and procedures relating to the handling of prisoners, and violations of those rules and procedures are treated extremely seriously... as a department, we do not and will not tolerate 'rough[ing]' up prisoners."

Lecia Brooks, Outreach Director for the Southern Poverty Law Center, stated that "it's disgraceful for anyone to advocate abuse against another human being."

183

Jeffery Robinson, deputy legal director at the ACLU stated:

"By encouraging police to dole out extra pain at will, the president is urging a kind of lawlessness that already imperils the health and lives of people of color at shameful rates."

***

In May of 2019, President Trump hosted one of the more bizarre foreign leaders. Viktor Orban, prime minister of Hungary, with just under 10 million inhabitants, uses overt racism and covert anti-Semitism in his election propaganda. He has "thumbed his nose" at the United States, and has aggressively welcomed a Russian bank that is thought to have espionage links and has undermined U.S. policy in Ukraine.

As Trump's ambassador David B. Cornstein to Hungary recently put it, in an interview in the Atlantic, stated, **"Trump would love to have the situation that Viktor Orban has, but he doesn't."**

What is Cornstein implying? That Trump would "love" to have a "situation" where you can be an "overt" racist and still not lose public support? WTF? How is this guy qualified to be an ambassador?

Figured Out?

There have been some things in my life that were hard to figure out…at first. For example, while in the Army, I wanted to know how I could do more pushups, sit-ups, and increase my 2-mile run. Why? Because your physical fitness score is a big deal when you are being judged. When all else is equal, and a slot opens up for some training you desire…the difference may be that score. The point is simply that you want that edge when you are looking to win, and it may come down to how well you have researched the event or your opponent. Politicians, both domestically and abroad, do the same kind of research…and have figured President Trump out.

David Ignatius, a writer for The Washington Post, wrote:

"Trump's problem is that, after two years, foreign nations seem to have figured him out. Rather than crafting quick deals that Trump could tout as wins, these adversaries have played a waiting game. They appear to sense in Trump an impatience and hunger for the spotlight that undermine his ability to negotiate."

In his 1987 book, Art of the Deal, Trump states, "My style of deal–making is quite simple and straightforward," he writes. "I aim very high, and then I just keep pushing and pushing to get what I'm after. Sometimes I settle for less than I sought, but in most cases I still end up with what I want."

He goes on to say, "I don't hire a lot of number-crunchers, and I don't trust fancy marketing surveys. I do my own surveys and draw my own conclusions." Throughout his campaign and into his presidency, Trump disputes statistics that come from traditional credible sources that don't support his agenda, but often tweets support for statistics that originate from sources that are less than credible.

In May of 2019, former Secretary of State Rex Tillerson told members of the House Foreign Affairs Committee that "Russian President Vladimir Putin out-prepared President Trump" during a key meeting in Germany. In the past, Trump has downplayed the importance of preparation, saying his "gut instinct and ability to read a room" are paramount for a successful summit.

President Trump was warned by his intelligence chiefs that North Korea was unlikely to surrender its nuclear weapons. His advisers worried that a deal was probably not going to happen, and that Trump might make an impulsive concession to make headlines. "I don't think I have to prepare very much," Trump stated ahead of his historic first meeting with North Korean leader Kim Jong Un.

Trump was determined to meet face-to-face with Kim Jong Un, due to what aides say is "…an unwavering faith in the power of the pen-pal relationship" he has cultivated with the North Korean leader. Trump, at a rally in West Virginia, stated, "He wrote me beautiful letters, and they're great letters…" and "We fell in love."

The "we fell in love" feelings is a long way from Trumps 2017 feelings about Kim when he stated, "North Korea best not make any more threats to the United States" or they will face "…fire and fury like the world has never seen." Had Kim figured Trump out, or did they both realize that the rhetoric was becoming more dangerous and getting out of hand?

Remember in the last chapter when President Kennedy and Soviet Union leader Nikita Khrushchev realized that they both needed to back down a bit in order to avoid a nuclear confrontation? Tamping down tensions between two countries that can kill millions of people within minutes, is probably a good thing.

There have been media reports that some people, who may hate his public persona, declare that Trump is very personable when you meet him in person and away from the media. Agree with some of his tactics or his behavior or not, nevertheless, you don't get millions of people to vote for you without possessing a degree of charisma.

It could be argued that Trump switched to utilizing his **Charismatic Leadership** skills when his **Forceful Leadership** style didn't work with Kim, but has also showed his **Narcissistic leadership** style by falsely believing that he did not have to prepare for meetings with world leaders.

Pseudo Training Mindlessness

When then General Stanley McChrystal took charge of the U.S. Joint Special Operations Task Force in 2003, he recognized that traditional tactics of warfare were failing in Iraq. He led an inter-service team which included Army Rangers, Navy SEALs, and Delta Force. He explained that he needed to find new ways to disrupt Al-Qaeda and *"get these disparate branches of elite U.S. soldiers to work cohesively."*

In McChrystal's book, *Team of Teams*, the General stated:

"I still believe in rehearsals, but I've learned they have a different value. When I joined the Army Rangers in 1985 we'd rehearse airfield seizure operations — we'd parachute in wearing night vision goggles, and take the field. It's a pretty complex thing, and we'd do it over and over. We'd have contingencies in case things went wrong, but we were always trying to make things as foolproof as we could. The longer we did it, the more I realized the value of rehearsal was not in trying to get this perfectly choreographed kabuki that would unfold as planned. The value of rehearsal was to familiarize everybody with all the things that could happen, what the relationships are, and how you communicate. What you're really doing is building up the flexibility to adapt. I've never been on an operation that went as planned."

In March of 2019, President Trump announced, following his "failed" summit with North Korean leader Kim Jong Un, stated that he was cancelling large-scale military exercises between U.S. and South Korean forces. Trump stated, "The reason I do not want military drills with South Korea is to save hundreds of millions of dollars for the U.S. for which we are not reimbursed." He went on to state, "That was my position long before I became President. Also, reducing tensions with North Korea at this time is a good thing!"

Apparently, they are eliminating massive springtime military drills and replacing them with smaller exercises in what they call an effort to support diplomacy aimed at resolving the North Korean nuclear crisis. That's like telling firefighters that fight major forest fires, to limit their training to garbage can fires in residential areas.

What do you think will happen when a massive forest fire breaks out? It will be a total ClusterPhuck! Let me put it this way…would you have a brain surgeon, that hasn't performed brain surgery in 2 years, but has worked on sprained ankles in that time period, perform brain surgery on your child?

Training, in order to be effective, must be as realistic as possible. I get the fact that Trump is essentially doing this to save money and convince North Korea to denuclearize. Well, in order to properly prepare for the war that most sane people don't want, you must conduct training…and that takes money.

It could be reasonably argued that Trump played right into Kim's hands, which is what many people, including allies of the United States, feared most. After the Singapore meeting, Kim pledged to return the remains of Americans from the Korean War and to also dismantle missile-launching sites.

American bodies were indeed returned to the United States, and Kim began dismantling missile sites and no test launches were made, which felt like, for good reason, some progress was being made. Then reality set in when Kim made it very clear that North Korea would NEVER give up its nuclear weapons.

There has always been skepticism about U.S. foreign policy as it relates to North Korea. One poll showed that 87 percent of respondents believe it is unlikely the Trump administration's strategy toward North Korea will lead Kim to give up its nuclear weapons, which is the stated goal of U.S. policy. As recently as May of 2019, intelligence reports show that not only is North Korea NOT denuclearizing, they are instead ramping up production of nuclear warheads.

And, by the way, North Korea, as of April 2019, has begun to test-fire a new tactical guided weapon, but Trump, on the 27th of May, gave cover to Kim as he directly contradicted his national security adviser, John Bolton, by arguing that North Korea had not launched ballistic missiles this month nor violated U.N. Security Council resolutions.

In two conflicting statements, Trump stated, "My people think it could have been a violation…I view it differently." He then added that he was not "personally" bothered by North Korea's short-range missile tests. Trump again displays his **Passive Leadership** style, as Kim is now in complete control of the relationship.

Dr. Gregory L. Cotton

Kim did get what he wanted, which was stature. What kind of stature? The kind of stature you receive when you meet not once, but twice, with the President of the United States…while the whole world is watching, and at the same time continue to work on their nuclear and short-range missile testing.

***

Tariffs, Trade Wars, and Foreign Policy Stupidity

Foreign Policy or **Foreign Relations** refers to how a government deals with other countries. It includes such matters as trade, defense and other matters. In an essay in Foreign Affairs magazine, it states:

"The president has proved himself to be what many critics have long accused him of being: belligerent, bullying, impatient, irresponsible, intellectually lazy, short-tempered, and self-obsessed. Remarkably, however, those shortcomings have not yet translated into obvious disaster."

The essay continued to state that President Trump has *"…outlined a deeply misguided foreign policy vision that is distrustful of U.S. allies, scornful of international institutions, and indifferent, if not downright hostile, to the liberal international order that the United States has sustained for nearly eight decades."*

In 2018, the Teaching, Research, and International Policy (TRIP) project, at the College of William & Mary, in collaboration with Foreign Policy magazine, surveyed international relations scholars at U.S. universities.

Among the findings, an overwhelming majority of international relations scholars surveyed said that the United States is less respected internationally today than in the past. Of those respondents, 99 percent agree that this loss of respect is a problem for the United States.

In another poll, 70% of the respondents, in 25 nations surveyed, said that they did not have confidence in Trumps leadership as it pertains to the handling of international issues. Only 27% said that they trusted him.

Regionally, 82% of Europeans surveyed said that they lacked confidence in Trump, while 18% were positively disposed toward him. 69% of French, Germans and Spanish; 56% of Swedes; and roughly half of Dutch and Greeks, say they had *no confidence at all* in Trump.

In the Asia-Pacific region, 32% see him favorably, while 54% lack confidence in

188

him. However, 78% of Filipinos view Trump favorably, but 66% of Japanese and Australians are not confident in him. In the three Latin American nations polled, overwhelming majorities say they have no confidence in Trump, including 78% of Mexicans, who say they have *no confidence at all*.

***

Some of the polling data shouldn't be that surprising to most of you. Trumps praise and embracement of dictators is just one of the reasons why his international polling numbers are so low around most of the world, but there are a lot more reasons behind the low numbers.

President Trump has been openly condescending of many multilateral institutions established by the United States and its allies to build and sustain the postwar international order. The expert views are utterly opposed to those of Trump. Scholars of international relations overwhelmingly believe that multilateral institutions benefit the United States.

Trump has been perhaps been the toughest on one multilateral institution…and that is the North Atlantic Treaty Organization or NATO. From its inception, the 29 country alliance, bordering the North Atlantic Ocean, **main purpose** was to defend each other from the possibility of communist Soviet Union taking control of their nation.

Trump, like his two most recent predecessors, has criticized the scale of U.S. contributions to NATO and the contributions of allied governments, albeit more diplomatically. However, unlike his predecessors, Trump has also threatened to withdraw from the pact. This **Forceful Leadership** style arguably may have some affect, but a 2018 NATO report estimates that only five out of the 29 nations will meet the spending standards that were agreed upon at the 2014 NATO summit in Wales.

If the United States did pull out of NATO, Trump would be handing a gift to Putin, who has longed for the day to break NATO apart. By the way, 92 percent of Americans agree that the treaty enhances U.S. security today, and 94 percent oppose U.S. withdrawal.

The reason for the other NATO partners concerns about Trump pulling out is due to his pension for cancelling or pulling out of agreements that has made the United States look more like bystander than the world's leader. It could be argued that Trump does at times present a **Laissez-faire** type of **leadership**, which has been defined as "the absence of leadership altogether."

Dr. Gregory L. Cotton

The Paris Climate Agreement

In case you didn't realize it…Climate Change is real and things are only going to get worse. It is NOT a "hoax" as Trump likes to call it. Some of you have perhaps noticed, in your respective states, that there have been more floods, fires, droughts, tornadoes, hurricanes, etc. You may have heard politicians and others utter sentences like, "we've never experienced anything around here like this."

Multiple studies published in peer-reviewed scientific journals show that 97 percent or more of actively publishing climate scientists agree Climate-warming trends over the past century are likely due to human activities. Here is a partial list of what some of these very credible organizations have publicly stated:

American Geophysical Union

"Human-induced climate change requires urgent action. Humanity is the major influence on the global climate change observed over the past 50 years. Rapid societal responses can significantly lessen negative outcomes."

American Meteorological Society

"It is clear from extensive scientific evidence that the dominant cause of the rapid change in climate of the past half century is human-induced increases in the amount of atmospheric greenhouse gases, including carbon dioxide ($CO2$), chlorofluorocarbons, methane, and nitrous oxide."

International Academies: Joint Statement

"Climate change is real. There will always be uncertainty in understanding a system as complex as the world's climate. However there is now strong evidence that significant global warming is occurring. The evidence comes from direct measurements of rising surface air temperatures and subsurface ocean temperatures and from phenomena such as increases in average global sea levels, retreating glaciers, and changes to many physical and biological systems. It is likely that most of the warming in recent decades can be attributed to human activities."

U.S. Global Change Research Program

"The global warming of the past 50 years is due primarily to human-induced increases in heat-trapping gases. Human 'fingerprints' also have been identified in many other aspects of the climate system, including changes in ocean heat content, precipitation, atmospheric moisture, and Arctic sea ice."

Statement on Climate Change from 18 Scientific Associations

"Observations throughout the world make it clear that climate change is occurring, and rigorous scientific research demonstrates that the greenhouse gases emitted by human activities are the primary driver."

Even with all of this evidence, both in scientific data, and with the average person seeing and feeling it up close, Trump is trying his best to convince the world that it is a "hoax." When Trump was elected President and pledged to withdraw from the agreement, the fact is that the US cannot formally withdraw until November 5, 2020, just days after the next presidential election, so perhaps the next President will take the lead on this issue.

Instead of relying on legal or economic sanctions, the Paris Climate Agreement looked to "harness the power of transparency and peer pressure." Think about this…under this agreement, each of the roughly 200 countries would come up with its own emissions-reduction pledge, its own "Nationally Determined Contribution," or NDC. It would be like your teacher telling you, the student, to come up with a suitable study plan that would suffice in adequately preparing you for a test. By the way, you would also determine your academic goal.

The Paris Climate Agreement does not sanction a country for failing to hit their targets. All the agreement was asking for was for each country to honestly tell the rest of the world how you're doing. However, if you fail to achieve your publicly proclaimed goals, you would have to deal with the public embarrassment and suffer through some reputational damage.

The idea behind making the agreement voluntary, with no risk of penalties, frees up countries to be less defensive. By just starting to set goals and moving forward, it is believed that each country will ***"learn and share, prompting a self-reinforcing cycle of rising ambition, driven by bragging rights and encouragement rather than shame and sanction."*** However, if you are a President that believes that climate change is a "hoax", the chances of Trump or the United States leading this effort is absolutely zero.

Trans-Pacific Partnership

If you have been paying attention, and I mean years before Trump became President of the United States, he had a habit of telling the American people how he would have made a better deal on this or that. In regards to the Trans-Pacific Partnership or TPP, Trump made such statements like, "And the Obama Trans-Pacific Partnership and fast track are a bad, bad deal for American businesses, for workers, for taxpayers. It's a huge set of handouts for a few insiders that don't even care about our great, great America." And, ***"The Trans-Pacific Partnership is an attack on America's business. It does not stop Japan's currency manipulation. This is a bad deal."***

The Trans-Pacific Partnership was the centerpiece of President Barack Obama's strategic axis to Asia…that is before President Donald J. Trump withdrew the United States in 2017. The TPP was set to become the world's largest free trade deal, covering 40 percent of the global economy.

Supporters of the deal believed that it would have expanded U.S. trade and investment abroad, spurred economic growth, lowered consumer prices, and created new jobs, while also advancing U.S. strategic interests in the Asia-Pacific region.

However, Trump, and its detractors, saw the deal as likely to accelerate U.S. decline in manufacturing, lower wages, and increase inequality.

The motivation for what became the TPP was a 2005 trade agreement between a group of Pacific Rim countries comprising Brunei, Chile, New Zealand, and Singapore. In 2008, it was President George W. Bush who announced that the United States would begin trade talks with this group, leading Australia, Vietnam, and Peru to join. As the talks proceeded, the group expanded to include Canada, Japan, Malaysia, and Mexico, for a total of twelve countries.

President Obama continued the talks when he took office in 2009, and in 2011, Secretary of State Hillary Clinton framed the TPP as the "centerpiece of the United States' strategic pivot." After nineteen official rounds of negotiations and many more separate meetings, resulting in the United States receiving more than 20 provisions that heavily favored the United States, the participating countries came to an agreement in October 2015 and signed the pact in early 2016.

So, Trump pulls out of the agreement in 2017, and in 2018 asked chief economic advisor Larry Kudlow and U.S. Trade Representative Robert Lighthizer, to consider trying to rejoin the TPP. What the ClusterPhuck!? This "fire, ready, aim" approach by Trump is the epitome of leading at the speed of stupid.

Did he even read the deal before he axed it? Of course not. The other countries have moved on without the United States, and have informed the President that they will NOT get the 20-plus provisions that heavily favored the United States in the original agreement, if they had any intentions of returning.

Have you ever left a job for what seemed like it would be a better opportunity for both pay and advancement? Did you get there and within a month or two you find out that you made a big mistake, and you go and beg for your job back? What are the chances of you getting that job back and at the same pay? I would say less than zero…especially when you consider that you cursed out your boss and slammed the door on the way out of his office!

Again, every decision has second and third order consequences to that decision, meaning that there are outcomes that are different than the first desired outcome, but are directly related to the initial decision. Trumps decision to pull out of the TPP will perhaps save a few manufacturing jobs, but it can't compare to what many believe would have put China in check, while at the same time increasing trade opportunities and positioning the United States into a more powerful global position.

That opportunity is now gone, and it seems Trump has again failed to consider the consequences of leaving the Joint Comprehensive Plan of Action (JCPOA), or what is best known as the Iran Nuclear Agreement.

Iran

The Iran Nuclear Agreement was signed in July 2015 and went into effect the following January. The five permanent members of the UN Security Council, China, France, Russia, the United Kingdom, United States, and Germany, negotiated the agreement with Iran over nearly two years that imposed restrictions on Iran's civilian nuclear enrichment program.

The Obama administration's intent was to set back Iran's nuclear program, which was producing enough fissile material for a weapon, that was reportedly a few weeks away from development at the time. Many of the nuclear provisions have expiration dates. After ten years, for example, centrifuge restrictions will be lifted, and after fifteen years, so too will limits on the low-enriched uranium it can possess, as well as the International Atomic Energy Agency (IAEA), access to undeclared sites. Iran would receive sanction relief, and other economic benefits, if they honored the agreement.

After Trump pulled the United States out of the nuclear deal, all of the other signatories decided to continue to observe the deal's terms, despite the fact that Trump reimposed unilateral sanctions in August and November, in 2018. Despite the fact that Tehran is bearing severe economic costs, they have continued to comply with the restrictions on its nuclear program under the Joint Comprehensive Plan of Action (JCPOA).

As the Trump administration pursues what it calls a "maximum pressure" campaign against Iran, it has increased tensions in the region. It is no secret that

National Security Advisor John Bolton has been a huge advocate of overthrowing the Iranian government. He has reportedly requested that administration officials draw up plans to send 120,000 U.S. troops to the Middle East to counter Iran's "threat" of plotting attacks on American troops in the Middle East.

Trump, who pledged to get the United States out of wars, had many in Washington feeling that Bolton, and others, were pushing Trump towards another war. However, a British general, Chris Ghika, contradicted the Trump administration's narrative that Iran was plotting attacks on American troops in the Middle East.

In May of 2019, the general told reporters that "there's been no increased threat from Iranian-backed forces" in the region. He went on to state, "We monitor them along with a whole range of others because that's the environment we're in...if the threat level seems to go up then we'll raise our force protection measures accordingly."

Within hours, the U.S. Central Command issued a statement disputing Ghika's comments and repeating John Bolton's unsubstantiated claim that American intelligence has "identified credible threats" from "Iranian-backed forces" in Iraq and Syria.

There is growing concern from many sides that the United States, led by Bolton, may be attempting to manufacture a false pretext to justify launching a war with Iran. U.S. officials are, without any concrete evidence, attempting to blame Iran for attacks on oil tankers in the Strait of Hormuz.

The New York Times reported that Trump administration officials are having a difficult time convincing America's European allies to join them on their march to war. The Times also reported that intelligence and military officials in Europe, as well as in the United States, said that over the past year, most aggressive moves have originated not in Tehran, but in Washington. Bolton has, according to reports, pressing President Trump into backing Iran into a corner.

Ladies and gentlemen, we've seen this movie before, and the ClusterPhuck continues to this day. Remember when The Bush administration wanted a regime change in Iraq? The administration legitimized the war on a state that did not threaten the United States. Remember the lead up to the war? Iraqi leader Saddam Hussein, according to the Bush administration, was linked to al-Qaida and was actively developing weapons of mass destruction which he might turn over to terrorists or use on their behalf, and in their minds represented an imminent threat to the US.

This is what the beginning of a 6th degree ClusterPhuck looks like. The same can be said about Trumps tariffs and trade wars.

Tariff it Forward

Imagine that you are the owner of a donut shop. I love donuts…especially from your particular store. I walk in and order my usual three dozen donuts for my office. This being my favorite place, and a frequent customer, I am pretty confident that I know what the total will be within a few pennies. However, this time something is different.

There is a 40% increase in the price of the donuts! I ask to have a quick word with the owner about what I perceive is an outlandish increase. He proceeds to tell me that the President put a 40% tariff, which is *"…a tax or duty to be paid on a particular class of imports or exports"* on his Canadian suppliers, and they responded by placing a 40% tariff on the ingredients that they use to make donuts. So, as a business owner…in business to make money…pass on the increase to the consumer.

Trump has proudly called himself "tariff man", and has promised the American people that he would reduce the trade deficit by *"…shutting out unfairly traded imports and renegotiating free trade agreements."* This goes counter to what U.S. scholars decisively support, which is free trade. It is not surprising they also believe, in large numbers, that Trump's tariffs on Chinese products and materials will hurt the U.S. economy. Trump may think of himself as showing **Strategic** Leadership, but in reality is displaying **Incompetent** Leadership. How?

Bob Woodward's new book titled "***Fear***", stated that Trump believes that "trade is bad." Trump has tweeted that "trade wars are good and easy to win." Tell that to companies like Harley Davidson, which is one of the most recognizable brands in the world.

In early 2019, they posted a 27% decline in earnings, specifically citing European tariffs that have been levied against them by the European Union in retaliation for tariffs levied on European goods by President Trump.

Once Trump viewed Harley Davidson as a company that was "on his side." Given his somewhat **Vindictive (**disposed to seek revenge, intended to cause anguish or hurt) style of leadership, Trump later encouraged consumers to boycott the motorcycle maker after it announced it was moving some of its production from the U.S. to Thailand, which they specifically cited the need to do so because of Trump's tariffs.

Harley Davidson was not alone in their criticism of Trumps actions. In April of 2019, Fox News, which typically sides with Trump, published an opinion piece explaining how President Trump's steel tariffs may hold the U.S. back from becoming the world's top crude oil exporter. During that same month, National Public Radio reported that the administration's metal tariffs have caused the cost of household appliances to rise.

Have you, as a consumer, noticed that the price of washers, dryers, fridges, freezers, dishwashers and other appliances increase since the imposition of metal tariffs? Some appliances saw price hikes of hundreds of dollars. Does this make you more or less likely to buy one of those appliances? I for one, wait a few months or longer to buy certain products, understanding that the price is likely to go down. I personally refuse to buy any non-emergency type products until this tariff war is over.

In a survey published by the Associate Press, 65 percent of Alaska-based seafood companies reported they immediately lost sales as a result of tariff increases. 50 percent said sales were delayed and 36 percent said they lost Chinese customers, which, by the way, is the largest export market and re-processor of Alaskan seafood.

The candidate Trump enjoyed the support of farmers during his 2016 presidential campaign. However, there are signs that his support is waning. For example, tariffs are harming soybean farmers in Ohio. In response to tariffs imposed on Chinese goods by the United States, China levied a 25 percent tariff on American soybeans. In response, Chinese purchases slowed, which sent a jolt through the American soybean industry.

As a business owner, how would you feel if your most lucrative customer decided to take their business elsewhere at no fault of your own? Can farmers expect to get China back once this is all over? Farmers are hurting and in 2018, Trump announced an aid program of as much as $12 billion to cushion their losses. Researchers at Iowa State University, by the way, estimated that tariffs imposed in 2018 on its "farm state", would cost the state as much as $2 billion in lost economic activity.

In March of 2019, CNBC reported that the Trump administration's tariffs cost American consumers $1.4 billion…per month. Additionally, according to experts at the Peterson Institute for International Economics, U.S. consumers and businesses are paying more than $900,000 a year for every job saved or created by Trump steel tariffs.

Trumps trade battles, according to a recent study, indicates that "…imports from targeted countries declined 31.5 percent while targeted U.S. exports fell by 11 percent. They also found that annual consumer and producer losses from higher costs of imports totaled $68.8 billion." The study goes on to say that the economy experienced $7.8 billion in lost gross domestic product in 2018.

If that's not enough to convince you that Trumps policies and erratic behavior is starting to affect the United States standing in the world, then perhaps you need to pay closer attention. For the first time in nine years, Singapore surpassed the United States and Hong Kong to clinch the title of the world's most competitive economy.

Singapore's "immigration laws, advanced technological infrastructure, availability of skilled labor and efficient ways to set up new businesses helped it advance to the top."

The analysis shows that what is hurting the United States is the "sense that closeness and avoiding globalization and trade hurts competitiveness." Keep in mind that the Republican Party was always seen as the "free trade" party until Trump got into office.

Historical Trade Deficit

A **Trade Deficit** is defined as *"...an economic measure of international trade in which a country's imports exceed its exports. A trade deficit represents an outflow of domestic currency to foreign markets. It is also referred to as a negative balance of trade (BOT)."* So, a trade deficit is a bad thing, and something Trump promised to fix.

Under Trumps leadership, the trade deficit rose to its highest level in history in 2018 to $891.3 billion. Although the increase was driven by some factors outside of President Trumps control, he had been warned several times by economists that the trade gap would increase due to his $1.5 trillion tax cut, which has been largely financed by government borrowing, along with the trade war he escalated. At its current pace, the "Goods" deficit could also hit $1 trillion in 2020.

Pattern of Racial Insensitivity

I spent a few years in military recruiting. It was required that we conducted background checks for potential law violations. In one particular case, a young man had accumulated 23 traffic tickets in less than three years. I was required to get a "waiver" approval from the command headquarters before he could be processed for enlistment. This individual did NOT have a drunk driving, driving under the influence, careless driving, or anything considered serious.

To my surprise, his waiver was denied and he was told he could not enlist in the Army. He was rejected due to "a pattern of misconduct." Apparently, the command felt, given his history, there was no reason to believe that he would change once he enlisted. They would however revisit his enlistment application after a year or two…if he didn't receive any more tickets.

My reason for bringing that particular story up is due to Trumps pattern of race related controversies. In 1973, The Justice Department filed a lawsuit against the Trump Management Company that focused on 39 properties in New York City. The government alleged that employees were directed to tell African American applicants that there were no open apartments. According to an employee, who was quoted in court documents, it was company policy to rent only to "Jews and executives." The company settled out of court and admitted no wrongdoing.

How would you feel if you spent between 6 and 15 years in prison for something you did not do? And, for good measure, even when you were clearly exonerated both by DNA testing and a confession from the real perpetrator, the man who would be President of the United States, still called for your execution. Yes, it happened.

The **Central Park Jogger** case was a major news story that involved the assault and rape of a white female jogger, and attacks on others in the North Woods of Manhattan's Central Park on the night of April 19, 1989.

On the night of the attack, five juvenile males, four African American and one Hispanic, were apprehended in the attack. Although they confessed, due to what they said were forced confessions (sleep deprivation, long interrogations, etc.), the FBI found that the DNA of the rape kit did not match to any of the tested suspects.

The five defendants, after spending several years in prison, had their convictions vacated in 2002 when Matias Reyes, a convicted murderer and serial rapist in prison, confessed to raping the jogger. DNA evidence confirmed his guilt, and he knew facts about the crime that only the offender could have known.

Before you criticize five teenagers for confessing to something they did not do, according to The Innocence Project, there have been more than 360 wrongful convictions overturned by DNA evidence that involved some form of a false confession. Researchers who study this phenomenon have determined that the following factors contribute to or cause false confessions:

• Real or perceived intimidation of the suspect by law enforcement.

• Use of force by law enforcement during the interrogation, or perceived threat of force.

• Compromised reasoning ability of the suspect, due to exhaustion, stress, hunger, substance use, and, in some cases, mental limitations, or limited education. Young people who do not understand their rights and are taught to please authority figures are particularly vulnerable.

• Devious interrogation techniques, such as untrue statements about the presence of incriminating evidence.

• Fear, on the part of the suspect, that failure to confess will yield a harsher punishment.

In October 2016, when Trump campaigned to be President, he declared that the Central Park Five were guilty and stated that their convictions should never have been vacated. Trump told CNN:

"They admitted they were guilty. The police doing the original investigation say they were guilty. The fact that that case was settled with so much evidence against them is outrageous. And the woman, so badly injured, will never be the same."

So 17 years after it was proven that the then teenagers didn't do the crime, Trump is using them as part of his campaign strategy. As usual, his statement attracted criticism from the Central Park Five themselves as well as others, including Republican U.S. Senator John McCain, who called Trump's responses "outrageous statements about the innocent men in the Central Park Five case", and cited it as one of many causes prompting him to retract his endorsement of Trump.

This was only the beginning of how Trump used Divisive Leadership to further his ambitions. It was reported that in the summer of 2005, Trump had the idea for the next season of his reality-TV show, *The Apprentice*. Apparently, he wanted to put "a team of successful African Americans versus a team of successful whites."

Trump thought the format would be a sort of social commentary "reflective of our very vicious world." Although the concept never made it to the air, you can clearly see a pattern forming.

The Pew Research Center conducted a survey of more than 6,600 adults on race relations in America. Among the findings were that 56 percent of Americans agree that Trump has made relations worse, while 28 percent believe he's made progress toward improving race relations or has tried but failed to make progress.

In contrast to Trump, 64 percent of respondents believed that President Barack Obama "…made progress toward improving race relations or tried but failed to make progress, while just 25 percent said Obama made race relations worse."

Additionally, 65 percent of Americans, including majorities across racial and ethnic groups, believe that it has become more common for people to express racist or racially insensitive views since Trump was elected President. 45 percent say that this has become more acceptable. A February 2018 Associated Press poll shows that nearly 6 in 10 Americans believe that the President Trump is a racist. The number is much higher among African-Americans.

This should not come as a surprise considering when that Trump launched his 2016 presidential campaign with a speech describing Mexican immigrants as criminals and "rapists." He also proposed a ban on all Muslims entering the US., and stated that a judge should recuse himself from a case involving Trump because of the judge's Mexican heritage.

Under Trump's watch, white nationalists and neo-Nazis held a rally in Charlottesville, Virginia, with attendees, including former KKK grand wizard David Duke. Duke stated, "We are going to fulfill the promises of Donald Trump. That's what we believed in. That's why we voted for Donald Trump, because he said he's going to take our country back." Counter protesters showed up to demonstrate against racism, and the racist protesters responded with violence.

One man rammed his car into a crowd of counter-protesters, killing a young woman, 32-year old Heather Heyer, and injuring dozens. The racist protesters chanted, "Jews will not replace us!" President Trump provoked outrage by declaring that there are "very fine people on both sides."

Trump, who was widely criticized, was seeking not to make the same mistake twice, issued a brief statement saying he condemned "in the strongest possible terms this egregious display of hatred, bigotry and violence on many sides." The "many sides" comment did not go over well because Trump seemed to be making an equivalency between white supremacists and those who resist them.

Military Leadership Speaks Out

The top commanders in the US military spoke out not only in the wake of the deadly violence that occurred at the white supremacist rally in Charlottesville, but also for Trumps weak response and lack of condemnation towards the white supremacists.

The statements were not directly addressing Trump's comments, but were instead presented as a message to the general public. The Chief of Naval Operations, Admiral John Richardson, was the first member to issue a statement, which read: *"Events in Charlottesville are unacceptable and mustn't be tolerated @USNavy for ever stands against intolerance & hatred."*

The Commandant of the US Marine Corps General Robert B. Neller stated, *"No place for racial hatred or extremism in @USMC. Our core values of Honor, Courage, and Commitment frame the way Marines live and act."*

The Chief of Staff of the Army General Mark Milley stated, *"The Army doesn't tolerate racism, extremism, or hatred in our ranks. It's against our Values and everything we've stood for since 1775."*

Air Force General Dave Goldfein stated, *"I stand with my fellow service chiefs in saying we're always stronger together-it's who we are as #Airmen."*

The Chief of the National Guard Bureau, Joseph Lengyel, stated, *"I stand with my fellow Joint Chiefs in condemning racism, extremism & hatred. Our diversity is our strength. #NationalGuard."*

In September of 2017, after being maligned in the press by Democrats, Republicans, Independents, and a host of religious leaders, Trump signed a resolution condemning white supremacy. Trump stated, "No matter the color of our skin or our ethnic heritage, we all live under the same laws, we all salute the same great flag, and we are all made by the same almighty God."

Why did the President wait until the issue reached a ClusterPhuctual level before he responded with the right message? It is obvious that he wanted the issue to fade out since it was affecting his pole numbers, but it did not keep in from contradicting his resolution later on.

In May of 2019, The United States broke with 18 governments and five top American tech firms, declining to endorse a New Zealand-led effort to curb extremism online. This was in response to the live-streamed shootings at two Christchurch mosques that killed 51 people in New Zealand. White House officials said that "free speech concerns" prevented them from signing the largest campaign to targeting extremism online.

When I use the term leading stupidly, I am referring to a situation like the one above. Why wouldn't you, as President of the United States, want to   L-E-A-D the effort in preventing extremism online, especially when a 2018 Quinnipiac University poll says that about half the people in America (49%) believe that President Trump is a racist.

By refusing to endorse the effort to curb extremism online, this leadership decision plays right into the hands of terror groups like ISIS…right? As reporter Audrey Alexander stated in her Foreign Affairs article:

"From Twitter to Telegram, Islamic State (ISIS) sympathizers continue to set up camp on social media platforms around the world. While some of the outlets are far-reaching and transparent, others are insular and protected. The range of platforms, the diffusion of sympathizers, and the sheer volume of content make it difficult for governments and private companies to contain the online ISIS threat."

A Lack of Moral Leadership

A Quinnipiac University Poll conducted in 2018, showed that 90 percent of voters believe that the President should be a positive influence on children. Only 29 percent said Trump is a positive influence on children, while 67 percent say he is not. The majority of voters across nearly every category, gender, education, age and racial group, deem Trump a bad role model.

As expected, the one notable exception found Seven out of 10 Republicans, 72 percent, say Trump is a good influence on children. Only 27 percent of American voters say they are proud to have Donald Trump as President, while 53 percent say they are embarrassed.

It doesn't get any better for Trump across the board. Six out of 10, 60 percent, say he is NOT honest, while 35 percent say he is. Nearly the same numbers, 59-38, say he doesn't have good leadership skills. 57 percent of respondents say he doesn't care about average Americans, while 40 percent say he does. Asked if Trump was level-headed, 61 percent said he wasn't, compared to 36 percent who said he was. Sixty-one percent also said he doesn't share their values; 34 percent said he did.

What do business leaders think? According to a 2018 CEO Summit, put on by the Yale School of Management's Chief Executive Leadership Institute, a survey showed that two-thirds of the CEOs feel that political instability, not trade, is the biggest threat to American business. Additionally, the same amount of respondents reported that they felt that Trump isn't effectively leading the country on national security issues, with a majority saying they think he's been outsmarted by Russia and North Korea.

The survey also showed that three out of four business leaders said that they often apologize for President Trump to their international business partners, while 88% of the top business leaders in the United States said that Trump's dysfunctional negotiating style has alienated our allies.

The "Fixer" Speaks

In February, 2019, in his testimony before the House Oversight Committee, Michael Cohen, former personal lawyer to Donald Trump, and vice president of the Trump family business, told the committee the following:

"Mr. Trump is a racist." He went on to give some examples, such as, "He once asked me if I could name a country run by a black person that wasn't a 'shithole.' This was when Barack Obama was President of the United States."

"While we were once driving through a struggling neighborhood in Chicago, he commented that only black people could live that way. He told me that black people would never vote for him because they were too stupid."

According to Cohen, Trump allegedly mistreated black workers in his casinos and, according to a former hotel executive, once said "laziness is a trait in blacks."

But for years, as it has been pointed out numerous times, Cohen didn't leave, and boasted that he would "take a bullet" for Trump. During the 2016 campaign, it was Cohen who visited predominantly black churches to try to convince congregants that Trump had their best interests in mind. You may recall the "what do you have to lose?" pitch by Trump.

Trump's alleged views, as you can see from his pattern of behavior, isn't anything new. However, Cohen, and others continued to support him, and ignore his comments and actions. Cohen is sitting in prison right now, probably wondering when it all turned to shit. Well, this was a slow-moving ClusterPhuck that he could have jumped off at any time. He decided to stay, and the blame rests squarely with him.

***

Pseudo Business Leadership Acumen

The Bureau of Labor Statistics uses surveys and statistical sampling to calculate how many Americans do or don't work. To calculate the unemployment rate, the agency "…divides the number of people who are out of work (counting only those who have recently looked for work) by the sum of the job-seeking and job-holding population."

On the 3ʳᵈ of May, 2019, the Aprils job report came out and showed that 263,000 jobs were added, and the unemployment rate fell to 3.6%, which was the lowest level in 50 years. All presidents want to take credit for the economy when its going good, but not when things are going bad.

Employment has actually grown for more than 100 months in a row, and the economy has created more than 20 million jobs since the Great Recession ended in 2009. Even though statistics will show that much of the increase occurred under Obama, President Trump will take credit for what he has at times called the greatest economy in history.

Some of you Dallas Cowboys fans may recall when Jimmy Johnson was the coach and led the team to back-to-back titles. After a "rift" developed between Johnson and owner Jerry Jones, Johnson left the team, and Barry Switzer took over as head coach. Switzer, who was out of coaching at the time he was hired, was a college coaching legend but had no prior NFL experience.

The Switzer led Cowboys nevertheless won the Super Bowl. Some will argue that Switzer won because Johnson left him with a fully intact Super Bowl team. However, it will go down in history as a win for Switzer, not Johnson. So Trump will be graded on the economy based on the day he took office, like all leaders are.

Although Trump touts his historic economic numbers, he insisted that the economic numbers under Obama were fake. As a candidate he made statements like, ***"I've seen numbers of 24 percent -- I actually saw a number of 42 percent unemployment. Forty-two percent."*** He continued, ***"5.3 percent unemployment -- that is the biggest joke there is in this country. … The unemployment rate is probably 20 percent, but I will tell you, you have some great economists that will tell you it's a 30, 32. And the highest I've heard so far is 42 percent."***

Of course these are untrue statements, but it did give Trump the kind of attention he wanted from the press, and it worked. However, now that he is President, has he made sound business decisions for the American people?

Tax Cuts That Hurt

The recent $1.5 trillion tax cuts by the Trump Administration is supposed to *"...spur the economy and drive new job growth."* However, both the nonpartisan Congressional Budget Office and the Joint Committee on Taxation estimated that, even if you assume that high levels of growth, the tax cuts will still add over a trillion dollars to the debt over the next 10 years. Furthermore, 38 leading economists unanimously agreed the GOP tax bills would cause the U.S. debt to increase substantially faster than the economy.

Even though President Trump and Congress sold it as a "middle class" tax cut, an analysis from the Tax Policy Center stated that even when the bill offers an across-the-board tax cut, in the first years of its implementation, upper-middle and upper-class Americans would receive most of the benefits. Nearly two-thirds of the benefits went to the richest fifth of Americans in 2018.

Additionally, by 2027, 53 percent of taxpayers will see a tax increase and 83 percent of the benefits will go to the top 1 percent. During Obama's presidency, Republicans constantly complained about the national debt and deficit spending, but since Trump took office, it's as if the Republican leadership has totally abandoned the concept of fiscal conservatism.

In April 2018, Republican Senator Marco Rubio told **Economist** magazine that there is "no evidence whatsoever" the law significantly helped American workers. He went on to state:

"There is still a lot of thinking on the right that if big corporations are happy, they're going to take the money they're saving and reinvest it in American workers...in fact, they bought back shares, a few gave out bonuses; there's no evidence whatsoever that the money's been massively poured back into the American worker."

Only time will tell how the American people will feel about the tax cuts. As of May, 2019, 56% of the people polled like the way the President Trump is handling the economy, which is largely based on the stock market, jobs report, and unemployment numbers.

When it comes down to it people are most concerned with their own personal economy...and there is evidence to be troubled about Trumps overall economic leadership actions like his tariff war, which will have far reaching consequences for American businesses and consumers.

Tarnishing The Trump Brand

In 2011, Donald Trump stated that his brand or name is worth $3 Billion. Forbes

Magazine disagreed and estimated that his brand name was worth about $200 million at that time. Branding is very important to Donald Trump. However, since 2016, the Trump name has been taking a beating. Trump spent years cultivating his brand, and affixing his name on everything from buildings, to golf courses, to water.

As you have read, there are plenty of reasons why the Trump name has become toxic. His name has been pried off of many buildings, and his golf resorts in Scotland posted millions of dollars in losses. Tech executive Gary Barrett stated, "People with enough cash to buy these units seem to be shying away from the Trump name," calling it "the Trump effect".

There were early signs that mixing politics and business was backfiring for the Trump brand. Calling Mexican immigrants crossing the border illegally "rapists," and then the release of the "Access Hollywood" tape of him arrogantly talking about grabbing women by the genitals, further eroded the brand. Macy's and Univision cut ties with his brand, and mattress maker Serta stopped licensing his name. NASCAR and the PGA booked events that used to be held at his Doral resort in Miami, to other locations. NBC, the TV network that aired the "Apprentice', ended its relationship with him.

Just how bad is it? A 2018 Associated Press analysis of sales data, shows prices per square foot have fallen in nine of the 11 Trump-branded buildings in Manhattan during the first 10 months of 2018. Since Trump has taken office, prices have fallen 9 percent on average and are now down to levels not seen in five years. In contrast, Manhattan condos overall have risen 29 percent.

Revenue at Trumps public golf course in the Bronx fell 9 percent in the first six months of 2018, on top of a 7 percent drop for all of 2017. Revenue from his Doral golf resort in Miami, which generates the bulk of Trump's golf revenue, is estimated by Forbes magazine to have plunged 26 percent in 2017.

In May of 2019, President Donald Trump's latest financial disclosure report shows he had at least $434 million in revenues last year. However, while the financial disclosure uses the term "income", the amounts in question are revenues, since they refer to gross receipts and not to profit. So, you have to make your own guess as to how much debt he accumulated, or profit Trump actually made.

Emoluments & Cascading ClusterPhucks

The **Emoluments Clause**, also called the foreign emoluments clause, is a *"provision of the U.S. Constitution (Article I, Section 9, Paragraph 8) that* *generally prohibits federal officeholders from receiving any gift, payment, or other thing of value from a foreign state or its rulers, officers, or representatives."*

In April, 2019, a judge ruled that Democrats in Congress can move ahead with their lawsuit against President Trump alleging that his private business violates the Constitution's ban on gifts or payments from foreign governments.

In January of 2017, President-elect Donald Trump said he would maintain ownership of his global business empire but give control to his two oldest sons while President. Trump said he would resign from all positions overseeing his hotels, golf courses and hundreds of other businesses and move his assets into a trust to help ensure that he will not consciously take actions as President that would benefit him personally.

However, unlike other U.S. government officials, the President is not required by law to steer clear of conflicts of interest. Trump stated, "I could actually run my business and run government at the same time. I don't like the way that looks, but I would be able to do that if I wanted to."

Well, now he is going to court because it appears that Trump has indeed violated the emoluments clause. In a 48-page opinion, the judge refused the request of the President's legal team to dismiss the case and rejected Trump's narrow definition of emoluments, finding it "unpersuasive and inconsistent."

A half-dozen House committees are seeking financial information related to the Trump organization, its accountants and lenders. The President and his family filed suit in New York against their biggest lender, and one of their banks, to try to stop them from complying with subpoenas from congressional committees. However, they lost their bid to block Deutsche Bank AG and the Capital One Financial Corporation from providing financial records to Democratic lawmakers investigating Trump's businesses.

Trump has gone out of his way to block any release of his tax returns or financial information concerning the Trump organization. What is he hiding from? The Mueller investigation showed that Trump was still negotiating to build "Trump Tower Moscow" even after he was elected. As you may recall, Trump made the following statements:

July 26, 2016: "I mean, I have nothing to do with Russia. I don't have any jobs in Russia. I'm all over the world but we're not involved in Russia."

July 26, 2016: "For the record, I have ZERO investments in Russia."

Oct. 6, 2016: During the second presidential debate, Hillary Clinton says Russia is trying to help elect Trump, "maybe because he wants to do business in Moscow." Trump calls this assessment "so ridiculous," adding, "I know nothing about Russia ... I don't deal there."

Oct. 24, 2016: "I have nothing to do with Russia folks, I'll give you a written statement."

Jan. 11, 2017: Trump tells reporters that he has "no deals that could happen in Russia because we've stayed away," adding that he could "make deals in Russia very easily" but "I just don't want to because I think that would be a conflict."

Jan. 11, 2017: "Russia has never tried to use leverage over me. I HAVE NOTHING TO DO WITH RUSSIA - NO DEALS, NO LOANS, NO NOTHING!"

Feb. 7, 2017: "I don't know Putin, have no deals in Russia, and the haters are going crazy."

May 11, 2017: Trump tells NBC News that he has "nothing to do with Russia," other than the fact that he "sold a house to a very wealthy Russian many years ago" and hosted the Miss Universe pageant there once.

In December, 2018, Chris Cuomo of CNN, announced that the network had obtained a letter of intent, personally signed by Donald Trump, to proceed with the Trump Tower Moscow project that would have provided his company with a $4 million upfront fee.

Yes, that signature on the letter of intent, which is dated October 28, 2015, five months after Trump launched his presidential campaign, and during a period in which he was lavishing praise on Russian President Vladimir Putin…which continues today. As you have read, Putin wanted Trump to win, and attacked the elections to help make it happen.

Trump has NEVER said a bad word about Putin, or has told him to stop attacking our elections. This, along with going over the head of Congress to sell weapons to Saudi Arabia, and defending the Saudi Prince, even after US intelligence believes that he was behind the assassination of a Washington Post reporter, are the main reasons behind the relentless investigations and lawsuits, that number in the teens, that Trump is facing.

Many of Trumps troubles are self-inflicted, and come from his leadership actions. For example, even though the Mueller Report found that the Trump campaign willing accepted help from Russia, and did not deter them in any way, Mueller did conclude that he couldn't find collusion/conspiracy between the campaign and Russia, but there is clear evidence that he tried to stop the investigation, dangled pardons, and intimidated witnesses, in plain sight.

Imagine if he would have just let the investigation take its course. Sure, he would have taken some heat for the unethical way his campaign operated, but he could have legitimately claimed exoneration.

That being said, there still would be a slew of investigations to contend with, like the hush money payments to two women, which could be campaign finance law violations, and part of the reason that Michael Cohen is in prison. Cohen's testimony indicated that Trump was aware of the payment and coordinated on how to portray it while serving as President.

Cohen presented a copy of a check signed by Trump for $35,000, and stated that the money was one installment of reimbursements he received for paying porn star Stormy Daniels. Cohen stated, "He asked me to pay off an adult film star with whom he had an affair, and to lie about it to his wife, which I did." Cohen recorded the conversation, by the way…which has been aired several times on national television.

During a question-and-answer session with reporters aboard Air Force One in April 2018, a reporter asked, "Mr. President, did you know about the $130,000 payment to Stormy Daniels?" "No" Trump replied.

So, the evidence shows that President Donald J. Trump has proven to be a shameless pathological liar. Now, some people will defend him and still think he is a great business man. That has been proven to be false as well. The New York Times, citing information from tax documents from 1985 to 1994, indicates that Trump's businesses reported losses of $1.17 billion.

Trump ran for President branding himself as a self-made billionaire, touting his financial success, but he has been steadfast in his refusal to release his tax returns to the public. It appears "Trump lost more money than nearly any other individual US taxpayer year after year."

Trump, starting at the age of 3, received at least $413 million in today's dollars from his father's real estate empire in order to bail him out of the many financial issues he created. Remember, Trump bankrupted six, yes 6 businesses, and there was not a US bank that would lend money to his business. What does that tell you? Again, we were warned well in advance, that Trump was a fraud.

Remember page 37…regarding persuasion? **Persuasion** is a "form of leadership" that is a powerful tool for forming both the expectations and beliefs in others." So, whether you like him or hate him, Trump has the ability to persuade a large group of people, even when the evidence is clearly against him.

Lastly, in May of 2019, Top House Republicans, who attended a presentation about China and trade, also received a psychological profile of President Trump. Larry Lindsey, a former economic adviser to President George W. Bush, who now runs a consulting business, was invited by Republican House Minority Leader Kevin McCarthy.

For some odd reason, Lindsey also came prepared with his own research on Trump's character. He told Republican lawmakers that he had asked two psychologists to evaluate the President from afar. The professionals found that Trump was a "10 out of 10 narcissist." Lindsey stated, "That's what he scored." He apparently wanted them to know that this wasn't just his opinion.

A person with a **narcissistic personality** disorder will exhibit such traits as a "grandiose sense of self-importance", "requires excessive admiration", "is interpersonally exploitative", and "shows arrogant, haughty behaviors or attitudes."

Lindsey also compared Trump's long-term planning ability to that of an "empty chair". The piece on Trump lasted about two minutes as part of a longer presentation on China. Lindsey was otherwise complimentary about how Trump has handled the trade conflict.

Many mental health professionals have tried to diagnose Trump from a distance, however the American Psychiatric Association's prohibits psychiatrists from "assessing public officials if they did not evaluate them in person." But, some have challenged what is known as the "Goldwater rule", arguing it is their "duty to warn" the public if they determine there's enough evidence to suggest Trump has a serious mental health issue. A petition to that effect was signed by 70,699 mental health professionals.

With the 2020 Presidential elections around the corner, just what are Trumps prospects for reelection? A January, 2019 Marist poll shows that 57% of registered voters said they would *"definitely vote against President Donald Trump."* If you break it down by party…10% of Republicans said they will not vote for Trump, while 21% aren't sure yet.

91% of Democrats and 62% of Independents said they would NOT vote for Trump for reelection. We are only two years into a Trump presidency. He has accumulated more investigations and created more turmoil, both domestically and internationally, than any President in history…including those that served eight years.

Only time will tell if President Trump will succeed in his effort to "stonewall" Congress, and at the same time completely transform the Republican Party from a party that believed in free trade, fiscal responsibility, and as NATO's most reliable partner, to a more anti-trade, anti-immigrant, and pro-far right party, that is only interested in its base.

Chapter 6

Institutional Moral Leadership Hypocrisy

Abuse of Power is defined as *"The act of using one's position of power in an abusive way. This can take many forms, such as taking advantage of someone, gaining access to information that shouldn't be accessible to the public, or just manipulating someone with the ability to punish them if they don't comply."*

When you cast your vote for a politician, judge, or have to deal with the government for a personal or business transaction, you, at the very least, expect to be treated fairly and ethically in their decision making process. Even if you are on the wrong end of a decision, you want to be able to walk away from the experience confident that the law, and the process, was followed, and that the decision was not influenced by a bribe or nepotism.

Earlier you read about a host of politicians that were removed from office or are currently in prison for violating their oath of office to basically use their positions to enrich themselves financially, or removed for some sex related offense. Their ethical lapses could possibly mean that you were a victim in the past, but it probably never occurred to you because the majority of us believe that people are honest and ethical…initially.

Institutions are led by human beings, and some human beings, unfortunately, are prone to exhibit unethical or abusive behaviors that lead to ClusterPhucks. As discussed earlier, there are degrees of "ClusterPhuckiness", in that some are more harmful than others…especially when it involves the leaders within major social institutions.

The term **Institution** commonly "applies to both informal institutions such as

211

customs, or behavior patterns important to a society, and to particular formal institutions created by individuals."

There are five major social institutions found in all societies, which are:

1. **Government**: which is an institution entrusted with making and enforcing the rules of a society as well as with regulating relations with other societies. In order to be considered a government, a ruling body must be recognized as such by the people it purports to govern.
2. **Family**: which is generally "regarded as a major social institution and a locus of much of a person's social activity. It is a social unit created by blood, marriage, or adoption, and can be described as nuclear (parents and children) or extended (encompassing other relatives)."
3. **Religious**: which are "the visible and organized manifestations of practices and beliefs in particular social and historical contexts. Like human emotions and attitudes, religious beliefs and practices project outward onto the social and historical plan. They create identities and representations, and determine attitudes, emotions, and behavior."
4. **Educational**: which are "places where people of different ages gain an education. Examples of some institutions are preschools, primary schools, secondary schools, and further and higher education. They provide a large variety of learning environments and learning spaces.
5. **Economic**: which are a "Network of commercial organizations (such as manufacturers, producers, wholesalers, retailers, and buyers) who generate, distribute, and purchase goods and services. Financial institutions are also included.

Moral Agent's & Institutions

A **Moral Agent** is a person who *"has the ability to discern right from wrong and to be held accountable for his or her own actions."* Moral agents have a moral responsibility not to cause unjustified harm, or knowingly create ClusterPhucks. Unfortunately, party affiliation plays a huge role as to whether it is important for the President of the United States to provide **Moral Leadership**.

In a 2018 Gallop poll, only 63% of Republicans say moral leadership is very important, which is down from 86% under President Clinton.

Gallup conducted polls twice regarding President Clinton's moral leadership during his presidency, and the results varied. In 1996, more Americans regarded his leadership in this area as strong (53%), rather than weak (45%). After Clinton's affair with former White House intern Monica Lewinsky his "strong" moral leadership numbers plummeted to 30%, while 68% said the President displayed weak moral leadership.

Democrats' opinions about Clinton's moral leadership in 1996 were similar to Republicans' views of Trump today. 78% of Democrats thought Clinton was a strong moral leader in 1996, while Republicans and independents were more likely to regard him as weak.

It can be argued that Trump and Clinton have had more character concerns than other recent Presidents, but their political allies stood by them. Doing so may have forced their supporters to "minimize the importance of having a President who is a strong moral leader."

At the same time, those who opposed the President may have played up the importance of that presidential responsibility. This type of "enabling" of bad behavior, hastens the decent into moral decay, until enough people speak out and do something about it…like, for example, Michigan Congressman Justin Amash.

"Do not follow where the path may lead. Go instead where there is no path and leave a trail." --Harold R. McAlindon

Amash became the first Republican lawmaker to say President Trump had "engaged in impeachable conduct." Of course, Trump responded to Amash, calling him a "loser" and "a total lightweight who opposes me and some of our great Republican ideas and policies just for the sake of getting his name out there through controversy."

Traditionally, moral agency is assigned only to those who can be held responsible for their actions. Meaning, those we elect to public office, school boards, or are appointed CEO's of major corporations, should know right from wrong. Children, and adults with certain mental disabilities, may, according to some experts, have little or no capacity to be moral agents.

Adults with full mental capacity, according to some, relinquish their moral agency only in extreme situations, like being held hostage for example. But, unfortunately, that does not hold true for even the most trusted institution in America, the military.

In one recent poll, 87 percent of the respondents said that they have **"a great deal or quite a lot of confidence"** in the military. However, it does NOT mean that military leaders are immune to creating or preventing ClusterPhucks.

Pressure & Duty to Country

On the 27th of January, in 1973, the military draft ended. As the Vietnam War drew to a close, the Selective Service announced that there would be no further draft calls. What that meant was that anyone joining the military from that point would either volunteer, or be recruited. Sure, an "all-volunteer" or "all-recruited" military force sounds good…but it is fraught with a relentless amount of ClusterPhuctual pitfalls, that have caused personnel to lose their careers, family, health, and even their lives.

Competition between military recruiters, at times, can get pretty intense. Remember, 71 percent of young adults in America don't qualify for military service, which puts added pressure on recruiters. Some of you are probably under the impression that the "all volunteer" military meant that anyone could walk into a recruiting office and join. That was exactly the feeling a National Public Radio (NPR) reporter thought when she interviewed me at a recruiting office in Syracuse, New York.

Most people, I explained, that walked into the office were unqualified. What disqualifies them? Not meeting the weight standards, law violations, and medical issues. The U.S. Army, had a 2018 recruiting goal of 76,500, which is the largest "mission" of all military services. Now, how many people are you going to have to call and interview to get to that number? The numbers range in the hundreds of thousands. Keep in mind that the soldiers sent to recruiting duty are typically Sergeants and Staff Sergeants, with many of them coming from combat or high-risk regions around the world. They overwhelmingly come from leadership positions, and are used to accomplishing missions.

Now, they are thrust into a position where they have no, or little control, in accomplishing their mission. An 18 year old can simply say "no" to an enlistment, and there is simply nothing you can do about it except call more people. Some of the more abusive leaders have used "motivation" techniques, such as keeping recruiters late into the night, threatened their careers, or told them that they "let down their country."

Army recruiting has always had a grueling pace with relentless deadlines. The environment came to a head in 2008, during the height of the war in Iraq, when the Army consistently had to recruit 80,000 new soldiers a year, and when the service investigated a trend of recruiter suicides, which totaled 17 since the Global War on Terror began. The investigation did force leaders to reduce hours to try and relieve the pressure on recruiters, but as of 2018, evidence suggests, due to shortages, that some services may have to resort to longer hours…including weekends, again.

The United States General Accounting Office (GAO), wrote in a report regarding military recruiting, that ***"Recruiters in all of the services generally work long*** *hours, take very little leave, and are under almost constant pressure until they achieve their assigned monthly goals. Successful recruiters are often required to make up for recruiters who do not perform well."*

Again, 71% of the 17 to 24 year olds that are the target ages for recruits are ineligible for military service. The military services designate personnel to screen and select recruiters. In general, prospective recruiters go through a process that includes conducting interviews, as well as checking their medical and personnel records.

Factors that may disqualify a person from recruiting duty, include average or low performance marks; recent alcohol or drug use; and financial health and legal problems.

Even with all of the thorough screening that went into finding the best possible recruiters, it still does not prevent some unethical behavior or recruiter improprieties. From 2007 to 2009, there were 1,119 substantiated allegations. The key word is **"substantiated"**, which means that the allegations were supported by proof or evidence.

In 2006, the U.S. Office of the Under Secretary of Defense, released a memorandum that focused on eight broad categories of recruiter improprieties, which are referred to as recruiter "irregularities." Reporting is required for cases involving allegations falling within one of these categories, including cases that may ultimately be **"unsubstantiated."** These categories and their definitions are as follows:

• **Criminal misconduct**: Behavior that can result in a court-martial or civilian conviction (and does not fall in another category).
• **Sexual misconduct**: A subcategory of criminal misconduct that includes rape, sexual assault, and statutory rape.
• **Sexual harassment**: Behavior that includes unwelcome sexual advances, requests for sexual favors, and other conduct of a sexual nature.
• **Fraternization or unauthorized relationship with an applicant**: Any personal relationship between a recruiter and an applicant that is unduly familiar, including dating, recreation, and dining.
• **Concealment or falsification**: Knowingly withholding, altering, or fabricating information, including using false diplomas, or advising an applicant not to disclose relevant information, including medical information.

Of the five categories, "Concealment or Falsification", showed the highest percentage of the 1,119 substantiated allegations. Recruiting environments are not the same as it pertains to attracting young men and women. The vast majority of casualties and injuries from the Iraq and Afghanistan wars are from the United

States Army. The Army is the largest military service and its overall mission is built for large-scale conflicts.

Recruiting Wars

In fiscal year 2018, the Army missed its goal, by 6,500, for the first time since 2005. The Army's leadership conclusions, like pretty much all other sales organizations that miss their numbers, were centered around bringing in more recruiters due to the increased goals, along with "marketing needs a complete overhaul, to include commercials, promotional events, research and social media; and "the recruiting focus must turn from mainstay Southern and Midwestern towns toward large, highly populated urban areas."

However, the Army did pour in an extra $200 million into bonuses, and approved some additional waivers for bad conduct or health issues. That being said, Congress is concerned about additional "waivers" that have allowed people into the service.

Why is Congress concerned? There is a fear that they are repeating the same mistakes made during the peak of the Iraq and Afghanistan wars, more than a decade ago, when it rushed to add soldiers to the ranks to meet deployment needs. At that time, the Army brought in more recruits with misconduct waivers, triggering discipline and other problems. Remember the "Garbage in, Garbage out" theory? Incidentally, shouldn't the same kind of scrutiny be leveled at the individuals that were granted security clearances to work in the White House, after they were rejected by career professionals? Just a thought.

So, if I'm reading this right, Congress is worried about another round of ClusterPhucks, due to the fact that not enough people are joining the Army. By the way, the Army National Guard and Army Reserves also fell far short of their goals, by more than 12,000 and 5,000 respectively. The Navy, Air Force and Marine Corps, meanwhile, all met their recruiting goals for 2018.

All services are exposed to high-risk situations at times. However, the Army has more personnel in places like Iraq and Afghanistan than any other service. The Army is built for ground wars. Now imagine trying to recruit a young man or young woman into the military, knowing that their parents, friends, guidance counselors, and a list of others, may be strongly against your decision to join.

Now add to the mix a President that makes threats, or insinuates, that the US may take "military action" if need be. If you are intent on joining a military service, safety always plays a role. However, there are those that join a particular service because of a family tradition, regardless of the perceived risks.

So, is the "root cause" of recruiter suicides, improprieties, and the overall negative culture in military recruiting, the fault of Army leadership, or politicians that won't reinstate the draft? After all, males still have to sign up for Selective Service when they turn 18 years of age. If Congress is so concerned about the quality of soldiers enlisting into the Army, why don't they do something about it? Why not start randomly enlisting some of those people on the Selective Service list?

To be sure, there is an argument to be made that a Selective Service type of draft would be full of people who didn't necessarily want to be there…making it harder for leaders to motivate service members.

However, there is another school of thought. My dad was in the Army during the Korean War. He volunteered, which was pretty common, from my understanding, for people who were raised in the south. Plus, volunteers could sometimes select their field of choice. My dad was in the artillery field, and did not reveal to me the horrors of war until I was 25 or 26 years old.

My question to him was, "how did the Army get people to do their jobs?" Meaning, what would prevent a person from doing absolutely nothing for their two year obligation? My dad clarified it very simply. He said that the Army was going to get "two GOOD years" from you, which meant, if, for example, that you thought you were going to get yourself thrown in prison for 6 months to get out of the war, they would just add 6 more months onto your enlistment. So, it was common to see days added to enlistments for soldiers not pulling their weight. It took some soldiers 3 or 4 years to get their two GOOD years before being discharged.

It is possible for this to work, but the political will is not there. It is much easier for Congress to bring in the Recruiting Commanding General and grill him on the decline in numbers, instead of addressing the real problem. This **Passive Leadership** style has worked since the draft ended, so why change it and risk being run out of office?

Military Leadership Failures

According to the Pentagon, sexual assaults across the US military increased by a rate of nearly 38% in 2018. 62% of the most serious sexual assaults involved "alcohol use by the victim and/or the alleged offender", and the vast majority of victims knew their assailant, the report said.

The Pentagon has established a sexual assault accountability task force that was assembled at the request of Arizona Republican Sen. Martha McSally in March, 2019.

In testimony before the House of Representatives, Defense Secretary Patrick Shanahan stated that he was going to issue a directive to the Defense Department that would "criminalize" sexual harassment in the military, and make it a stand-alone crime under military law. I wouldn't hold my breath, given the historical record.

Tell Them What They Want To Hear

In 1997, then Air Force Secretary Sheila Widnall, testified before Senate Armed Services Committee, in a hearing on sexual harassment, stating:

"The success of our missions depends in large measure on the degree of trust and understanding that exists among the people in our units... Anything that might erode that trust is just not tolerable. We will maintain it, and we will enforce it. We will ensure that our people are treated with the human respect and dignity that they deserve."

In 2013, Army Chief of Staff Ray Odierno, on the same sexual harassment subject to Congress, stated:

"Our profession is built on the bedrock of trust — the trust that must inherently exist among soldiers, and between soldiers and their leaders to accomplish their mission... these acts ... will not be tolerated. This is about inculcating a culture that is in line with our values, specifically treating all with dignity and respect."

With regards to who is responsible for fixing the mess…Widnall stated,

"The most effective way of ensuring accountability in military organizations is to give commanders the direct responsibility ... 'Commanders' demonstrated leadership and personal commitment ... must be visible and unequivocal."

General Odierno stated,

"Command authority is the most critical mechanism for ensuring discipline and accountability, cohesion and the integrity of the force…It is imperative that we keep the chain of command fully engaged and at the center of any solution."

Critics say that the military is unwilling or incapable of dealing with the issue, and that they are in "denial" thinking that they can solve the problem themselves. Clearly, regardless of what was said and done in the past, has failed.

Sex has been the downfall of Presidents, members of Congress and is also among the chief reasons that senior military officers are fired.

At least 30 percent of military commanders fired over the past several years lost their jobs because of sexually related offenses, including harassment, adultery, and improper relationships. For good reason, there are growing concerns over the declining ethical values among U.S. forces, and came into sharp focus with the resignation of one of the Army's most esteemed generals, David Petraeus, and the investigation of a second general, John Allen, at the time, the top U.S. commander in Afghanistan.

The statistics from all four military services show that adulterous affairs are more than a four-star weakness. From sexual assault and harassment to pornography, drugs and drinking, ethical lapses are an escalating problem for the military's leaders. With all those offenses taken together, more than 4 in every 10 commanders at the rank of lieutenant colonel or above who were fired fell as a result of behavioral missteps.

However, as former Army Secretary John McHugh stated, *"I think the narrative comes out of many soldiers who rightfully or wrongfully believe that the Army doesn't hold senior leaders, senior military officers accountable in the same fashion they hold junior officers or enlisted."*

Holding senior leaders accountable is always a good thing, but how do you explain a 38% increase in sexual assaults? The fact is, the military's top leadership has failed year after year. Yes, military personnel get relieved, fined, jailed, etc., but for some reason it's not deterring bad behavior.

Do As I Say

There is an expectation that younger military personnel will experience some growing pains and will get into a little trouble every now and then. Depending on the offense, they can expect anything from a written counseling, extra duty, or a fine. The goal is to send a message without ruining the first enlistment of an individual that may prove to be valuable in the future. That cannot however be said for those in positions of leadership, that have been around long enough to know better. Unfortunately, leading stupidly has no rank limitations.

Since 2013, military investigators have documented at least 500 cases of serious misconduct among its generals, admirals and senior civilians. Roughly half of those instances involved personal or ethical lapses. Many cases involved sex scandals, including an Army general who led a "swinging lifestyle", and another who lived rent-free in the home of a defense contractor after his affair fell apart, while another was relieve for sending "steamy" Facebook messages to the wife of an enlisted soldier on his post.

In early 2018, Navy leadership officials relieved all three members of the command triad for Naval Mobile Construction Battalion Four, deployed to Okinawa, Japan, after an embarrassing incident in which the unit's executive officer was reportedly found drunk and naked in the woods.

Nancy Parrish, President of Protect Our Defenders, an advocacy group for military sexual assault victims, stated, ***"This epidemic has persisted for at least 20 years and probably four decades…nothing has changed."***

So, even when America has consistently voted the military as the institution they most have "confidence" in…there will always be a few that initiate ClusterPhucks, due to pressure, greed, or just plain old stupidity. If you can't trust the top leadership to police its own…who can you trust? Politicians? Really?!

ClusterPhuckers & Official Corruption

"I always did let ethics beat me out of money and I suppose I always will."

President Harry S. Truman

Ok, you now have a pretty good grasp as to what a ClusterPhuck is and how they are formed. ClusterPhuckers are people employed by the government (federal, state, county, local), to serve the people, but use their positions for personal gain.

In 2017, The Chapman University Survey of American Fears, polled 1,207 U.S. adults on their level of fear across 80 different categories ranging from crime to personal anxieties and natural disasters. At the very top of the list was "corruption of government officials", by a significant margin, with 74.5 percent of U.S. adults saying it makes them either "afraid" or "very afraid".

There are multiple ways to categorize corruption, which are:

1. **Administrative Corruption**: alters the implementation of policies and has some traces of the previous spoils system.
2. **Political Corruption**: influences the establishment of laws and regulations.
3. **Grand Corruption**: otherwise known as kleptocracy — typically involving substantial amounts of money and high-level officials.
4. **Petty Corruption**: relates to the abuse of entrusted power by public officials in their day-to-day conduct with average citizens trying to access

basic guarantees such as hospitals and schools; this can occur on a state, county, or local level.

Political corruption is present on both the federal and state level. At the national level, according to a survey conducted by Transparency International, "44 percent of Americans believe that corruption is pervasive" in the Trump White House. Remember the 30 individuals that were initially "rejected" by the security screening department, but were overruled by Trump loyalist, Carl Kline?

Kline does not only fit the ClusterPhucker role, but is now attached to whatever the "rejected-30" does to cause a ClusterPhuck. Kline is not the only ClusterPhucker out there of course. According to the Justice Department, in the last two decades more than 20,000 public officials and private individuals were convicted for crimes related to corruption.

State Integrity Investigation's, which provides a comprehensive assessment of state government accountability, revealed some disturbing information. For example, 13 states received a grade of **F**, 34 received a grade of **D**, and three passed with a **C**. Forty-seven states have thus "failed to maintain state integrity in areas such as budget transparency, government scandals, and crime by cabinet officials."

ClusterPhuckers are enticed by the economic gain via corruption, in order to fund personal interests and allows for wealthy citizens within the community to easily sway local politics.

One study concluded that higher levels of corruption lead to "increased inequality and poverty", meaning lowered incomes for those impoverished. For states that have larger income inequalities, it can be expected, according to the study, there is a higher rate of corruption in that area.

You may have heard of the term **"Pay-to-Play"**, which is a phrase used for "a variety of situations in which money is exchanged for services or the privilege to engage in certain activities."

Crony Capitalism is a term that describes how success in business depends on close relationships between business people and government officials. It may be exhibited by favoritism in the distribution of legal permits, government grants, and special tax breaks. Crony capitalism is believed to arise when political cronyism spills into the business world. It is marked by self-serving friendships and family ties between businessmen and the government.

Well respected billionaire Warren Buffett put it best when he stated:

"We've got K-Street, we've got lobbyists, we've got money on our side in terms of lobbyists." He went on to state that his secretary, Deb, *"...does not have a lobbyist. She doesn't have anybody remotely that's representing her. But, believe me, plenty of rich families have lobbyists that are working like crazy to get rid of estate taxes, lower capital gain taxes, whatever it may be. So, if there has been a war going on, the war has been waged by the people who are very well to do who are trying to shift the burden onto people like that and away from themselves."*

When the government can deliver favors to businesses, the latter have an incentive to devote resources to acquiring the favors. Firms often approach the government with the claim that they have unfair foreign competition, and they seek protection in the form of tariffs, quotas, or regulations that protect domestic firms.

It's not often that a high ranking government official admits to being a ClusterPhucker. Mick Mulvaney, the acting director of the Consumer Financial Protection Bureau and head of the Office of Management and Budget, did just that.

Mulvaney, a former South Carolina representative, said he would only meet with lobbyists who had donated to his campaign, stating, *"We had a hierarchy in my office in Congress."* And added, *"If you're a lobbyist who never gave us money, I didn't talk to you. If you're a lobbyist who gave us money, I might talk to you."*

Of course he tried to clean it up later, but it's like telling your wife that it looks as if she'd gained a few pounds over the winter. No, there is no fixing that folks.

Pseudo Moral Agents

If you are a New England Patriots football fan, you may have heard from news reports that all head coach Bill Belichick asks of his players is for each one of them to do their jobs. It seems like such a logical request, but as you have seen, thousands upon thousands of politicians, can't seem to just do the job they campaigned for.

The job of a congressman or congresswoman, each representative is, among other duties, is to " introduce bills and resolutions, offer amendments and serve on committees." Prior to establishing the permanent select committee in 1977, the House of Representatives established the "Select Committee on Intelligence".

It is the primary committee in the U.S. House of Representatives charged with the oversight of the United States Intelligence Community. Devin Nunes was the chairman of the Select Committee on Intelligence until January 3rd, 2019.

Nunes, who was also a member of President Trump's transition team, failed miserably in leading the investigation into Russia's attack on the 2016 presidential elections. He actually went from criticizing the investigation into Russian interference, to strategizing about how to minimize its impact should it imperil President Trump.

He even released a memorandum accusing the intelligence community of conspiring against the President, and sought documents from the Justice Department as part of his investigation into the law enforcement officials leading the Russia inquiry.

At a closed-door fundraiser for a Republican colleague, Nunes tied the investigation to the midterm elections. He was recorded stating, *"I mean, we have to keep all these seats...we have to keep the majority. If we do not keep the majority, all of this goes away."*

His "party over country" leadership behavior didn't go unnoticed. Ted Lieu, also of California, called on Nunes to resign, saying his comments ran counter to the oath of office he had taken upon entering Congress.

University of Texas Law School professor Steve Vladeck, tweeted, *"After all, this has been the only explanation — for quite some time — for his ridiculous behavior on everything from the unmasking scandal"* to the "Rosenstein impeachment." Yes, he pushed for the impeachment of Rod Rosenstein of the Justice Department, in order to stop him from investigating Trump.

In a September, 2018, Fox News poll, 52% of the respondents saw the Republicans putting their party's interests above the nation's interests, while only 36% of likely voters believed Republicans sincerely want what's best for the country.

The poll showed that 44% saw the Democratic party as wanting what was best for the country, while 43% saw them as wanting what was best for the party. Still, this is not particularly bad news for the Democrats, considering that Fox News is widely considered a Republican dominated network.

Remember, it was only a few years ago, when Obama was President, that Senate Majority Leader Mitch McConnell's biggest fear was having a handful of Senate Republicans voting for the Affordable Care Act and then, according to

McConnell, praising Obama's commitment to bipartisan ideas and governance. He suggested that the campaign ads would have been so powerful that Obama's approval ratings would have soared.

So, regardless of how overwhelming Democratic and Republican voters want the two parties to work together to solve problems, like healthcare, there will always be ClusterPhuckers that will place their party needs over the country's.

Then again, you do, now and then, have someone step up against their own party to try and **UnPhuck** a situation that has gotten out of hand. You may recall when Senator John McCain, during his often heated campaign against Obama, "in the face of constituents spouting racist conspiracies about the then-senator from Illinois", during a town hall, cut off a lady from Minnesota, who stated, *"I can't trust Obama. I have read about him, and he's not, um, he's an Arab."*

McCain responded, grabbing the microphone from the woman, *"No, ma'am, he's a decent family man [and] citizen that I just happen to have disagreements with on fundamental issues, and that's what the campaign's all about. He's not [an Arab]."*

That ladies and gentlemen, is what REAL LEADERSHIP is about. I didn't vote for Senator McCain, but I had the utmost respect for his service to the country and the way he handled that situation. He could have easily fed into the woman's fears, but took the high road instead.

Some of you may remember when Mitt Romney's son, Tagg, during an interview with a North Carolina radio station, said Obama's comments questioning his father's truthfulness, made him want to "jump out of my seat and ... rush down to the debate stage and take a swing at him."

Of course, there was an uproar in some circles, but if you would have heard it, you could tell by the playful tone, that he wasn't serious at all. I said that then, and I will say it again…he was NOT serious.

Now, when people pounce on your kid, it hurts you as a parent. Tagg more than likely didn't expect that kind of backlash, I'm assuming. Fast forward to the third and final debate between Obama and Romney. If you get a chance, go to YouTube and watch the end of the debate, when all of the family members come up on stage, shaking hands, smiling, etc.

If you watch the video closely, you can see Tagg Romney, reach over and "whisper" an apology to President Obama. Having spent years in military recruiting, including interviewing people for positions that require an advanced security clearance, you tend to be able to read mannerisms. From my standpoint, Tagg was sincere in his apology when he told President Obama that he was "just joking".

Given Obama's character, did you really think he wouldn't accept his apology? I was more interested in Governor Romney's mannerisms. He was fully engaged in what was going on between the two. As a father, I would be hoping that the President would take some of the pressure off of my son, which Obama did.

In May of 2019, now Senator Mitt Romney, was the only Republican to oppose the nomination of Michael Truncale, a President Trump pick for the U.S. District Court for the Eastern District of Texas. Romney's stated reason, "He had said some things disparaging of President Obama and having been a Republican nominee in 2012, I couldn't sign on to that for a district judge." Truncale had called Obama an "un-American imposter." Really?

Truncale, attempting to rationalize what was truly unbecoming of a person looking to serve the ALL the people, responded by stating that at that time he was "merely expressing frustration by what I perceived as a lack of overt patriotism on behalf of President Obama." Interesting enough, he had nothing to say about President Trumps praising the "love letters" he received from North Korea's brutal dictator Kim Jong Un, or for refusing to tell Russia's Vladimir Putin to quit attacking US Presidential elections.

Then there is Trumps defense of Saudi Crown Prince Mohammed bin Salman, who, according to the Central Intelligence Agency (CIA), ordered the assassination of Washington Post journalist Jamal Khashoggi. Of course, you haven't heard a peep out of "judge" Truncale, who, like Nunes, will be placed in a position of power, and will more than likely side with party over country.

As you have seen from the thousands of convictions, hypocrisy is deep and rampant when it comes to government officials. However, there are some good ones out there, even in this "tribal" environment we find ourselves in today. Let's take Robert S. Mueller as an example of good.

Robert Swan Mueller III, is lawyer and government official who served as the sixth Director of the Federal Bureau of Investigation from 2001 to 2013. Mueller, a registered Republican, was appointed and reappointed to Senate-confirmed positions by Presidents George H. W. Bush, Bill Clinton, George W. Bush and Barack Obama. Let that sink in.

He served as a Marine Corps officer during the Vietnam War, receiving a Bronze Star for heroism and a Purple Heart. On May 17, 2017, Mueller was appointed by

Deputy Attorney General Rod Rosenstein as special counsel overseeing an investigation into allegations of Russian interference in the 2016 U.S. Presidential elections, as well as any obstruction of justice matters that may have been committed by President Trump.

From the moment Mueller was chosen as special counsel, I was more than a little confident that he wouldn't be tainted by politics and get to the truth, because…now get this…he has a history of being a man of INTEGRITY. If he exonerated Trump or his campaign, I would fully accept his conclusions, because he was leading the investigation.

As Mueller pointed out on the 29th of May, 2019, in his first public appearance since the investigation started, "If we had confidence that the President clearly did not commit a crime, we would have said that." Mueller's remarks also made clear how heavily his office relied on, as mentioned earlier, a long-standing legal opinion from the Justice Department's Office of Legal Counsel that a sitting President cannot be indicted.

He went on to state, "the Constitution requires a process other than the criminal justice system to formally accuse a sitting President of wrongdoing." Meaning, it is up to Congress to investigate and decide if Trump obstructed justice, which, more than 900 former federal prosecutors, believe Trump did.

Mueller's remarks has also shown the world that Attorney General Barr lied, or at the very least, misled the American people and Congress when he stated, "The Special Counsel's decision to describe the facts of his obstruction investigation without reaching any legal conclusions leaves it to the Attorney General to determine whether the conduct described in the report constitutes a crime."

In March of 2019, Barr reviewed the evidence and concluded Trump did not break the law, which again, is NOT up to him to decide. As many experts and pundits have pointed out, Barr is clearly acting as if he is Trumps personal lawyer instead of the top justice official in the United States. There have been calls for his removal through impeachment, due to his obvious lack of integrity. This shouldn't surprise anyone though…he has stated that his job is to protect the presidency.

Former Attorney General Jeff Sessions was berated and eventually forced out by Trump because he recused himself from inquiries related to the 2016 elections. Now, Sessions views and actions on illegal and legal immigration, bordered on the extreme. However, in this particular situation, he did what was ethically right. Barr, seemingly does not want to get on Trumps bad side, and stated he would not recuse himself, even though he had already prejudged the Mueller investigation by basically auditioning for the position, with his 19 page unsolicited letter to the White House.

In a 2010, a study investigating the **moral hypocrisy** of the powerful, by researchers at Tilburg and Northwestern university's, found that when people are assigned to powerful positions, or even if they are merely put in the mindset of having power, they cheat more and think of their own transgressions as less bad. At the same time, they tend to hold their underlings to higher standards. Again, the mentality is, do as I say…and not as I do.

***

One of the major findings that came out of the Mueller Report was the fact that the Trump campaign welcomed the help from the Russian's, even though there was not enough evidence to bring criminal charges. It would be like you receiving a stolen playbook from someone who wanted to see your team win. Now, YOU didn't plan the theft or conspire with the thieves, but the head coach did make a statement like, "If anyone's listening, I would really appreciate any advice on how we may defeat our next opponent."

Adlai Stevenson II was a popular governor of Illinois between 1949 and 1953. He was known as a "witty, articulate and smart politician." He was the Democratic nominee for President, but lost twice to Republican Dwight D. Eisenhower.

During the 1956 campaign, he advocated a ban on the testing of hydrogen bombs, a stance that led to accusations of Stevenson being "soft" on national security issues.

The Soviet Union took notice of this and believed that Stevenson might be someone they could work with. Does this sound familiar? Stevenson had publically stated he would not seek the nomination again in 1960, but Soviet ambassador Mikhail A. Menshikov, hoped he would reconsider. On January 16, 1960, Menshikov invited Stevenson (**Charismatic Leadership** style), to supposedly thank him for helping negotiate Soviet premier Nikita Khrushchev's visit to the U.S., but there was an ulterior motive.

At one point, the Soviet ambassador pulled notes from his pocket and began delivering Stevenson a message he said came directly from his boss, Soviet premier Khrushchev, encouraging Stevenson, (**Strategic Leadership** style), to seriously consider another run for President. In a memorandum dictated a week later, Stevenson recounted Ambassador Menshikov's speech, which stated:

"Before returning last week from Moscow, he [Menshikov] had spent

considerable time alone with Premier Khrushchev. He [Khrushchev] wishes me [Menshikov] to convey the following: When you met in Moscow in August, 1958, he [Khrushchev] said to you that he had voted for you in his heart in 1956. He says now that he will vote for you in his heart again in 1960. We have made a beginning with President Eisenhower and Khrushchev's visit to America toward better relations, but it is only a beginning. We are concerned with the future, and that America has the right President. All countries are concerned with the American election. It is impossible for us not to be concerned about our future and the American Presidency which is so important to everybody everywhere.

"In Russia we know well Mr. Stevenson and his views regarding disarmament, nuclear testing, peaceful coexistence, and the conditions of a peaceful world. He has said many sober and correct things during his visit to Moscow and in his writings and speeches. When we compare all the possible candidates in the United States we feel that Mr. Stevenson is best for mutual understanding and progress toward peace. These are the views not only of myself—Khrushchev—but of the Presidium. We believe that Mr. Stevenson is more of a realist than others and is likely to understand Soviet anxieties and purposes. Friendly relations and cooperation between our countries are imperative for all. Sober realism and sensible talks are necessary to the settlement of international problems. Only on the basis of coexistence can we hope to really find proper solutions to our many problems.

"The Soviet Union wishes to develop relations with the United States on a basis which will forever exclude the possibility of conflict. We believe our system is best and will prevail. You, Mr. Stevenson, think the same about yours. So we both say, let the competition proceed, but excluding any possibility of conflict.

"Because we know the ideas of Mr. Stevenson, we in our hearts all favor him. And you Ambassador Menshikov must ask him which way we could be of assistance to those forces in the United States which favor friendly relations. We don't know how we can help to make relations better and help those to succeed in political life who wish for better relations and more confidence. Could the Soviet press assist Mr. Stevenson's personal success? How? Should the press praise him, and, if so, for what? Should it criticize him, and, if so, for what? (We can always find many things to criticize Mr. Stevenson for because he has said many harsh and critical things about the Soviet Union and Communism!) Mr. Stevenson will know best what would help him."

Although Stevenson lost twice in his bid to become President, he didn't let that cloud his ethics. Stevenson declined the offer, and repeated that he would not be running for the nomination. He did admit that the offer rattled him, which is understandable.

"A person cannot do right in one area while attempting to do wrong in another area. Life, therefore, is one indivisible whole."

Mahatma Gandhi

Unlike members of the Trump campaign, Stevenson shut the foreign adversary down quickly. By the way, what did Nixon do to turn them to Stevenson? Trust me…I'm going somewhere with this…and it will leave a trail that leads directly back to the Russian playbook.

The Kitchen Debate

In late 1958, the Soviet Union and the United States agreed to set up national exhibitions in each other's nation as part of their new emphasis on cultural exchanges. The Soviet exhibition opened in New York City in June 1959; the U.S. exhibition opened in Sokolniki Park in Moscow in July. Ok, it sounds like a good idea…right?

I have been to several military recruiting exhibitions, air shows, etc. Each service will display their most advanced weapons, aircraft, etc., to not only show their military might, but as an impressive recruiting "tool". The bottom line, the world will be watching, so you want your best on display.

Vice President Richard Nixon served as the host to Soviet leader Khrushchev, for the Moscow exhibition. Before the exhibition was officially opened to the public, Nixon led Khrushchev through the American exhibition. It was there that Khrushchev's "famous temper" flared.

When Nixon demonstrated some new American color television sets, Khrushchev launched into an attack on a resolution, "Captive Nations", that was passed by Congress just days before. The resolution condemned the Soviet control of the "captive" peoples of Eastern Europe and asked all Americans to "pray for their deliverance".

Khrushchev then mocked the U.S. technology on display, proclaiming that the "Soviet Union would have the same sort of gadgets and appliances within a few years."

Nixon, who had a reputation of never shying away from a debate, provoked Khrushchev by stating that he should "not be afraid of ideas", and "after all, you don't know everything." Khrushchev snapped back at Nixon, "You don't know anything about communism—except fear of it."

Now imagine yourself being one of the reporters and photographers following them as they continued their argument in the middle of the model kitchen. With voices rising and fingers pointing, the two men went at each other hard. Nixon suggested that Khrushchev's constant threats of using nuclear missiles could lead to war, and Khrushchev, perhaps seeing this as a threat, warned of "very bad consequences."

Have you ever got into a heated or passionate discussion, and are so focused that you tuned out everything, including the fact that your voice has gone up 6 decibels since the start of the conversation? Well, perhaps Khrushchev and Nixon got the feeling that the exchange had gone too far. Khrushchev pulled back and stated that he simply wanted "peace with all other nations, especially America." Nixon, rather awkwardly, stated that he had not "been a very good host."

Both leaders displayed a **Forceful** style of **Leadership**, which is not a bad thing...given the circumstances. Khrushchev obviously wanted to show his displeasure about the "Congressional Resolution" thing, but it looks as if the modern "kitchen of America" showed him just how far behind they were when compared to the United States. Remember his comment that the Soviet Union will have the "same sort of gadgets and appliances within a few years..."? That told you all you needed to know.

More broadly, it showed Khrushchev that he would much rather have someone else in the White House that perhaps wouldn't be as confrontational, and yes, strong, as Nixon appeared to be. That is why they wanted Stevenson to run. It would have at least given them a President, in Stevenson, that advocated for the banning of hydrogen bomb testing.

Putin's Hate For Hillary Clinton

The Mueller Report established that the, "...Russian government perceived it would benefit from a Trump presidency and worked to secure that outcome..." The first attempt by Russia's military intelligence service to compromise Clinton's personal office came within about five hours of Trump publicly asking Russia to find "30,000 emails" that had been deleted from the former secretary of state's personal email server.

Mueller brought charges against 13 Russian nationals accusing them of waging "information warfare" against the U.S. through an *"elaborate network of social media accounts and astroturfed groups, using techniques that included posting racially divisive messages on Facebook and staging political rallies on U.S. soil."*

Why target Hillary Clinton? Clinton, like Nixon, took a hard line regarding Russian aggression. Clinton also did the one thing that triggered the attack on Clinton, at that was challenging Putin's legitimacy.

In December of 2011, there were mass protests against President Putin. Putin made it clear that Secretary of State Hillary Clinton was behind the protests. Clinton stated that the elections were "dishonest and unfair", which prompted Putin to public remark that Clinton gave "a signal" to demonstrators working "with the support of the U.S. State Department" to undermine his power. Putin went on to declare, "We need to safeguard ourselves from this interference in our internal affairs." And there you have the motivation behind Russia's attack on Hillary Clinton and the 2016 presidential elections.

Both Clinton and Putin, like Nixon and Khrushchev, displayed a **Forceful Leadership** style. However, Putin, a former intelligence officer, displayed **Strategic** and **Operational Leadership** in targeting Clinton, by arguably, utilizing "useful idiots", such as Julian Assange and WikiLeaks, along with members of the Trump campaign.

Useful Idiot is a derogatory political term, utilized for "a person perceived as a propagandist for a cause, the goals of which he or she does not fully comprehend, and who is used cynically by the leaders of the cause."

WikiLeaks, for example, under the guidance of founder Julian Assange, has published more than 10 million documents on war, spying and corruption. The group received infamy for its leaking of footage of an American airstrike that killed Iraqi journalists. It later dumped more than 250,000 classified U.S. diplomatic cables, and hundreds of secret files regarding Guantanamo Bay military prison.

The group held itself out as an "equal opportunity, no-holds-barred anti-secrecy" outfit. However, after WikiLeaks amplified Russia's 2016 election interference, there were suspicions that they had acted as Russia's co-conspirator. According to the U.S. intelligence community, WikiLeaks played a key role in Russia's 2016 election interference.

In other words, WikiLeaks targeted Clinton, not Trump. Their credibility as being an "equal opportunity" outfit is gone. The timing of the WikiLeaks releases coincided with bad publicity concerning Trump, like the **Access Hollywood** video, in order to basically drown out any negative press aimed at Trump.

Trump and some of his campaign members behavior during his campaign has convinced many people that Trump himself was not simply a "useful idiot", but a "clueless pawn manipulated to Russia's ends." Trumps greed had no bounds as he lied repeatedly and openly to the American people about how he hoped Vladimir Putin would deliver hundreds of millions of dollars, namely "Trump Tower Moscow, to his personal family business.

At the same time his campaign manager and senior campaign staff were carrying out three separate, unrelated criminal conspiracies even as they have claimed to be working on his behalf. The term "unpatriotic" comes to mind when the Trump campaign fielded numerous inquiries and offers of help from Russia, without ever once contacting law enforcement or US intelligence. Trump swore to "uphold the Constitution" at his inauguration, but despite the Mueller Report concluding that he or his campaign did nothing that they could charge criminally with regards to collusion/conspiracy, his first instinct was to obstruct the investigation.

***

Scorched Earth Leader Stupidity

The most appropriate definition for the term **Scorched Earth** is *"…directed toward victory or supremacy at all costs."*

In December of 2018, President Trump stated, "I'll be the one to shut it down. I will take the mantle. And I will shut it down for border security." Well, Trump did shut the government down, and it turned out about as well as previous shutdowns have, as total failures. It is estimated that the shutdown cost the economy $11 billion due to lost output from federal workers, delayed government spending and reduced demand.

According to an analysis from the nonpartisan Congressional Budget Office or CBO, the total delayed federal spending due to the impasse stood at about $18 billion.

But what about the average worker? How did this Trump "manufactured" ClusterPhuck affect them? Well, an estimated 800,000 federal employees and hundreds of thousands more federal contractors and support staff, missed paychecks. Those of you out there that live paycheck to paycheck understand

232

that this is one burden you cannot handle for more than a couple of weeks…at best.

The lapse in funding for U.S. Department of Agriculture (USDA) programs, meant that millions of families faced uncertainty in meeting their nutritional needs. The Supplemental Nutrition Assistance Program (SNAP), the nation's largest anti-hunger program, reaches roughly 40 million low-income individuals, with about two-thirds of whom are children, seniors, or people with disabilities.

The U.S. Department of Housing and Urban Development (HUD), also closed, which provides federal rental assistance and safe housing for more than 5 million low-income households, with nearly 90 percent of which contain seniors, families with children, or people with disabilities, were put at considerable risk of major funding lapses.

Smaller, lower-income, and more geographically isolated communities, many of which already had to contend with inadequate resources and services, were also hurt by the massive federal employee furloughs and funding suspensions. Additionally, a number of domestic violence programs were preparing to curtail services as funding dried up. How bad could a shutdown for one day impact services?

On a single day, over 70,000 survivors access lifesaving services from domestic violence programs across the country. A significant portion of domestic violence and sexual assault programs heavily rely on federal funds.

When the 35-day government shutdown ended, Trump received no money for a border wall, but $1.375 billion for 55 miles of border fencing, which is well shy of the $5.7 billion and 200 miles in wall funding he demanded that led to the shutdown.

As a matter of fact, the amount of funding is actually shy of the original deal Republicans and Democrats reached a few months earlier that Trump rejected. Again, Donald J. Trump is NOT the great dealmaker he convinced voters that he was.

Trumps core supporters and former aides were said to be "furious" and "melting down." One White House official stated, "President Nancy Pelosi, she runs the country now…we went from indefinite shutdown, to down payment, to cave — all within a span of 24 hours"

By the way, Trump's approval ratings dropped to record lows, his much-touted economy lost steam because of the shutdown and conservative immigration activists "rolled their eyes" over his fixation with building a wall.

Opinion writer Bill Press may have summed it up best by stating:

"When it was all over, what was the Trump Shutdown all about? A giant, cruel, unnecessary, ill-considered, and ineffective nothing burger. Nobody got helped, and everybody involved got hurt."

Not My First Shutdown Rodeo

Trumps shutdown was not the first one to result in a negative backlash. In 1995 and 1996, United States federal government shutdown for a total of 27 days. It was the result of conflicts between Democratic President Bill Clinton and the Republican Congress over funding for Medicare, education, the environment, and public health, not over a border wall that both Republicans and Democrats didn't want.

Like Trumps shutdown, government workers were furloughed and non-essential services were suspended. A 1995 ABC news poll had Republicans receiving the brunt of the blame with 46% of respondents compared to the 27% that blamed President Clinton. The shutdown impacted all sectors of the economy. Health and welfare services for military veterans were curtailed; the Centers for Disease Control and Prevention stopped disease surveillance; new clinical research patients were not accepted at the National Institutes of Health; and toxic waste clean-up work at 609 sites was halted.

Other impacts included: the closure of 368 National Park sites resulted in the loss of some seven million visitors; 200,000 applications for passports and 20,000 to 30,000 applications for visas by foreigners went unprocessed each day; U.S. tourism and airline industries incurred millions of dollars in losses; more than 20% of federal contracts, representing $3.7 billion in spending, were affected adversely.

One would think that avoiding another ClusterPhuck of this magnitude would be a good thing for politicians. However, the same stupidity was repeated again in 2013.

The Re-Phuck of 2013

This shutdown occurred after Congress failed to enact legislation appropriating funds for fiscal year 2014. Again, approximately 800,000 federal employees were indefinitely furloughed, and another 1.3 million were required to report to work without known payment dates.

According to an initial analysis from the rating agency Standard & Poor, the 16-day government shutdown was a $24 billion hit for the U.S. economy. Of course there was plenty of blame and finger pointing about who caused the shutdown. One poll, conducted by NBC News/Wall Street Journal survey, showed by a 22-point margin, more people blamed the GOP in Congress rather than the White

House for the shutdown. And only 24% approved of the job congressional Republicans were doing, which was 12 points lower than the approval rating for their Democratic counterparts.

The shutdown strategy, which was an effort to defund President Obama's health care expansion, was not embraced by all Republicans. Senator John McCain called the effort "a fool's errand." However, a CNN/ORC International poll shows that no one came out ahead.

The House Republicans voted 70 times to repeal or otherwise undermine the Affordable Care Act (Obamacare), and it has failed to pass every single time. That being said, regardless of what side of the political fence you sit on, would you keep or fire a group of executive leaders that lost your company $24 billion in 16 days?

Desperately Seeking Relevance

Government officials, in a desperate effort to get a "win" for their city, party, or constituents, throw all logic out of the window and proceed down a path to destruction. Take the Fast Ferry Fiasco in Rochester, New York.

The Rochester, New York area has been on several "best places to raise a family" lists during the past several years. Although the weather can be brutal in the winter it is still a great place to live. It has minor league baseball, hockey, basketball and even soccer.

Unfortunately, there is no major sports franchise (i.e., NFL, NBA, and NHL) that could potentially create hundreds of new jobs and millions in tax revenue. Add that to the fact that the city had lost 41 percent of its manufacturing jobs over the last several years and you can see why city officials were scrambling to find something that could help fill its $30 million budget deficit.

A high speed ferry service between Rochester and Toronto, Canada, had been discussed for years by local politicians and business leaders. The city of Rochester built a ferry terminal in speculation of such a service being implemented. A group of investors formed a U.S. company named Canadian American Transportation Systems (CATS) which then entered into a contract to build ***Spirit of Ontario*** *I* in 2003.

CATS promoted the new service, aiming to begin operations in early May 2004. Unfortunately, the startup didn't go as planned. Problems included:

- Hull repairs in New York City in April, pushing back the delivery date.

- Unexpected engine repairs in May and early June, 2004 after arriving on Lake Ontario.
- A dispute over payment for Canadian customs services in Toronto. The federal government of Canada passed a law in the 1990s whereby any privately owned new border crossing point (such as a ferry service or private toll bridge) must pay for its customs services at no cost to Canadian taxpayers.
- Ongoing construction of a ferry terminal in Toronto. A temporary terminal building and parking lot was rushed to completion for the spring startup of operations while construction of a permanent passenger terminal began.

When the operations began, the ferry performed its daily service between Rochester and Toronto, which was one or two round trips daily, and by most accounts, went very well. The ridership was initially relatively low due to the uncertainties associated with the start-up, poor marketing, and a lack of highway signage in Toronto.

Unfortunately, CATS suspended the ferry service indefinitely on September 7, 2004, citing financial problems related to the delays in getting the vessel operational and missing its first service launch date in May. However, there were reportedly more contributing factors to the financial difficulties, such as:

- Slow progress by the Toronto Port Authority in constructing a permanent ferry terminal in Toronto. The delays in getting even temporary terminal facilities built in Toronto during the spring of 2004 was another reason for forcing a delay in starting the service until mid-June.

- CATS felt that it was being charged excessive Canadian customs and immigration costs. U.S. port of entry services were being provided in Rochester at no cost to CATS whereas Canadian port of entry services had to be completely covered by the company, resulting in a hidden charge on each ticket price.

- CATS blamed U.S. customs for not giving approval for the Spirit of Ontario I to carry freight trucks and express cargo, claiming that this altered the original business plan.

- CATS endured criticism from both nations for a decision to have Spirit of Ontario I registered under the flag of Bahamas, a flag of convenience nation, allegedly for taxation purposes. CATS was able to do this since the vessel was operating in an international service; additionally, since the

Spirit of Ontario I was a foreign-built vessel, CATS would have had to pay significant penalties were it to register the vessel in either Canada or the U.S. (particularly the U.S., given the domestic-content restrictions of the Jones Act).

- Because of the foreign flag registry for Spirit of Ontario I, CATS was required to pay for pilotage services on every crossing (approx. $6000 per crossing). Canadian and U.S. registered vessels exempt from requiring the services of pilots while navigating on the Great Lakes.

In 2004 CATS declared bankruptcy and the Spirit of Ontario I was seized by the United States Marshals Service for resale to pay creditors. Although CATS was rightfully blamed for its share of mistakes, but were they the root cause of this ClusterPhuck?

Doomed Prior To the Start

The State of New York, Office of the State Comptroller, performed an audit of the ferry fiasco, and released its final report in July, 2006. It is apparent that the project had no chance of success. The report stated:

"…there were a variety of clear warnings that were known, or should have been known, by City officials during the approval process of the ferry project. These red flags should have alerted City officials to the extremely risky nature of this venture, and should have caused them to increase their review of various aspects of the Project's plan before proceeding and committing public funds to the Project."

The report went on to state:

"City officials obtained two reviews of CATS' plan from outside consultants that contained several critical and cautionary statements, yet we found no evidence that City officials heeded the warnings in the evaluations. Those evaluations highlighted a number of concerns with the plan, including the mismatch between vessel capacity and demand, serious deficiencies in the financial model included in the proposal, concerns about CATS' existing equity, low profit margins, **the lack of enthusiasm by the Toronto market, and unrealized time savings in comparison with other transportation options. Despite these strong cautions, City officials did not perform any further analysis of the subsequent plans."**

A Root Cause Analysis, like the one performed on the ferry project, is usually a reactive method of identifying event(s) causes, revealing problems and solving them. Analysis is done after an event has occurred, which defeats the purpose of recognizing and responding to Red Flag situations.

However, insights in RCA may make it useful as a **preemptive method**, so that ClusterPhucks, like this, can be dealt with prior to a catastrophic event.

Pseudo Leader Proactivity

Perhaps some of you have heard of a company called **Kodak**. They were once the most recognized brand name in photography, and not that long ago emerged from bankruptcy. Because cameras are now digital, and most photos taken today are snapped with smartphones, film is pretty much obsolete. Consumer choice directed the evolution from film to digital by shunning the use of film. Digital is simple and instant.

Interestingly, digital technology was developed in an Eastman Kodak applied research lab. From its discovery, the first digital camera appeared in 1974. Although Kodak developed the technology and invested billions of dollars in digital imaging, its business model failed to recognize and transition the foundation of the company into a brand that could claim the creation of a whole new category of imaging.

Leadership failed to understand how consumers ultimately wanted their memories to be captured, shared and stored, and they would not adapt to the changes happening around them until it was too late. Since 2003, Kodak has eliminated 47,000 employees and restructure the company. Businesses that have been sold or spun off during the bankruptcy includes their digital and photographic film patents, photo kiosks, online photo-sharing, consumer printing and document scanners. They could have saved themselves a big headache if they, the leadership at Kodak, would have been more proactive in their product development efforts.

Several of you likely have heard of the company *Blockbuster*, a provider of home movie and video game rental services, originally through video rental shops. At one time they employed about 60,000 people and had more than 9,000 stores. Poor strategic planning and mismanagement pretty much doomed the company. **Netflix**, a provider of on-demand Internet streaming media, as of January, 2019, had 139 million subscribers and has become the ideal model for streaming movies, television shows, documentaries, etc..

Blockbuster, like Kodak, had a significant jump on the competition, but its leadership failed to capitalize on their market dominance, by investing in new technology, when they had the money, dedicated customers, opportunity. Remember, it only takes a handful of individuals to Phuck things up. How? *Groupthink*.

Groupthink & Leadership Stupidity

Groupthink is a *"type of thought within a deeply cohesive in-group whose members try to minimize conflict and reach consensus without critically testing, analyzing, and evaluating ideas. It is a second potential negative consequence of group cohesion."*

It was Irving Janis that studied a number of American Foreign policy "disasters", such as the failure to anticipate the Japanese attack on Pearl Harbor (1941); the Bay of Pigs fiasco (1961), when the US administration sought to overthrow Cuban Government of Fidel Castro; and the Vietnam War (1964–67) by President Lyndon Johnson.

Janis concluded that in each of these cases, the decisions were made largely due to the "cohesive nature of the committees" which made them. That cohesiveness prevented contradictory views from being expressed and subsequently evaluated.

Have you ever been in a room full of people and tried to get them to decide on what food to order? Someone will invariably say something like, "why don't we get pizza?" If 15 of the 20 people say "that sounds good", it immediately puts pressure on the rest of the group to conform. It's even worse when there is one dominant voice, perhaps the CEO, who says "let's get pizza", resulting in the conformity effect.

When people are in this mode of thinking, and are deeply involved in a cohesive in-group, their zeal to reach for unanimity can override their motivation to realistically appraise alternative courses of action.

Individual creativity, uniqueness, and independent thinking are lost in the pursuit of group cohesiveness. Meaning, there may have been a good restaurant across the street that had a variety of dishes, including a vegan menu, that would have satisfied each person there, but no one dared to even bring the place up. Why is that?

There are several motives for not interjecting. We all have a desire to avoid being seen as being foolish, as well as being embarrassed or angering other members of the group. However, the problem with groupthink may cause groups to make hasty, irrational decisions, where individual doubts are set aside, for fear of upsetting the group's balance, which, as you have seen throughout this book, leads to ClusterPhucks.

On the other end of the spectrum is **Polythink**, which is characterized by a ***"plurality of opinions and divergent policy prescriptions, resulting in a disjointed decision-making process or even decision paralysis.***

The 2003 invasion that started the Iraq War, has been used as an example of Polythink. Experts contend that there was no policy process leading to that decision, as well as any discussions or debates inside government about whether launching the war was a good idea.

Richard Armitage, then deputy secretary of state, would later comment that ***"There was never any policy process....There never was one from the start. Bush didn't want one, for whatever reason."***

Well then…no policy process for what is now the longest war in US history??? I am willing to bet that some of you are surprised by this…while some of you may have experienced it before. It actually happens more than you think, and is even more disturbing when money dictates who will run some of the most important, high-level positions in the country.

Rich People Leadership Placement & Institutional Stupidity

Trump, the wealthiest man ever elected to the White House, has appointed the wealthiest Cabinet in history. How could it arguably be the most unqualified and inept as well? Well, you've already read about Carson, Pruitt, and a few more. In February 7, 2017, Betsy DeVos was confirmed by the Senate by a 51–50 margin, with Vice President Mike Pence breaking the tie in favor of her nomination.

This was the first time in U.S. history that a Cabinet nominee's confirmation was decided by the Vice President's tiebreaking vote. When Education Secretary Betsy DeVos was interviewed on "60 Minutes" in 2018, it showed just how incompetent, unqualified, and ill prepared she was to lead the Department of Education.

Under questioning by Lesley Stahl, DeVos didn't know the answers to some questions and statistics like the "reading and math scores of American schoolchildren have increased and not decreased over the past several decades, or that for many students the charter school expansion in her native Michigan has led to poorer educational outcomes."

DeVos's qualifications for the job of education secretary were based simply on the fact that she came from a family that is worth $5.4 billion, and donated to the Trump campaign. No, she wasn't a self-made billionaire like, let's say, Oprah was; DeVos inherited her fortune. Trump made it very clear that a person's wealth was a key qualification for his Cabinet picks, stating, "I want people that made a fortune because now they're negotiating with you." I guess those that inherit their fortune are great negotiators too?

The Pew Research Center ranked the US in 38th place out of 71 countries when it comes to math scores and 24th place when it comes to science. The biggest surprise of the study is just how far the US has fallen in the rankings. In 1990, the US ranked sixth in the world for its levels of education and health, 21 spots ahead of where it is now.

So, what happened in the last 30 years? One explanation is the decline in US spending on elementary and high school education, which fell by 3% from 2010 to 2014, even as its student population grew by 1%. This is a sharp contrast to developed nations like the UK or Portugal, where education spending rose by more than 25% from 2008 to 2014. Turkey is the nation with the most dramatic improvement in education, increasing its spending by 76%.

A **Transformational Leader** is a leader that *"works with teams to identify needed change, creating a vision to guide the change through inspiration, and executing the change in tandem with committed members of a group."* Most parents and educators realize that a transformation in our educational system is needed. How has DeVos' leadership led to change? Has she addressed the shortfalls in investing more into education like others countries have?

Has she spoken to researchers that have published studies showing how parent involvement with their children, no matter their background, are more likely to have higher grades and test scores, attend school regularly, have better social skills, show improved behavior, and adapt well to school? Has she put forth a plan that could improve the "parent-school" connection? No.

DeVos instead proposed cutting millions of dollars in special education funding, including $17.6 million intended for Special Olympics, as well as $20 million in cuts to programs for blind and deaf students. There was universal outrage, of course, especially since DeVos had found money to support her own pet projects.

Trump, in typical fashion, threw DeVos under the bus and stated, "I heard about it this morning. I have overridden my people. We're funding the Special Olympics." Trump, as you have seen time and time again, can only take so much negative public pressure before giving in.

DeVos, after Trumps announcement, stated, "I am pleased and grateful the President and I see eye to eye on this issue and that he has decided to fund our

Special Olympics grant." And…"This is funding I have fought for behind the scenes over the last several years." WTF?

In a prior heated exchange with Sen. Dick Durbin, D-Ill., DeVos said she "wasn't personally involved" in pushing for elimination of the funding, but she nevertheless defended it as her agency seeks to cut $7 billion for the 2020 budget. Not "personally involved" in the decision to cut billions of dollars? Yes, call it **Bad Leadership** to sum up her stint thus far…but don't forget that 51 so-called leaders, confirmed her appointment. Blame them for their leadership stupidity as well.

As Nicole Jones Young, an assistant professor of organizational behavior at Franklin & Marshall College stated, " ***Well-connected individuals who feel like they were born to rule the world or, at the very least, leapfrog over Kevin in accounting, make appearances in politics, academia, and cubicles and boardrooms across the land.***"

Go back to the chapter on how "money" equals "social inclusion", and it will show just how easy it is for people, like DeVos, to get into a position that she is grossly unqualified for.

The Intertwined Institution of Family & Religion

Studies indicate, in one way or another, that the family is the place where the *"intergenerational transmission of religious beliefs and practices takes place and thus is of crucial importance for the persistence and continuation of religious traditions and communities."*

Parental Influence:

1. Most people stick to the denomination they were brought up in or they abandon faith altogether. This indicates that religious preferences, beliefs and affiliation are determined early in life as a result of parental influences.

2. Although parents are not the only factor in this respect, they are by far the most influential. Religious transmission may also occur in religious schools or in the religious community, but compared to the influence of parents, the influence of the religious school or the religious community is weak.

3. Religion is but one aspect of the value complexes parents may transmit to their children. Parents may for instance also transmit life style characteristics, sex roles, political party affiliation and general political orientation. However, parental influence is most noticeable in the field of religion.

For the record, I was raised as a Roman Catholic from grades K thru 12. I was an "altar boy", which is "a boy who acts as a priest's assistant during a service, especially in the Roman Catholic Church", for at least 4 or 5 years. I also served a wedding and even the Midnight Mass, which scared me to death.

The worst thing that ever happened to me was being slapped in the 5th grade, by the principal, Sister Mary Editha, for acting up in class. I recall running down the hall crying to my oldest sister, Patricia, who was in the 8th grade. She told me, "Don't worry, we will get her back!" I am still waiting for that day…but it made me feel good that my older sister had my back.

For the longest time I thought the schools that my brothers and sisters attended were free of charge. It didn't dawn on me that the reason why my dad was working two jobs, was to support a family of ten. Apparently, they had made a pledge prior to getting married, that we, the children, would always come first, and they would make whatever sacrifice they had to in order to keep that promise…which they did.

So you can imagine my utter shock and horror when cases of child sexual abuse by Catholic priests, nuns and members of religious orders, came to light. A Church-commissioned report in 2004 said more than 4,000 US Roman Catholic priests had faced sexual abuse allegations in the last 50 years, in cases involving more than 10,000 children, mostly boys, between the ages of 11 and 14…while church officials covered it up.

Members of the Church's hierarchy have actually argued that the media coverage was "excessive and disproportionate", and that such abuse also took place in other religions and institutions. I grew up in the Roman Catholic church believing that church leaders were of impeccable integrity. Instead, the church was led in a way that can only be described as a display of **Callas** and **Evil Leadership**.

Yes, there is a feeling of betrayal, but my belief in God has not changed. I won't go into it, but there are just too many experiences that have occurred in my life that has made my belief even stronger today than it was when I was an altar boy. But I refuse to justify, or make excuses for the individuals that raped children, and for those that covered it up. They should ALL be in prison.

During a summit in February 2019, Pope Francis promised an end to cover-ups, saying that "all abusers would be brought to justice."

The followers of the Catholic Church are not the only ones still feeling a sense of betrayal...like some Evangelicals do, when it comes to defending President Trump.

Liberty University is regarded as the largest evangelical Christian university in the world. The private institution was founded by the late televangelist Jerry Falwell in 1971, and claimed to be committed to developing "Christ-centered men and women with the values, knowledge, and skills essential to impact the world."

Liberty's current President, Jerry Falwell, Jr., who assumed leadership after his father died in 2007, publicly endorsed Donald Trump's Presidential bid, stating that he would "lead our country to greatness again." Since the election, Mr. Falwell, utilizing both **Spiritual** and **Charismatic Leadership**, has been an unapologetic supporter of Trump, even defending him when Trump failed to condemn the white supremacist rally and deadly car attack in Charlottesville, Virginia, which could be deemed as a show of **Callas Leadership**, and totally against the teachings that millions have become accustomed to.

As a result, for many alumni, these incidences have become an affront to their faith and to their association with the university. In the days after Charlottesville, a private Facebook group was created called "Return your diploma to LU," urging alumni to mail their diplomas back to Liberty with letters explaining their decision.

Hundreds of former students returned their diplomas. Some went into great detail as to why they were distancing themselves from the university. Laura Honnol, a 2013 graduate, also returned her diploma along with this convicting statement:

"In light of the incidents in Charlottesville, in Liberty's backyard, I can no longer grieve privately when you repeatedly and uncritically escalate your commitment to adulation of our sitting President as a hero to the faith and to the cause of Christ – a man who refuses to unequivocally call out the blatant, blasphemous sin of racism in the face of clear and incontrovertible evidence of white supremacist, Neo-Nazi incitement. There is no moral equivalency to be made between the KKK and counter-protestors. Racism is an outright denial of the image of God in His creation and should be repudiated swiftly, decisively, and thoroughly – full stop."

Emily Gibbs left the university after completing her undergraduate and graduate programs, and after working there as a full-time staff member for three and a half years. She stated:

"As Christ followers, our first priorities must be to love God (Matthew 22:37) and to fulfill the Great Commission by making disciples of all nations (Matthew 28:19–20). As a Christian university representing the name of Jesus Christ, Liberty University's priorities must be the same. It has become evident through the words and actions of Mr. Jerry Falwell, Dr. Ronald Hawkins, and the leadership of Liberty University as a whole that the priorities of the university are political power and earthly wealth. For this, I call Liberty University and its leadership to repent and return to the gospel... We must take Jesus' words seriously. Therefore, we cannot celebrate 'ending' our enemies, we cannot shy away from calling evil by its name, we cannot place our hope in political leaders, and we cannot spit in the face of those who call us to repentance."

An April, 2019 Pew Research poll found that 69 percent of white evangelicals approve of how Donald Trump is handling his job as President of the United States. This number is slightly lower than previous polls, some of which had white evangelical support for Trump as high as 78 percent.

Trump is a far from the sort of leader white evangelicals say they admire. His personal life is not nearly aligned with Christian teachings on fidelity, honesty, humility and charity. According to some, evangelicals have put their morals on hold and put their trust in political saviors, like Trump, to "advance God's work" in the nation and around the globe.

Their political playbook requires evangelicals to elect an attentive President who, in turn, will appoint socially conservative federal judges, as Trump did. Now that the judges are in place, evangelicals believe that they are better positioned to win the battles over these key issues.

The Christian right remains focused on the Supreme Court, which many evangelicals see as the chief impediment to their agenda on issues ranging from school prayer to LGBTQ rights to abortion. Many white evangelical churchgoers now see the fight to overturn **Roe v. Wade** as equivalent to their call to share the Gospel with unbelievers.

There are of course "never-trump" evangelicals that lack the household names. One of them, Doug Pagitt, stated:

"These conservative leaders are willing, at all costs, to make a moral trade – anti- abortion laws and court decisions in exchange for basic human dignity...This impulse for self-preservation allows them to champion an administration that runs afoul of America's commitment to be a place of protection, that violates the call of the parable of the Good Samaritan, in

which Jesus calls his followers to let go of our religious agendas to care for the harmed stranger."

This strange mix of "biblical Christianity and conservative talking points empowers an incompetent and immoral President." Some believe it will likely have disastrous consequences for the future mission of born-again Christianity in the United States, as the message of the Gospel becomes little more than a political agenda that turns off those who otherwise might be longing for spiritual solace.

Praying for Time

These are the days of the open hand
They will not be the last
Look around now
These are the days of the beggars and the choosers

This is the year of the hungry man
Whose place is in the past
Hand in hand with ignorance
And legitimate excuses

The rich declare themselves poor
And most of us are not sure
If we have too much
But we'll take our chances
'Cause God's stopped keeping score

I guess somewhere along the way
He must have let us all out to play
Turned his back and all God's children
Crept out the back door

And it's hard to love, there's so much to hate
Hanging on to hope
When there is no hope to speak of
And the wounded skies above say it's much, much too late
Well, maybe we should all be praying for time

These are the days of the empty hand
Oh, you hold on to what you can
And charity is a coat you wear twice a year

This is the year of the guilty man
Your television takes a stand
And you find that what was over there is over here
So you scream from behind your door
Say, "What's mine is mine and not yours"
I may have too much but I'll take my chances
'Cause God's stopped keeping score

And you cling to the things they sold you
Did you cover your eyes when they told you
That he can't come back
'Cause he has no children to come back for

It's hard to love, there's so much to hate
Hanging on to hope when there is no hope to speak of
And the wounded skies above say it's much too late
So maybe we should all be praying for time

Songwriter: George Michael

Chapter 7

Wanted: Red Flag Action Leaders

As you may recall in an earlier chapter, a "**Red Flag**" is basically a "**warning of danger or a problem.**" Unfortunately, red flags are ignored or fall through the cracks at an alarming rate, which often leads to devastating consequences. At the center of red flag leadership is **Proactivity**.

Why Proactive Leadership?

Being proactive simplifies leadership and increases your chances for positive results. Although **Proactive Leaders** expect some situations to be beyond their control, they are secure in their problem-solving capabilities and in the capabilities in their team. Take the terrorist attacks that occurred in the United States on the 11th of September, in 2001.

In 2002, FBI Special Agent Coleen Rowley alleged that the agency failed to act on information provided by agents from the Minneapolis, Minnesota FBI Field Office concerning Zacarias Moussaoui. Moussaoui had been suspected of being involved in preparations for a suicide-hijacking several years earlier. Rowley testified in front of the Senate and for the 9/11 Commission about the FBI's internal organization and mishandling of information related to the September 11,

2001 attacks.

There is no doubt that this was a Red Flag situation. It is debatable as to whether or not Rowley's information, if acted upon, would have stopped some of the attacks. However, it did force a major reorganization that helped to create a better flow of intelligence, which is a **reactive** approach to a catastrophe.

Reactive Leaders are individuals that *"fail to stop and think about the bigger problem when faced with an issue."* They generally act on impulse hoping that the problem will just go away and not return. Proactive leaders, on the other hand, are focused on the long term benefit to the company or organization. They bring in key staff members and other experts in order to tackle the issue from all angles. They also understand that temporary fixes are just that, temporary.

A **Proactive Leadership** approach could have possibly rescued the Republican Party from Donald J. Trump, or at the very least given the public a clearer picture of his financial dealings and motivations if it weren't for a series of **Passive Leadership** actions.

Rules Committee Leadership

The Rules Committee has the power to review and amend all of the rules of the Republican Party, pending ratification by the full convention. If it wanted to, it could vote to force **all candidates** to release their tax returns. However, the 112 member committee did not enact the change.

If the rules committee had enacted the change, Trump would have likely refused to release his tax returns, and, as he often threatened, run as an Independent Candidate.

It would have also given Trump a way to bow out of the race without losing face. He could then spend the rest of his life claiming how much better he would have done than Clinton, Cruz or whatever candidate became President. Instead, he is under several investigations that could result in impeachment or the dismantling of the Trump organization.

Red Flag Issues & Warnings

Red Flag warnings can come from individuals, committees, or organizations involved in business, media, politics, academia, entertainment, or even in the world of sports. As was pointed out earlier, there were many, many people, and even groups of Republicans, that warned the American voting public that Trump was not qualified to occupy the highest office in the land.

There are several examples of Red Flag warnings that you may have forgotten. Do you remember the former owner of the Los Angeles Clippers basketball team, Donald Sterling? Back in 1983, prospective Clippers coaching candidate Rollie Massimino, says that Sterling used the N-word in an impromptu interview at the Los Angeles International Airport.

So there was Donald Sterling, looking at coach Massimino, and allegedly stated: "I wanna know why you think you can coach these niggers."

In February 2003, the Housing Rights Center of Los Angeles (HRC), filed a housing discrimination case against Sterling on behalf of 18 tenants. The lawsuit featured several racist statements allegedly made by Sterling to employees, such as that "black people smell and attract vermin" and "Hispanics just smoke and hang around the building". Sterling allegedly only wanted to rent to Korean tenants because, "they will pay the rent and live in whatever conditions I give them".

Sterling agreed to pay an undisclosed amount in a lawsuit that alleged Sterling tried to force non-Koreans out of apartments in Koreatown. In 2009, Sterling paid a then-record $2.73 million Justice Department penalty for rental housing discrimination.

In 2014, he was fined $2.5 million for his racist comments, was forced to sell the team, and was banned for life by NBA Commissioner Adam Silver. What took so long to oust Sterling? He did have a history of racist behavior.

So what prompted the commissioner to act so swiftly and decisively? The Clippers' were in the playoffs with one of what is now one of the most dominant and popular basketball teams in history, the Golden State Warriors. The players had planned to walk out if Silver's punishment had not been severe. As superstar Stephen Curry stated:

"It would have been our only chance to make a statement in front of the biggest audience that we weren't going to accept anything but the maximum punishment." And ***"We would deal with the consequences later, but we were not going to play."***

Imagine, just before the tipoff of a nationally televised basketball game, each player walked off the court. What would you think if you were the commissioner? What could you possibly do? What if you were a sponsor…paying perhaps millions of dollars in advertising during the playoffs?

Yes, Adam Silver did make the decision to come down hard on Sterling, in an excellent display of **Crisis Leadership**, but it was the players, with their united threat to boycott games, that pushed Silver to move so quickly.

Pee Wee Reece & Jackie Robinson

There have been several examples of Red Flag leadership displays over the years, both by individuals and corporations, that took a stand to show the world where they stood, despite the backlash. Professional baseball player and Hall of Famer, Jackie Robinson, who became the first African American to play in Major League Baseball in the modern era, broke the baseball color line when the Brooklyn Dodgers started him at first base on April 15, 1947.

Cincinnati fans were spewing racist rhetoric as Robinson took the field. In a show of support, Pee Wee Reese, a white teammate, temporarily left his position at shortstop and traveled over to Robinson at first base and put his arm around Robinson. His act silenced the crowd. This is what Red Flag leadership looks like. Its stepping in and taking a stand for what you know is right. Keep in mind that Reese was a very popular player and an All-Star, which carries a lot of weight.

At the dedication of Jackie Robinsons statue, his widow, Rachel Robinson, stated:

> *"It's a historic symbol of a wonderful legacy of friendship, of teamwork, of courage -- of a lot of things we hope we will be able to pass on to young people. And we hope they will be motivated by it, be inspired by it and think about what it would be like to stand up, dare to challenge the status quo and find a friend there who will come over and support you."*

There were of course other athletes, owners, and others that stood up to racism, and the United States participation in wars. Boxer Muhammad Ali, refused the military draft citing his religious beliefs and opposition to the Vietnam War. He was arrested, found guilty of **draft** evasion, and stripped of his boxing titles.

However, on the 28th of June, 1971, The Supreme Court held that the conviction was invalid and must be reversed. Ali was of course branded a draft dodger. But, what you must keep in mind that the very rich were keeping their sons out of the war, by sending them to college or using their political clout, to give them some type of deferment, that ensured that they would never see the front lines (see Donald Trump's 5 deferments).

The other thing you have to understand, is that not only was the Vietnam War unpopular, the man behind it, Former Defense Secretary Robert McNamara, would eventually state:

"We of the Kennedy and Johnson administrations who participated in the decisions on Vietnam acted according to what we thought were the principles and traditions of this nation…we made our decisions in light of those values. Yet we were wrong, terribly wrong."

McNamara will not go down in history as a Red Flag leader…especially when you consider the war took the lives of over 58,000 American troops, for what you later called a "mistake".

There are also other Red Flags in history that perhaps few people know about. Take former Secretary of the Interior Stewart Udall, who worked for both John F. Kennedy and Lyndon B. Johnson in the 1960s. He became involved in the civil rights movement through his intervention with a Washington Redskins football franchise that refused to integrate.

The Redskins owner, George Marshall, staunchly refused to sign black football players. Despite the pleading of the press and fans, it wasn't until Udall stepped in and threatened retribution on the federal level did the Washington Redskins become the last team in the NFL to integrate. How did he convince the owner? The Redskins' new stadium was on federal land, and Udall informed Marshall that if he continued to refuse to be integrated, the team would not be allowed to use it.

Now, make no mistake, it helps that a Red Flag leader, is in a position to implement big changes, as Udall did. However, a simple act, like Pee Wee Reese did with Jackie Robinson, can go a long way.

Don Barksdale was the first African American to represent the US on the Olympic basketball team in 1948. During an exhibition game, when his teammates passed a water bottle down the bench, each man took a sip. After Barksdale took his sip of water, he passed it to a teammate, "Shorty" Carpenter of Arkansas, who drank from the bottle without hesitation.

The water bottle drew the attention of all those in attendance, many of whom felt that Carpenter could have made a statement by refusing to drink, especially true given that whites and blacks in the South rarely, if ever, drank from the same glass or from the same water fountain at the time. Another Red Flag leader moment that could have just reinforced the divide between the races…but instead strengthened it.

You may find it difficult to believe, but before 1967, no woman had officially run in the Boston Marathon, and the Boston Athletic Association (BAA) did not willingly issue "bib numbers" to women who applied. The Amateur Athletic

Association (AAU) did not formally accept women as participants in distance running, fearing that "their bodies could not handle the rigors" of long distances.

Roberta Gibb ran the Boston Marathon in three consecutive years (1966–1968), but did so without a bib number, having to hide in the bushes at the race's starting line to avoid being spotted. However, in 1967 Kathrine Switzer became the first woman to officially run the Boston Marathon.

Switzer was issued a bib number because she did not clearly identify herself as a female entrant and signed her entry form as "K.V. Switzer." She started the race unnoticed, but around the fourth mile, the press bus caught sight of her. This caused a "stir", and race officials, once were notified, tried to rip off her bib number and physically remove her from the race before another runner, and then boyfriend, "Big" Tom Miller, a nationally ranked hammer thrower and former All-American football player, pushed an official aside. Switzer officially finished the race and helped clear the path for female participation in distance running events.

As Switzer would later state many years later, "I wasn't trying to prove anything. I loved running and knew that for others who had run Boston, it was a great experience." What if her boyfriend, Tom Miller, wasn't there to push the official away and she was removed from the track? How many years would it have taken to finally allow women to "officially" run the race?

Al Davis was the brash owner of the Oakland Raiders football team. Even though his football legacy was somewhat tarnished during the last decade of his life due to zero appearances in the playoffs since their Super Bowl win in 2002, he was still a man that fought for civil rights.

In 1963, Davis refused to play a preseason game in Mobile, Alabama as a protest against the state's laws on segregation. He also implemented a policy stating that the Raiders would not play in cities in which players would have to stay in different hotels due to race. There are just certain issues that Red Flag leaders won't back away from. However, your position of power or influence, and whether or not you have positive or negative enablers on your side.

Positive and Negative Enablers

Let's say that Al Davis, owner of the football team, decided that he would, after all send his team to Alabama, despite his concerns about his black players being treated like second class citizens, or worse. Let's say he decided to go because the National Football League (NFL) threatened to impose a hefty fine, and perhaps take a draft pick or two from the team.

Although the NFL didn't take such action, they proved to be a positive enabler, in that they didn't try to prevent Davis from making the decision to avoid Alabama. **Positive Enablers** are a must in this 24/7 ClusterPhucktual world we live in. How far down the marathon track do you think Switzer would have made it if her boyfriend would have stayed on the sidelines?

There are a number of Red Flag leaders out there that provide warnings to their bosses or to the authorities, but they often fail to act in many cases. Bernie Madoff's $65 billion fraud could have been severely curtailed if the Securities & Exchange Commission (SEC) would have taken Harry Markopolos's waving of the Red Flag in front of the faces, for years by the way, seriously.

Because of the SEC's failure to act, they became **Negative Enablers** to Madoff, resulting in tens of thousands of retirees being financially ruined. His fraud forced charities to close, made hospitals cut back on the care they could give, and wiped out people who'd never even heard of Bernie Madoff.

Take Lehman Brothers, who had the largest bankruptcy in the history of the United States, valued at $691 billion. Emails showed that the investment banks Risk Managers were sounding Red Flag alarms all over the place, but to no avail. How would you like to be known as one of the three or four individuals (CEO, CFO, COO, etc.), that totally ClusterPhucked a 169 year old company? As you have seen, some leaders fail to take advice from the very people they pay to provide them with actionable business intelligence. Some leaders, however, take action very quickly to ensure that the issue does not escalate.

On the 6th of June, 2019, National Basketball Association (NBA) commissioner Adam Silver, banned Golden State Warriors investor Mark Stevens for one season and has fined him $500,000 after the team executive shoved Toronto Raptors guard Kyle Lowry, and repeatedly cursed at him during Game 3 of the NBA Finals at Oracle Arena. His decision came less than 24 hours after the incident. His **Forceful**, yet inclusive style of leadership, reinforces to owners, players, and fans, that certain types of behaviors won't be tolerated.

Silver has gained a reputation as a "progressive, forward-thinking leader", and the NBA has become by far the "most politically outspoken" of the major U.S. sports leagues. At a sports-business event in 2018, Silver encouraged attendees to "not stick to sports" and stated, ***"I think there's never been a time when sports has been more impactful on society then it is today."***

Think about this…the NBA actually has a leader that fully understands that players are actually more than just a collection of individuals dribbling a basketball for the purpose of entertaining the fans and making money. There are also a few coaches who are paying close attention to more than their next opponent. They too see bad behavior by politicians, and social issues that can't be ignored, and they speak out…sometimes forcefully.

One of the most inspiring **Leader-Positive Enabler** interactions occurred within a company called **Salesforce**. The San Francisco-based cloud computing company that sells customer relationship management tools, has more than once held the top spot on the "Companies That Care" list.

Now, it was chief personnel officer Cindy Robbins, who first raised the issue with CEO Marc Benioff, of a pay gap between men and women. Benioff told 60 Minutes that he was "stunned" that the pay gap was *"through the whole company, every department, every division, every geography."*

Not only did Benioff fix the problem by dedicating $3 million immediately to correct the discrepancy, he added another $3 million in 2017 to correct compensation differences by gender, race, and ethnicity across the company. He also created a new rule that would make it more likely that women would be promoted and seen as leaders.

Servant Leadership is a leadership philosophy in which the main *"goal of the leader is to serve"* and places the *"needs of the employees first"* and helps people develop and perform as highly as possible. Benioff seems to be a prime example of a leader that truly values his workforce.

What if all CEO's and politicians responded the way Benioff did when presented with issues like immigration or climate change…do you think there would be a greater chance of the problems being solved, instead of being put on the back burner? Benioff simply made the issue a **Non-Negotiable** item.

Non-Negotiables

I first heard the words, **"My Non-Negotiables"**, from one of my former Army Commanding Generals. The Business Dictionary definition is as follows:

1. Not able to be bought, sold, exchanged, or transferred.

2. Not open to negotiation. "The terms of this contract are absolutely non-negotiable; the company will not budge."

However, the General was not referring to any business related terms. He was basically letting us know that there were certain matters that were etched in stone, and there would be no movement on his part. For example, driving under the influence of alcohol or drug use was a non-negotiable, and meant that if you got caught, you could expect the harshest punishment allowed by the Uniform Code of Military Justice (UCMJ).

After all, driving under the influence was something you could control. If you were stupid enough to take the chance of hurting others or yourself, you deserved whatever punishment came your way.

Anyone who has spent more than a day in the military understood that the military is NOT joining YOU…YOU are joining THEM. There are rules, regulations, and policies that you either follow or you simply get pushed out. By most accounts the Republican Party was positioning themselves to be a more inclusive party, but Trump changed all of that with what many consider racist rhetoric.

Trumps resistance to inclusiveness, the "Access Hollywood" tape that showed him bragging about how he could grab women in their private areas, along with his refusal to release personal taxes, should have been non-negotiable items. These were glaring Red Flags. The problem was, there were no Red Flag action leaders in sight.

Keep in mind that a Red Flag leader, or leaders, must be in positions of influence in order to take action to prevent a ClusterPhuck. Think back to the space shuttle *Challenger* disaster. There were two engineers that attempted, unsuccessfully, to stop the launch. One engineer felt so strongly that the launch be cancelled that he refused to sign a document recommending the launch. His ***pseudo red flag*** supervisors, overruled him.

I bring this up because Reince Priebus, at the time, Chairman of the Republican National Committee, had two chances to save the party from Donald Trump. The first was to call Trumps bluff and encourage him to run as an Independent instead of appeasing him. As you may recall, Trump threatened many times that he would run as an Independent.

However, instead of taking a **Forceful Leadership** stance, Priebus demonstrated a somewhat **Passive Leadership** style by stating, "Donald Trump can make his own decision about whether to release his tax returns before the general election."

Priebus', who was under constant threat by Trump to run as an Independent if he was "not treated fairly", responded, "Those kinds of comments, I think, have consequences...and so when you make those kinds of comments and you want people to fall in line for you, it makes it more difficult." Huh? Could he have displayed a weaker leadership tone than that?

Yes, I fully understand that Priebus, in his political calculus thinking, felt that a split vote would have given Clinton an easier path to victory. However, the Republicans did expect Clinton to win after all, and they would have saved the party, and its reputation, if they would have employed a non-negotiable strategy.

Gene C. McKinney, was the first and to date the only African American to reach the rank of Sergeants Major of the Army (SMA). Those of you who have never served in the Army may not fully understand that there is only one person in that position at a time.

The holder of this rank and position is the most senior enlisted member of the Army, unless an Army Sergeants Major is serving as the senior enlisted advisor to the Chairman of the Joint Chiefs of Staff

In 1998, he was court-martialed on a variety of charges including sexual harassment and obstruction of justice. He was convicted of the obstruction of justice charge and demoted to the rank of master sergeant.

That sent a very strong signal to every enlisted soldier in the Army. After all, McKinney held the top enlisted position in the entire Army, and was busted and humiliated. What chance would I have of skating on a charge? How about ZERO. My point is that Priebus, and others, that had the power to take action, failed. They should have stood up to him and demanded his tax or run as an Independent.

If you haven't noticed by now, Trump is more bluster and threats than taking coherent, measured, leadership actions. He did not have the money to run as an Independent, and would have saved face by tweeting about how he was not being treated fairly, and how the "deep state" was out to get him. He would have bowed out, like when he failed to buy the Buffalo Bills football team, and continued on with the network venture he was planning. AND, the party would have survived.

Republican Influencer Exodus

We all have our breaking point which either causes us to quit our jobs, leave a spouse, or even a political party. My dad once told me a story about growing up in Mississippi. As a young boy he picked cotton on a plantation. The plantation owners son, a young boy as well, harassed him to the point that my dad threw a rock and hit him in the mouth.

Later that evening, the boy came to the door with a couple of his friends. My grandmother opened the door and said they were there to "whip" my dad. My grandmother told them to go home, and they left. Now, I was in my mid-thirties at the time, and understood the potential ramifications of my dad's act against, of all people, the plantation owners son.

I looked at my dad and said, "Dad, you could have been killed!" I knew fully about the history of hangings, dragging's, and house burnings in Mississippi during that period of time. In my mind, there were only two scenarios that could have occurred, which are:

1. The plantation owners son didn't tell his dad about the incident and decided to take care of it himself, but couldn't get past my grandmother, and decided to drop it.

2. The plantation owners son did tell his dad, and perhaps told his son he shouldn't have been harassing my dad in the first place and deserved what he got.

I'm not sure what happened, but he never harassed my dad again. My dad was strong, silent, and worked for the government at the Rock Island Arsenal for almost 40 years, with an "exceptional" record of achievements. He came from a family of 16, and although he had some flexibility about him, there was a code of conduct that would not be compromised.

The exodus from the GOP includes conservative columnist, George Will, and former congressman and "Morning Joe" host Joe Scarborough. Lifetime Republican and Washington Post columnist Max Boot, campaign adviser Steve Schmidt, and Peter Wehner, who served former Presidents Ronald Reagan, George H.W. Bush and George W. Bush, have also left the party.

Wehner, may have perhaps summed it up perfectly for what most Republicans felt when they decided to leave the party, stating:

"I saw in the Republican Party a commitment to human freedom, Democratic capitalism, and a traditional social order; to upward mobility through self-reliance; to the dignity of work; to the cultivation of character and respect for the Constitution; and to a foreign policy that placed a high priority on human rights, a strong national defense, and American leadership. Republicans argued for limited government, economic growth, and free trade. The party respected the role of religion in public life and envisioned America as a welcoming society to immigrants and the unborn. It was hardly a perfect party. Like all political institutions, it fell short of its ideals; it was also led by some deeply flawed individuals. Yet in the main, it stood for principles that I believe promote human flourishing... The party

257

of Reagan has been fundamentally transformed...It's now Donald Trump's party, through and through."

Speaking of being fed up. There are also several reporters and expert contributors that have left Fox News due to the "direction" of the network.

Retired United States Army lieutenant colonel and longtime Fox News analyst Ralph Peters, severed ties with the network, which he accused of "wittingly harming our system of government for profit." Peters went on to state:

"Four decades ago, I took an oath as a newly commissioned officer. I swore to 'support and defend the Constitution,' and that oath did not expire when I took off my uniform...Today, I feel that Fox News is assaulting our constitutional order and the rule of law, while fostering corrosive and unjustified paranoia among viewers."

Peters had gotten fed up with the situation, and took action. Dr. Jeffrey A. Kottler, in his research, suggested that life-changing alterations take place in daily life, when you are going about your usual routines. For example, several years ago I would flip on the television to "Fox and Friends", while I was getting ready for work. I enjoyed the lighthearted banter, and it became part of my normal routine.

I can't give you the exact day or year, but the tone started changing, and then there were some blatant lies that totally turned me away from the channel permanently.

Dr. Kottler went on to state, concerning his research, that *"the vast majority of cases occurred after recovering from a challenging or even traumatic event—the death of a loved one, a major failure or disappointment, a crisis or catastrophe, a relationship or job ending, a threatening illness, or something similar.*

ClusterPhucktual events do get people to make changes...some even create national movements in order to address the issues, such as:

The **Me Too Movement,** is a movement *"against sexual harassment and sexual assault."* The movement began to spread virally in October 2017 as a hashtag on social media in an attempt to demonstrate the widespread prevalence of sexual assault and harassment, especially in the workplace.

Tarana Burke, an American social activist and community organizer, began using the phrase "Me Too", and the phrase was later popularized by American actress Alyssa Milano, who encouraged victims of sexual harassment to tweet about it, which prompted a number of high-profile posts and responses from American celebrities Gwyneth Paltrow, Ashley Judd, Jennifer Lawrence, and Uma Thurman, among others, soon followed.

Black Lives Matter (BLM), is an international activist movement, originating in the African-American community, that campaigns *"against violence and systemic racism towards black people."* BLM regularly holds protests speaking out against police killings of black people, and broader issues such as racial profiling, police brutality, and racial inequality in the United States criminal justice system.

The movement began in 2013 using the hashtag **"#BlackLivesMatter"** on social media after the acquittal of George Zimmerman in the shooting death of African-American teen Trayvon Martin in February 2012. Black Lives Matter became nationally recognized for its street demonstrations following the 2014 deaths of two African Americans.

Time's Up is a movement *"against sexual harassment"* and was founded on January 1, 2018, by Hollywood celebrities, in response to the Weinstein effect and #MeToo. As of December 2018, it had raised more than $22 million for its legal defense fund, and gathered nearly 800 volunteer lawyers.

There are of course other movements that are focused on the "Right to Life" or "Abortion Rights", as well as many dealing with the environmental security, immigration, prison reform, gun reform, "LGBTQQ" (lesbian, gay, bisexual, transgender, questioning, queer), and many more.

Whether you agree with a movements goals and objectives or not, you should at least understand what the movement is about, and have your *for* or *against* arguments ready for debate.

Decision Making & Judgement

One of my former Army company commanders told a story about the then, brigade commander. As is customary, eight or so company commanders met the brigade commander for dinner. As the story goes, he didn't smoke or drink, and was an avid runner. Most telling, he told the company commanders something like, "I will have a hard time giving you a one block under judgement, if you are a smoker."

A "one block" check mark in the Army Officer's Evaluation Rating (OER) system, meant that you were among the "most qualified" officers in the Army, and very competitive for promotion to the next highest rank. You may not think that a "two block" was that bad, but in a sea of "one blocks", a two block could be very detrimental to your career.

Field-grade officers are majors, lieutenant colonels and colonels. As they move up in grade, the competition for advancement increases, and promotion percentages decrease substantially. For example, roughly 80 percent of captains reach the rank of major. However, in 2016, nearly one-fifth of the 4,000 Regular Army captains screened by retention boards were put on notice that they would be involuntarily separated or retired later that year.

According to the Centers for Disease Control & Prevention (CDC), cigarette smoking is responsible for more than 7 million deaths worldwide per year, including 480,000 deaths per year in the United States, including more than 41,000 deaths resulting from secondhand smoke exposure. This is about one in five deaths annually, or 1,300 deaths every day.

Some of you may be thinking that the brigade commander uttered a subtle threat to the company commanders...but was it really a threat, or a Red Flag warning? The evidence was clearly on the brigade commanders side with regards to the hazards of smoking.

As you've seen throughout this book, people make decisions to initiate a ClusterPhuck even though they know from the start, what the result will be. So, is it logical for the highest ranking officer in the brigade to award bad behavior that will, in all likelihood, cause you, the smoker, some serious health concerns down the road that could hinder your units readiness?

Would this be any different than a general manager of a chemical plant telling his employees that he or she, would have a difficult time giving a shift supervisor high marks under judgement if they allowed employees to enter a highly toxic area without ALL of their hazardous chemical protection gear on?

There is no doubt that smoking not only kills the individual smoking, but innocent people, including children, that happen to be near them. Now, let's say, for arguments sake, that a couple of the company commanders spotted the brigade commander behind the restaurant smoking. Does that change the nature of his threat? Not really. Although they may view him as a hypocrite, he still has the power to "two block" them on their evaluations.

I recall one of my former First Sergeants telling a deputy brigade commander, that his sideburns were too long. The commander looked at him and said, "you wanna fucking cut them for me?" Needless to say, although he was the senior First Sergeant in the 9 state area, it was comments such as this, that resulted in him not getting promoted to the next rank. What I did like about him was that although he yelled and screamed a lot at you, he rarely put it down on paper. Ask any soldier which method they would prefer. I guarantee you that 99.9 percent would rather take the yelling and screaming than a negative mark on your official evaluation report.

The Decision Making Process

President Trump talks about making a lot of his decisions using his "gut" instead of the experts around him that have years of experience and data to back them up. The Army has a regulation or policy for everything. During my first year in recruiting, I made the decision to bypass the process of looking up answers to questions myself, which, by the way, the Army had taught me how to do at the recruiting training course.

I would instead ask a recruiter who had been in the station longer for answers. Well, come to find out, they were giving me wrong answers, at least a quarter of the time. My impatience, and yes, laziness, could have gotten me into a lot of trouble. When I took over my first office and my recruiters asked me questions, I literally threw the regulation at them.

I told them to look for the answer, and if they couldn't find it, to come back in and we would find it together. They were frustrated and resistant at first, because they were always "in a hurry" and needed the answer right then, but quickly found out that this was one of my non-negotiable items.

It was widely known that President Obama was a reader. Meaning, that he actually read briefings and reports prior to making a decision. Some politicians even tried to use that as a criticism. Have you ever watched politicians, both Democrats and Republicans, criticize the contents of, let's say, the over 2,000 page federal budget proposal, within hours of its release?

I find it amazing when reporters ask, "have you read the budget proposal?" And their response is, "No, but I know what's in it." I won't go into how many levels of incompetence was displayed in that one response, but it is safe to say that leaders make better decisions when they adhere to the decision making process.

Bad Decisions can be traced back to the failure of clearly defining alternatives, the collection of useless information, and that the costs and benefits were not properly considered.

A leaders success hinders on the day-to-day decisions they make or approve.

261

Leaders can increase his or her decision-making effectiveness by:

1.   Viewing a problem from a variety of perspectives instead of sticking with the first option that comes to mind.

2.   Examining the problem yourself first to avoid being tied to outside suggestions.

3.   Seeking information from a variety of sources and people in order to widen the frame of reference.

4.   Considering how your objectives will be served by the status quo.

5.   Being careful when others recommend decisions, and examine the way they framed the problem and challenge them with different frames.

Leaders must consider a wide variety of sources and influences in order to increase the probability of making a successful decision. Parents make decisions for their children and for the overall welfare of the family. Yes, parents are leaders, and like executives, they typically seek outside sources for information concerning day care, schools, vacation locations, doctors, employment opportunities, etc. Why? So that they can reduce the risk of a ClusterPhuck occurring.

However, one could argue that the information that is provided to and executive, or parent, could be flawed or inaccurate, and can lead making ill-advised decisions, which, by the way, they will be held accountable. The secret to success is simple, just question the validity of the information that is presented, and it will substantially reduce the possibility of a failed decision.

Strategic Deception & Protecting Yourself

"...All warfare is the way (Tao) of deception. Therefore, when capable, feign incapacity; when active, inactivity. When near, make it appear that you are far away; when far away, that you are near. Offer the enemy a bait to lure him; feign disorder and strike him..."

Sun Tzu.

President Trump is the "Master of Deception." He is not the only one, of course, but no doubt has the largest megaphone in the world. Some may argue that he is the master of "strategic" deception, which is "aimed at misleading rivals from the true strategic intent of the firm or the environment."

Deceptive strategies may range from "perfectly legal competitive strategies" to "illegal practices of lying" to gain an advantage. If you are a National Football League fan, you may have witnessed some deception demonstrated by team executives, days or weeks leading up to the draft. It is not unusual for teams to give off the impression that they are not interested in a certain player, in order to give them a trade or draft advantage.

Trump, has no problem "lying" to obtain a political advantage, or using deception to shine a light away from a negative story about him. Watch closely when a negative story about him hits the airwaves. He will, usually within hours, make an outlandish statement or controversial policy announcement, or send a tweet with an obviously controversial video attached, claiming that it was all true.

In the early days of his administration, some of the media was reluctant to say that Trump lied. They often used the term "misleading statements" or say something like "the President is simply wrong" about his numbers. Gradually, more media outlets were calling them "lies", and fell into the trap of focusing on the lie instead of understanding that he was utilizing a deceptive strategy in order to move the media away from a negative story.

Victor Lipman, a Contributor for **Forbes**, wrote that there are 4 principles of Trump's deceptive, but "effective communication", which are:

1. **Say exactly what you want to without regard for the truth**. Meaning, Trump won't let the facts get in the way of a good story, like saying that he was "totally exonerated" by the Mueller Report.

2. **Distill it to a short, media-friendly sound bite**. He is great at planting, in the minds of his supporters, and others, a "core message", "take home message", or "key message", like "no obstruction", "crooked Hillary", "Lock her up", "build a wall", etc.

3. **Recognize the sound bite will be amplified exponentially by "friendly" media**. Trump utilizes a "razor-sharp" message like "DOJ report proving exoneration and no collusion or obstruction", and it gets "amplified exponentially" by "friendly" media, like Fox News.

4. **Never ever admit fault**. "Give credit, take responsibility" is the "old management" motto learned back in business school. Not learned by Trump, however.

In Trump's own book, **Crippled America: How to Make America Great Again**, he states: *"if you say outrageous things and fight back, they love you."*

The free publicity that results from deliberately provoking controversy is invaluable, especially for someone like Trump that is truly an expert on bringing attention on himself. During his campaign, it is estimated that Trump received, according to data from tracking firm ***mediaQuant***, $5.6 billion throughout the entirety of his campaign, which was more than Hillary Clinton, Bernie Sanders, Ted Cruz, Paul Ryan and Marco Rubio combined.

It's like that old saying about how anyone can become a millionaire…if they are willing to lie, cheat, steal, or sell their soul. There are people out there, unfortunately, that have no conscience about stealing your money, regardless if you are elderly and on a fixed income.

I met an elderly woman at a local Mall a few months ago in the food court. She saw me wearing my Army hat and asked me a question. She was on ***Facebook*** and had "friended" a few of what she thought were military personnel. As I soon discovered, they were asking her for money, and she had been sending them money for quite some time, until she couldn't send anymore, and they were angry. I told her, after reading their messages, that they were NOT in the military, and that she was being scammed.

So here was this elderly woman, who admitted that the reason she was sending money is because she was lonely and loved companionship. She never realized that it was a scam. She thought that she was helping military people out.

You may be asking why Donald Trump is mentioned a lot in this book. Because, like I stated before, he is in the most powerful position in the world, and can literally ClusterPhuck millions of people before they even know it happened.

One of his biggest campaign promises to voters was that he would leave Medicaid, Social Security, and Medicare untouched. His exact statement during the campaign was, ***"I'm not going to cut Social Security like every other Republican and I'm not going to cut Medicare or Medicaid."***

Over the next 10 years, Trump's 2020 budget proposal aims to spend $1.5 trillion <u>less</u> on Medicaid, instead allocating $1.2 trillion in a block-grant program to states, $25 billion less on Social Security, and $845 billion less on Medicare. Yes, he, along with his enablers, are going to make your lives worse.

So how do you protect yourself in the future? First, P-L-E-A-S-E stop casting "protest" votes! I get it! You want to show your distain for the system or the fact that you didn't like either major candidate. Got it! What did it get you? It got you Donald J. Trump.

There were literally millions of voters that did not care for Mr. Trump or Mrs. Clinton when it came to the 2016 elections, and decided to use their protest vote power. A **Protest Vote**, according to the English Dictionary, is defined as *"...a vote against the party you usually support in order to show disapproval of something they are doing or planning to do."*

There were 137,125,484 cast during the 2016 Presidential elections. Although Mrs. Clinton received almost 3 million more popular votes than Trump, she lost the electoral vote count 304-227. If you are one of the many people, whether Conservative, Democrat, Independent, etc., that prior to the election, felt that Trump was unqualified to be President and had a strong distaste for Hillary Clinton and decided to cast a Protest Vote for Jill Stein, Gary Johnson, or Evan McMullin, or didn't bother to vote at all, you may have contributed to what is now considered by many to be a Cascading ClusterPhuck of an administration.

Have you ever worked a long night shift and had to drive 45 minutes or longer to get home...and you started sleeping at the wheel? I have...and it's a scary feeling. I rolled down the window, blasted music, and did whatever I needed to do to make it home safely.

Yes, we all are aware that Washington, D.C. is full of partisan hypocrites that are more interested in retaining their own personal power than solving the really tough problems. Somehow, we went to sleep at the wheel, and woke up with Donald J. Trump as President.

Trumps victory did however, get people off the couch...including a diverse group of candidates that dominated the 2018 midterm elections. Yes, millions of people fell for his act, and we are now feeling the ramifications of electing someone to the most powerful office in the world, who would be fired within a week if he was at a *Fortune 500* company.

So how do we protect ourselves from not just choosing the wrong presidential candidate, but also from those running for Congress and the Senate...or for that matter, from any scam or situation that may lead you into a ClusterPhuck?

Managing ClusterPhucktual Risk

If you want to avoid or reduce the chances of starting or being in the middle of a ClusterPhuck, the best and surest way is to barricade yourself in your home and stay away from people. Don't work or socialize with anyone, and you should be ok, right? Actually, there is a better way, and it starts with understanding and then applying the principles associated with **Risk Management**.

Risk always involves the possibility of some kind of loss. If there is no possibility of loss, there is no concern about risk because it cannot affect you. However, sometimes we fail to recognize the "2nd and 3rd order consequences" of taking action, or NOT taking action. Like staying home instead of casting a vote.

Ok, show of hands…how many of you know how your Congressman or Congresswoman, voted on issues like abortion rights, healthcare, immigration, etc.? Now, how many of you know where to look to find that information? Why is this important? Because we make plenty of false assumptions.

In 2008, then Senator Barack Obama, outscored his Republican rival, Vietnam veteran John McCain, in a report card issued by an influential, nonpartisan veterans' group, called *The Iraq and Afghanistan Veterans of America (IAVA's)*. The group gave McCain a "D" on his congressional report card. Obama received a "B" from the group.

Much of IAVA's scoring revolves around legislation to boost education benefits for Iraq and Afghanistan veterans, known as the *"Post 9/11 GI Bill: Fair Education Benefits for Veterans."* Because of campaigning, McCain missed six votes on the issues the group rated, out of which four were the votes regarding the GI Bill. IAVA has about 105,000 members and makes no political contributions or endorsements.

I had nothing but respect for Senator McCain as a person, and how he served his country. The results did however surprise me, as well as some veteran friends of mine. My point is simply that you have to look deeper for answers, instead of making assumptions.

Each year the U.S. Senate and House of Representatives take thousands of votes, some to pass bills, resolutions, nominations, and treaties, and others on procedural matters such as on cloture and other motions. Go to a website like "GovTrack", and it will tell you how your representative voted on ANY issue.

Some politicians will say publicly that they are for "preexisting conditions" as it relates to healthcare insurance. How did they actually vote? Some politicians are hoping that you don't dig too deeply. Don't let them play you for a sucker…do your research. There is NO middle ground when it comes to a politicians vote. Either you voted for something I was in favor of , or you didn't.

Not all news is "fake news" as President Trump likes to say when something negative is published about him or his administration. But how do you minimize the risk of knowing what's real and what's fake?

According to a survey conducted by the University of Missouri's **Reynolds Journalism Institute**, the most trusted news source in the U.S. is *the Economist* , which is weekly magazine published in the U.K. The second most reliable news source, according to respondents, is public television, with the Public Broadcasting Service (***PBS***), separately ranking sixth.

Reuters, ***BBC***, and National Public Radio (***NPR***), placed just ahead of PBS in 5th place. ***The Guardian*** was ranked number 7, and ***The Wall Street Journal***, the *Los Angeles Times* and the ***Dallas Morning News***, rounded out the list of the 10 most trusted brands.

Fox News has taken a considerable amount of heat for acting like a "state-owned" media outlet that protects Trump at all cost. The truth is, there are legitimate anchors like Bret Baier, Shepard Smith, and Chris Wallace, who hit both Democrats and Republicans, including Trump, hard.

Judge Andrew Napolitano, a legal commentator, who seems to be "disappearing" from Fox News altogether as he's grown more and more critical of the Trump administration.

However, they get drowned out by the likes of Laura Ingraham, Jeanine Pirro, Tucker Carlson, Sean Hannity and Lou Dobbs. Tucker Carlson saw his 2018 fourth quarter ad revenue total drop to $13.6 million, a 45% decline from the previous year. Why? For making "misogynistic, homophobic and racially insensitive remarks."

Laura Ingraham lost many of her sponsors in 2018 after joking on Twitter about Parkland high school shooting survivor David Hogg being rejected by several colleges.

Melissa Joskow of Media Matters, stated in May, 2019:

"Fox News in its current incarnation is operationally a propaganda network for Donald Trump, using any amounts of racism, sexism, and bigotry necessary to push his message, whatever the cost. Media Matters *has repeatedly documented the network's increasing and dangerous promotion of extremism, its embrace of white nationalism, and more. Sean Hannity, Laura Ingraham, Jeanine Pirro, Tucker Carlson, Lou*

Dobbs, and Fox & Friends *are the tip of the spear, but the entire network is culpable."*

Edward Luce, the U.S. national editor of the *Financial Times*, stated:

"The most effective thing Americans can do is boycott companies that advertise on Fox."

Max Boot, a right-wing columnist, called on companies to *"boycott Fox News until they pull back from the hate."*

You may be asking yourself why the executives at Fox News would keep such toxic and divisive personalities on air. The answer is simple…they are making hundreds of millions of dollars with this format, and they will continue to do so until it fails to become profitable.

So where does that leave you when you're trying to get to the truth? If you are a Fox News viewer, record what Hannity and the other say, and then go check with Bret Baier, Shepard Smith, and Chris Wallace to see what they have to say on the same subject. Then, check with the most "trusted brands" list, and see who is lying, and who is giving it to you straight.

***

Conducting research from credible sources, is how to reduce your risk of getting duped. A few months ago my neighbor was looking to buy a second car. They found a "soldier" online that was selling his car, because he was getting shipped overseas. He told my neighbor that the government would ship his car to them. That's when they called me.

I told them that the government will ship a military members car in certain circumstances, but NOT to the buyer of his or her vehicle. Now, the vehicle was about $3200. I said to my neighbor, "Do you really think that the government would spend $845, of taxpayer money, to ship a car that someone is selling?" By the way, they were going to supposedly buy the car from a "soldier" in North Carolina, and have it shipped to New York. WTF?

Anyway, all of this was being done online, and I told them what questions to ask, which caused the "seller" to become agitated, because typically scam artists have answers to the first 2 or 3 questions you are likely to ask, but after that, they start to struggle.

Within an hour, I found the Army regulation governing the transport of vehicles for military personnel…and sent it to my neighbor. That finally convinced him that it was a scam. How did I know it was an $845 cost to taxpayers if the deal was in fact real? I researched it.

Remember, the goal is to keep you out of a ClusterPhuck, like the scenario above. Former Green Beret Sergeants Major Karl Erickson, who has an extensive background in finding out if a person is lying or not, provides us with an easy to follow eight step road map.

1. "Do some fast research prior to the conversation and learn some truths about this person. Go to their social media pages and find some easy things you know they won't lie about: vacations, celebrations -- easy stuff like that. Then look for some other stuff that might make them uncomfortable to talk about."

2. Watch their body language as they answer easy questions that you know the truth about. 'Do anything fun this summer?' If they answer truthfully about a vacation and seem jittery, you now know that they're just nervous and the jitteriness doesn't mean they're lying. Watch where their eyes go, note if they clear their throat before they speak, do they lean back or forward?"

3. "Then move on to topics that you think they might lie about, that you know the answer to. This may be some information you read about their company online. If they lie, watch and listen for what changed in their tone or mannerisms."

4. "At this point, you should have a good baseline for their body language and speech patterns when they are telling the truth. Now you can get into the questions that you don't know the answer to. Using what you now know about their behavior, you'll have a better chance of ascertaining if they are lying or not."

5. "If you think someone is lying, ask them the same question in three different ways. You might think that it is to catch any differences in their response, but what I'm telling you to look for just the opposite: is there a scripted aspect to their response? Do they use the same careful phrasing over and over again? Politicians are amazing at this. It allows them to answer the question without revealing anything they don't want you to know. If it feels like a prepared and scripted response, that is a sign that they're either lying or not telling you the whole story."

6. "Take note of how quickly they answer a question. Did they immediately respond without giving much thought? Think about a teenager standing in front of his parents. If the parents ask him a question and the kid immediately launches into an answer without thinking, he is prepared.

7. "When possible, have another observer in the room. Have someone pretending to be an assistant sitting off to the side working on a laptop, or someone pretending to be an IT person. Your interview subject will quickly forget that they are in the room. That gives you another set of eyes paying attention strictly to this person's mannerisms, someone who can help you catch changes that you might have missed. While you're watching their eyes, you might not notice that they started tapping their foot on the ground."

8. "What this all allows is for you to make better decisions on partnerships. For the most part, you don't want to link up with liars, but you also don't want to pass on a great opportunity because the guy had shifty eyes and it turns out he was just nervous. This method can help prevent that from happening."

As a military recruiter, asking an applicant about their drug use was routine. However, I didn't ask the question the way the applicant expected me to ask it, which is "Have you ever used illegal drugs, including marijuana?" I asked them, "Ok, when was the last time you smoked marijuana?"

The ones that had used the drug recently would pause, look in the air, searching for the most recent time. However, the applicants that were not frequent users, would say something like, "I haven't smoked since the 10th grade."

The funniest response I ever had to the question concerning "the last time you smoked, when an applicant stated, "What time is it?".

ClusterPhuck Mitigation

To **mitigate** means to "make something less severe", and is perhaps the reason why mitigation planning is the most powerful action plan an individual, business or any organization can develop to stave off a potential ClusterPhuck. Mitigating a risk is therefore tied to prevention planning.

Take Captain Chesley Sullenberger, the pilot of US Airways Flight 1549, that crash-landed into New York's Hudson River a few years ago. When birds disabled both engines Captain Sullenberger stated:

"I think, in many ways, as it turned out, my entire life up to that moment had been a preparation to handle that particular moment."

Sullenberger, a former Air Force fighter pilot, spent nearly 30 years flying commercial aircraft, specializing in accident investigations. He also instructed flight crews on how to respond to emergencies in the air. Is it really so surprising that he was able to adapt to an emergency situation that would save the lives of all of his passengers?

Sure, there is an expectation that having several years of experience should reduce the chances of a ClusterPhuck. But didn't the ***Challenger*** bosses at NASA have years of experience? Didn't the top people at Lehman Brothers have years of experience?

The objective of risk management is to preserve the operating effectiveness of the organization. However, if you, as a leader, fail to adhere to the principles of risk management, you are destined to eventually, knowingly, by the way, cause a ClusterPhuck.

Eleven people died a few short years ago when British Petroleum's (BP), Deepwater Horizon rig exploded and caused the worst accidental oil spill in US history. The US Presidential Commission investigating the disaster reported that BP had been told weeks before the explosion that the cement slurry that would be used for the well, was unstable. In other words, this was an AVOIDABLE ClusterPhuck.

Some organizations have people in leadership positions that have little or no training solving problems, but must react to unexpected disruptions as best they can. **Project Trouble-Shooting**, which is used to characterize a deductive effort to discover the root-cause of a problem, is often used as an effective tool for contingency planning.

Contingency Planning is sometimes referred to as "Plan B", because it can be also "used as an alternative for action" if expected results fail to materialize. Think of it as having a backup plan in case your family reunion gets rained out.

Although it makes good business sense to bring in trouble-shooting experts to help solve unexpected disruptions, the most effective risk management programs invest in training programs for managers as well as its employees. The most successful organizations set high performance standards for safety, productivity, quality and service.

An effective training program uses role playing, case studies, discussions and other participative exercises that relate to the organizations current environment. There is nothing worse than sitting through a training session that has nothing to do with how your company or organization operates.

Training should include such topics as identifying risks, assessing risks, preventing risks, managing risks, financing risks, and evaluating risks. Without training, individuals will argue about what is really a risk, will have no means of determining a risk's likelihood, and will fail in developing effective risk management plans.

Think about some of the business and politically related ClusterPhucks you've read about thus far. Risk management only serves a real purpose if Leadership embraces it as a necessary part of an overall strategy. Although it is the risk manager that is charged with developing and implementing the risk management plan, it is the top level leaders that establishes the risk policy.

It is they who are accountable for deciding what level of risk the organization is willing to incur. However, some individuals that have no business being in leadership positions, do end up Phucking it up. Who ends up paying? Usually, it is the employees or the consumers.

One Last Thing

So, now that you have a good understand of both **Groupthink** and **Polythink**, I would like you to be aware of two more, newly created, "think" definitions, which are:

PhuckThink (plural), *"Characterized by a group of people that decide an issue devoid of any real logic, values or critical thinking. Decisions are based on what is politically feasible at that moment in time, and do not consider 2nd and 3rd order consequences of their initial decision. When the initial decision does result in a ClusterPhuck, the group members will typically point fingers, vehemently continue to justify their decision with false or misleading information, or simply hide until another controversy takes its place.*

*PhuckThinkers (*singular*), Are individuals that highlight certain areas of a policy, regulation, law, or study, and only use those particular passages to make their argument. They purposely create controversy as a way to bring the kind of national attention that will benefit them politically or monetarily. They often contradict themselves and are willing to put their values on hold when necessary.*

Now, as far as preparing and planning for the next ClusterPhuck…I want you to remember this quote when you believe that you have a detailed plan that is strong enough to withstand cuts in social security, layoffs because of tariffs, scams, and stupid bosses.

"Everyone has a plan 'till they get punched in the mouth."

Mike Tyson

REFERENCES

Abuse of Power Definition
http://www.businessdictionary.com/definition/abuse-of-power.html

Ackoff, R. (1981). On the use of models in corporate planning. Strategic Management Journal, *2*(4), 2–3.

Adams, S. (2005). Learning the lessons of Katrina for the unexpected tomorrow. Risk Management, *25*(12), 24.

Ainsley, J., Silva, D. ACLU: Trump admin's 2-year timetable for reuniting separated migrant families is too long. NBC News, 16 April, 2019.

Alexander, A. How to Fight ISIS Online, Why the Islamic State Is Winning on Social Media, Foreign Affairs, 7 April. 2017.

Anderegg, W. R. L. "Expert Credibility in Climate Change," Proceedings of the National Academy of Sciences Vol. 107 No. 27, 12107-12109 (21 June 2010); DOI: 10.1073/pnas.1003187107.

Anonymous. (2006). When the levee breaks . . . again. Risk Management, 53(5), 9.

Andone, D. The warning signs almost everyone missed about the Parkland shooter. CNN (26 February, 2018).

Appelbaum, S., & Goransson, L. (1997). Transformational and adaptive learning within the learning organization: A framework for research and application. The Learning Organization, 4(3), 23–36.

Argyris, C., & Schon, D. (1978). Organizational learning, Reading, MA: Addison-Wesley.

Army psychiatrist's reviews were sanitized, study finds The Associated Press (20 January, 2010).

Arond-Thomas, M. (2004). Resilient leadership for challenging times. Physician Executive, 30(4), 1–5.

Associated Press. (2006). Death toll from Katrina likely higher than 1300. Retrieved September 13, 2008, from http://www.editorandpublisher.com/eandp/news/article

display.jsp?vnu_content id=1003593.

Associated Press. The Latest: Police chief apologizes to men from Starbucks (19 April 2018).

Association of State Floodplain Managers. (2000). National program review. Madison, WI: Author.

Astor, M. Aaron Persky. Who Gave a 6-Month Sentence for Sexual Assault. New York Times (6 June 2018).

Atkinson, K., Sukin, G. Timeline: The major developments in the college admissions scandal. Axios, 15 May, 2019.

Augustine, N. (1995). Managing the crisis you tried to prevent. Harvard Business Review, 73(6), 16–21.

Austin, D. Our Long History of Presidential Lies. Gallop, 14 March, 2019.

Avolio, B. J., & Gibbons, T. C. (1988). Developing transformational leadership: A life span approach. Journal of Occupational & Organizational Psychology, 75(2), 195–216.

Axson, D., & Hackett, G. (2006, May). Identifying business risks. Financial Executive, 55–57.

Bai, M. How Gary Hart's Downfall Forever Changed American Politics (18 Sep, 2014).

Baker, P. (2005, September 9). Director replaced as head of relief effort. Washington Post, p. A2. Retrieved October 15, 2008, from www.csc.sagepub.com/cgi/reprint/72/169.pdf.

Baker, A., Brinke, L., & Porter, S. Will get fooled again: Emotionally intelligent people are easily duped by high-stakes deceivers The British Psychological Society (2012).

Barbara C. Crosby and John M. Bryson Public Integrative Leadership the Oxford Handbook of Leadership and Organizations (May 2014).

Baertlein, L. Simpson, I. Black men arrested at Starbucks hope scandal sparks change. Reuters (19 April 2018).

Baldor, L. Army misses 2018 recruiting goal. Associated Press, 21 September, 2018.

Barbaro, M. After Obama, Christie Wants a G.O.P. Hug. New York Times (19 November, 2012).

Barrett, T., Borak, D. Senate votes to roll back parts of Dodd-Frank banking law. CNN (14 March, 2018).

Barrett, D., Dawsey, J. Mueller's statement highlights key differences with Barr on investigation of President Trump. The Washington Post, 29 May, 2019.

Barr, J., Murphy, D. Nassar surrounded by adults who enabled his predatory behavior ESPN (16 Jan, 2018).

Bass, B. M. (1986). Implications of a new leadership paradigm. Binghamton: State University of New York, School of Management.

Bass, B. M. (1998). Transformational leadership: Industry, military, and educational impact. Mahwah, NJ: Erlbaum.

Bass, B., Avolio, B., Jung, D., & Berson, Y. (2003). Predicting unit performance by assessing transformational and transactional leadership. Journal of Applied Psychology, 88(2), 24–29.

Bass, B., Waldman, D., Avolio, B., & Bebb, M. (1987). Transformational leadership and falling dominoes effect. Group & Organization Studies, 12(1), 32.

Battaglio, S. Bill O'Reilly reportedly paid $32-million harassment settlement before signing new contract. Fox News, 21 Oct 2017.

Battaglio, S. Fox News courts advertisers after brands flee Tucker Carlson and Laura Ingraham. Los Angeles Times, 13 March, 2019.

BBC News. Catholic Church sex abuse scandals around the world. 14 September, 2010.

BBC News. Donald Trump admits President Obama was born in US. 16 September, 2016.

Becker, I.S. Devin Nunes, in secretly recorded tape, tells donors GOP majority is necessary to protect Trump: 'We're the only ones. The Washington Post, 9 August, 2018.

Belluz, J. How Andrew Wakefield's shoddy science fueled autism-vaccine fears that major studies keep debunking. Vox, 5 March, 2019.

Belvedere, M. Trump asks why US can't use nukes: MSNBC. CNBC, 3 August, 2016.

Bendix, A. The US was once a leader for healthcare and education — now it ranks 27th in the world. Business Insider, 27 September, 2018.

Benen, S. Poll: Americans see Republicans putting party over country. MSNBC, 25 September, 2018.

Bennis, W. G. (2001). Leading in unnerving times. MIT Sloan Management Review, 42(2), 29–30.

Bennis, W. G., & Nanus, B. (1985). Leaders: The strategies for taking charge. New York: Harper & Row.

Benen, S. Souter warned of a Trump-like candidate in prescient remarks. 21 October, 2016.

Berman, M. Trump tells police not to worry about injuring suspects during arrests. Washington Post. 28 July, 2017.

Bieler, D. NBA's Adam Silver reportedly approached by 'several NFL owners' to run their league. The Washington Post, 14 February, 2019.

Bilmes, l. & Stiglitz, J. The Three Trillion Dollar War: The True Cost of the Iraq Conflict: (2008).

Blackledge, Brett J. (November 6, 2009). "Who is Maj. Nidal Malik Hasan?". Fox News. Retrieved April 2, 2013.

Blackledge, Brett J. (November 6, 2009). "Details emerge about Fort Hood suspect's history". Associated Press. Retrieved November 6, 2009.

Blake, A. Trump's failed shutdown strategy produced an even worse deal than he started with. The Washington Post, 12 February, 2019.

Blanchard, K., Zigarmi, D., & Nelson, R. (1993). Situational leadership after 25 years: A retrospective. Journal of Leadership Studies, 1(1), 13–17.

Blitzer, W. (Executive Producer). (2005a, September 7). CNN: The Situation Room [Television broadcast]. Retrieved January 10, 2009, from www.cnn.com/2005/US/09/06/katrina.impact/.

Blitzer, W. (Executive Producer). (2005b, September 15). *CNN* [Television broadcast]. Retrieved January 15, 2009, from www.cnn.com/2005/POLITICS/09/15/bush.transcript/.

Bloomberg BusinessWeek, "Please Pray For Me", Hank Paulson on Facing the Abyss. Retrieved 22 December, 2013 from Capella University database.

Block, R. (2005, September 6). Power failure: Behind poor Katrina response. The Wall Street Journal, p. A1. Retrieved January 3, 2009, fromwww.online.wsj.com/public/article_print/0,,SB112597239277632387-xYOQX_P04Q8UyBopbzTsXfSE_oA_20051007,00.html.

Bobic, I. Mitt Romney Voted Against A Trump Judge Who Made Disparaging Remarks About Obama. Huffington Post, 14 May, 2019.

Boin, A., Hart, P., Stern, E., & Sundelius, B. (2005). The politics of crisis management: Public leadership under pressure. MA: Cambridge University Press.

Boren, C. NBA players were "ready to boycott" games if NBA hadn't acted against Donald Sterling. The Washington Post, 30 April, 2014.

Bostock, B. Vladimir Putin refused a salute from a North Korean general, which Trump controversially accepted. Business Insider, 30 April, 2019.
Briceno, S. (2007). Global early warning systems needed. UN Chronicle, 2, 73–75.

Bova, D. Use This Secret Military Trick to Tell if Someone Is Lying. Entrepreneur, 30 January, 2019.

Brooks, B. Former Brazilian tycoon Batista gets 30-year corruption sentence. Reuters Staff (3 July 2018).

Brown, A. (Executive Producer). (2005, September 5). CNN Reports: Katrina: State of emergency [Television broadcast]. Retrieved January 10, 2009, from www.thefreelibrary.com/CNN+reports%3B+Katrina--state+of+emergency.(Brief+article).

Brown, P., Westwood, S., Zeleny, J., Diamond, J., Acosta, J. Kelly says report he called Trump an idiot is 'total BS'. CNN (1 May 2018).

Bucher, R, Ex-NBA Player Cliff Robinson on North Korea Trip: 'What Are We Doing Here?' Bleacher Report, 28 January, 2014.

Budowsky, B. George Will, Joe Scarborough lead midterm exodus from GOP. The Hill, 6 July, 2018.

Bump, P. Trump's 'rogue killers' line is a reminder of his consistent bad faith in demanding proof. The Washington Post, 15 October, 2018.

Bump, P. Trump's 2018 midterm rebuke came from the most diverse electorate in history. The Washington Post, 23 April, 2019.

Bureau, US Census. "American Community Survey (ACS)". census.gov. Retrieved 2017-04-22.

Burnett, M. (Executive Producer). (2005, September 1). Good Morning America [Television broadcast]. Retrieved December 11, 2008, from www.medlibrary.org/medwiki/Timeline of_Hurricane_Katrina.

Bush R. & Wardell H.S. 1900, Stoke Industrial School, Nelson (Report of Royal Commission On, Together With Correspondence, Evidence and Appendix) Government Printer; Wellington, 8.

Caldeira, S., & Does, D. (2006). Effective leaders champion communication skills. Nation's Restaurant News, 40(13), 27.

Calamur, K. Nine Notorious Dictators, Nine Shout-Outs From Donald Trump. The President of the United States continues to heap praise on the world's most reviled rulers. 4 March, 2018.

Carmon, I. Donald Trump's Worst Offense? Mocking Disabled Reporter, Poll Finds. NBC News, 10 August, 2016.

Carns, A. (2005, September 1). Long before flood, New Orleans system was prime for leaks. Wall Street Journal, p. 21.

Carroll, J., & Hatakenaka, S. (2001). Driving organizational change in the midst of a crisis. MIT Sloan Management Review, 42(3), 71–76.

Cassidy, J. Trump University: It's Worse Than You Think. The New Yorker (2 June, 2016).

Catholic Church child sexual abuse scandal. BBC, 26 February, 2019.

Centers for Disease Control & Prevention https://www.cdc.gov/tobacco/data_statistics/fact_sheets/fast_facts/index.htm.

Chase, G., & Reveal, E. C. (1983). How to manage in the public sector. Reading, MA: Addison-Wesley.

Chang, S. These are the most — and the least — trusted news sources in the U.S. Market Watch 31 August, 2017.

Chicago Tribune wire reports, Timeline: Boeing 737 Max jetliner crashes and aftermath, 29 April, 2019.

Chmielewski, D., Patten, D. Netflix Fired Comms Chief Jonathan Friedland Over His Use Of The N-Word, Deadline, 22 June, 2018.

Chuchmach, M. Kreider, R. Ross, B. ABC News Tracks Missing iPad To Florida Home of TSA Officer. ABC News (27 Sept. 2012).

Cillizza, C. Melania Trump's 'I really don't care. Do U?' jacket was no mistake. CNN (22 June 2018).

Cillizza, C. Why Mitt Romney's "47 percent" comment was so bad CNN (4 March 2013).

Cillizza, C. The utter collapse of Donald Trump's 'best people' boast. CNN, 13 August, 2018.

City of New Orleans. (2004). *Comprehensive emergency management plan*. Retrieved December 10, 2008, from www.cityofno.com/pg-46-18-general-evacuation-guidelines.aspx.

Claycomb, W., Huth, C., Flynn, L., McIntire, D., Lewellen, T., (2013). Chronological Examination of Insider Threat Sabotage: Preliminary Observations, CERT Insider Threat Center.

Cleveland, W. PMI Industries employee accused of forging reports for SpaceX rocket parts appears in court. Rochester Democrat and Chronicle, 23 May, 2019.

CNBC, America's Top States for Business 2017, 11 July, 2017.

Cohen, M. (2005). A month after Katrina: Lessons from leadership. Knowledge@Wharton, 3. Retrieved October 8, 2008, from www.knowledge.wharton.upenn.edu/article.cfm.

Cohen, M., & Palmer, G. (2004, February). Project risk identification and management. AACE International Transactions, 3, 37.

Cohen, Z., Starr, B. US military leaders condemn racism after Charlottesville violence. CNN, 16 August, 2017.

Cohen, E. America's Long Goodbye The Real Crisis of the Trump Era. United States Foreign Policy, Essay January/February 2019 Issue.

Col, M. (2007, December). Managing disasters: The role of local government. Public Administration Review, 67, 114.

Collinson, S. From the GOP with love -- Trump gets gift from Russia panel. CNN (13 March, 2018).

Collinson, S. Trump is not the first US President to bemoan NATO spending ... but no one did it like this. CNN, 4 July, 2018.

Comfort, L. (2007, December). Crisis management in hindsight: Cognition, communication, coordination, and control. Public Administration Review, 67, 189.

Congleton, R. (2006). The story of Katrina: New Orleans and the political economy of catastrophe. Public Choice, 127(5), 18–32.

Cook, P. (2005). Formalized risk management: Vital tool for project and business success. Cost Engineering, 47(8), 12.

Cook, J. et al, "Consensus on consensus: a synthesis of consensus estimates on human-caused global warming," Environmental Research Letters Vol. 11 No. 4, (13 April 2016); DOI:10.1088/1748-9326/11/4/048002.

Cook, J. et al, "Quantifying the consensus on anthropogenic global warming in the scientific literature," Environmental Research Letters Vol. 8 No. 2, (15 May 2013); DOI:10.1088/1748-9326/8/2/024024.

Cook, J. FAA orders emergency inspections of 352 engines following deadly Southwest incident (20 April, 2018).

Cooper, D., & Schindler, P. (2006). Business research methods (9th ed.). New York: Hill Irwin.

Costa, R. Balz, D. Delreal, J. Trump campaign chairman Paul Manafort resigns Reuters (19 August 2016).

Couric, K. (Executive Producer). (2009, February 8). 60 minutes [Television broadcast]. New York: Central Broadcasting Service.

Cowan, D. (1991). The effect of decision-making styles and contextual experience on executives descriptions of organizational problem formulation. Journal of Management Studies, 28(15), 166–173.

Crane, Michael (2004). The Political Junkie. SP Books.

Crawford, J. Military sexual assaults increase sharply, Pentagon report finds. CNN, 2 May, 2019.

Crotty, W. Presidential Policymaking in Crisis Situations: 9/11 and Its Aftermath. The Policy Studies Journal (2003).

Crowley, Mark. How The Wrong People Get Promoted And How To Change It. (29 April, 2015).

Crowley, M. Why Putin hates Hillary. Politico, 25 July, 2016.

Cunningham, J. What Papa John Didn't Get About Being A CEO (12 July 2018).

Da Costa, P.N. EX-REAGAN ADVISOR: Trump's cabinet could go down as the worst in history (2 Oct 2017).

Daley shocked at federal snub of offers to help. (2005, September, 2). Chicago Tribune. Retrieved August 5, 2008, from www.chicagotribune.com/topic/katrina/archives .html.

Daley, J. How Adlai Stevenson Stopped Russian Interference in the 1960 Election. Smithsonian.com, 4 January, 2017.

Da Silva, C. More Than 80% Of Americans Want Undocumented Immigrants To Have The 'Chance To Become U.S. Citizens'. Newsweek, 2 April, 2019.

D'Antonio, M. Trump on '60 Minutes': A master class in deception and denial. CNN, 15 October, 2018.

De Alessi, L. (2001). Property rights: Private and political institutions. In W. F. Shughart II & L. Razzolini (Eds.), The Elgar companion to public choice (pp. 33–58). Northampton, MA: Elgar.

Delreal, J. Ben Carson, outsider with no government experience, confirmed to lead HUD. The Washington Post, 2 March, 2017.

Denning, S. Why The Trump Organization Now Risks Being Charged As A Criminal Enterprise. Forbes, 29 May, 2018.

Denzin, N., & Lincoln, Y. (1994). Handbook of qualitative research. Thousand Oaks, CA: Sage.

Deadline.com "Two More Complaints Against Matt Lauer: Report". Retrieved November 30, 2017.

Demirjian, K. Russia favored Trump in 2016, Senate panel says, breaking with House GOP. The Washington Post (16 May 2018).

Dennis Rodman Talks Recovery, The Fix, 3 January, 2018.

Derthick, M. (2007, December). Where federalism didn't fail. Public Administration Review, 67, 36.

Desta, Y. Paramount TV Chief Is Latest Exec to Be Fired Over Alleged Racist Remarks, Vanity Fair, 20 July, 2018.

Dier, A. 4th Person Connected to Madoff Commits Suicide. Newser Staff (28 Mar 2017).

Donnan, S., Singh, S. Trump's Trade War Is Hurting Farmers, But They Still Think He Can Win It. Bloomberg, 11 April, 2019.

Doran, P. T. & Zimmerman, M. K. "Examining the Scientific Consensus on Climate Change," Eos Transactions American Geophysical Union Vol. 90 Issue 3 (2009), 22; DOI: 10.1029/2009EO030002.

Douglas, M. Tampa Bay area police, firefighters, engineers buy fake college diplomas. News Channel 8, 20 November, 2017.

Downs, A. (1967). Inside bureaucracy. Boston: Little, Brown.

Drucker, P. (2004). What makes an effective leader? Harvard Business Review, 82(6), 58–63.

Duclos, R., Wan, E., Jiang, Y. (2013). Show Me the Honey! Effects of Social, Exclusion on Financial Risk-Taking Journal of Consumer Research.

Durkee, Alison. Judge in Brock Turner rape case speaks out for first time. MIC. (2 July, 2017).

Drum, K. How Many Threats Can the FBI Evaluate on a Daily Basis? Mother Jones (18 February, 2018).

Earl, J. Politicians caught padding their resumes, from fake diplomas to biographical discrepancies. Fox News, 22 September, 2018.

Economic Impact of Immigration. https://www.fb.org/issues/immigration-reform/agriculture-labor-reform/economic-impact-of-immigration

Edwards, F. (2007). Recovering from Katrina: A work in progress—2007. Public Manager, 36(4), 7.

Eisenhardt, K. (1989). Building theories for case study research, Academy of Management Review, 14(4), 532–550.

English Dictionary. Protest Vote definition.

EL-ERIAN, M. (2013, July-August). THE NEW NEW NORMAL, After Bernake, Foreign Policy.

Enten, H. How Trump Ranks In Popularity vs. Past Presidents Pollapalooza (19 Jan, 2018).

Essay January/February 2019 Issue United States Foreign Policy.

Eversley, M. Trump tells law enforcement: 'Don't be too nice' with suspects. USA Today, 28 July, 2017.

Farazmand, A. (2007, December). Learning from the Katrina crisis: A global and international perspective with implications for future crisis management. Public Administration Review, 67(1), 149–159.

Fahrenthold, D., Partlow, J. 7 questions about Trump's use of undocumented workers at his golf courses. The Washington Post, 24 May, 2019.

Farrow, R. From Aggressive Overtures to Sexual Assault: Harvey Weinstein's Accusers Tell Their Stories. (19 March 2018).

Fea, J. Why do white evangelicals still staunchly support Donald Trump? The Washington Post, 5 April, 2019.

Federal Emergency Management Agency. (2004). Hurricane Pam exercise concludes. Retrieved November 16, 2008, from www.fema.gov/news/release.fema.

Firefighters who start fires: a look at the phenomenon of 'firefighter arson'". Edmonton Journal. 2016-05-03. Retrieved 2016-06-27.

Fiedler, F. E. (1993). The leadership situation and the black box in contingency theories. In M. M. Chemers & R. Ayman (Eds.), Leadership, theory, and research. Perspectives and directions. New York: Wiley.

Fiedler, F. E., & Chemers, M. M. (1974). Leadership and effective management. Glenview, IL: Scott, Foresman.

Feng, Y. (2010). Toyota Crisis: Management Ignorance? School of Business and Engineering, Halmstad University, Sweden.

Finkelstein, S., & Jackson, E. (2006). Reducing risk. Leadership Excellence, 23(4), 9.

Fisk, M., Hanna, J. Boeing Crash Fight Will Set Price on Victims' Minutes of Terror. Bloomberg, 11 May, 2019.

Fottrell, Q. Incompetent, rich people are more likely to get ahead than smart people with no money. Market Watch, 1 June, 2019.

Fox, J. Jr. Impact of the Oklahoma City Bombing 20 Years Later Newseum (17 Apr, 2015).

Frank, R. Warren Buffett is the most charitable billionaire CNBC (21 Sept 2017).

Frankel, T. Fisher-Price invented a popular baby sleeper without medical safety tests and kept selling it, even as babies died. The Washington Post, 30 May, 2019.

Friedersdorf, C. & Lemarque, K. These 23 Republicans Passed on a Chance to Get Trump's Tax Returns. Reuters. 15 Feb, 2017.

Frieden, T. Fort Hood shooting report faults FBI handling of accused shooter's e-mails. CNN. 20 July, 2012..

Galoozis, C. It's the Economy, Stupid. Harvard Political Review. 17 Oct, 2012.

Gaouette, N., Miller, A. C., Mazzetti, M., McManus, D., Meyer, J., & Sack, K. (2005, September 11). Put to Katrina's test: After 9/11, a master plan for disasters was drawn. Los Angeles Times. Retrieved November 18, 2008. fromwww.emeraldinsight.com/Insight/ViewContentServlet?Filename=/publishe d/emeraldfulltextarticle/pdf/0420190406_ref.html

Garcia, H. (2006). Effective leadership response to crisis. Strategy & Leadership, 34(1), R.

Gardner, H. (1995). Leading minds: An anatomy of leadership. New York: Basic Books.

Garvin, D. (1993). Building a learning organization. Harvard Business Review, 71(4), 5.

Gearan, Anne (November 6, 2009). "Army: Shooting suspect was bound for Afghanistan". Boston Globe. Retrieved November 6, 2009.

Gee, T., Griffiths, B., Kenna, R. Trump's Transition of Untruths, Exaggerations and Flat-out Falsehoods.

Geller, E. Collusion aside, Mueller found abundant evidence of Russian election plot. Politico, 18 April, 2019.

"Gene McKinney sentenced to reduction in rank and reprimand". CNN, 16 March 1998.

Gerstein, J. Supreme Court overturns Bob McDonnell's corruption convictions (27 June 2016).

Gertz, M. How Fox News uses "news side" anchors like Shepard Smith to save its brand. Salon, 24 March, 2019.

Getha-Taylor, H. (2008, Summer). Learning indicators and collaborative capacity: Applying action learning principles to the U.S. Department of Homeland Security. Public Administration Quarterly, 125–126.

Gibson, K. Your MD may have a phony degree MoneyWatch (May 9, 2017).

Gill, M & Theakston, K. Rating 20th-Century British Prime Ministers.

Gilsinan, K., Trying to Kill the Iran Deal Could End Up Saving It. The Atlantic, 17 March, 2019.

Gillespie, E. Sorry About the President: 75% of CEOs Apologize for Trump to Their International Business Partners, Survey Finds. Fortune, 18 December, 2018.

Glick, S. & Koehl, S. Why the Rescue Failed. 14 September, 2012.

Glover, J., Friedman, H., & Jones, G. (2002). Adaptive leadership: When change is not enough (Part 1). Organization Development Journal, 20(2), 15.

Glover, J., Rainwater, K., Jones, G., & Friedman, H. (2002). Adaptive leadership (Part 2): Four principles for being adaptive. Organizational Development Journal, 20(4), 18–38.

Golway, T. "Nothing Innocent About Pay-to-Play". The New York Observer.26 August, 2001.

Goodman, H.A. 4,486 American Soldiers Have Died in Iraq. President Obama Is Continuing a Pointless and Deadly Quagmire. (6 Dec, 2017).

Goleman, D. (2004). What makes a leader? Harvard Business Review, 82(1), 13–15.

Golshan, T. Trump said he wouldn't cut Medicaid, Social Security, and Medicare. His 2020 budget cuts all 3. Vox, 12 March, 2019.

Goodwin, B. (2005). Business continuity. A third of companies have no plan for ensuring business continuity. Computer Weekly, 3(4), 17.

Goodkind, N. Trump Officials Acknowledge Sixth Migrant Child Death in U.S. Custody in 6 Months After None the Previous Decade. Newsweek, 23 May, 2019.

Gorman, B. (2006). Four crucial steps to setting up a crisis-response plan. Strategic Communication Management, 10(4), 14.

Gottschalk, P., Arnulf, J. Heroic Leaders as White-Collar Criminals: An Empirical Study Norwegian Business School, Journal of Investigative Psychology and Offender Profiling Department of Leadership. 12 August, 2012.

GovTrack https://www.govtrack.us/congress/votes

Graff, G. Mueller Makes It Clear: Trump Was Worse Than a 'Useful Idiot'. Wired, 22 April, 2019.

Graham, D. Trump's Surreal Phone Call With Vladimir Putin. Once more, the President has failed to press the Russian President on electoral interference. The Atlantic, 3 May, 2019.

Greening, D., & Johnson, R. (1997). Managing industrial and environmental crises: The role of heterogeneous top management teams. Business and Society Journal, 36(4), 334–361.

Green, Jason. Effort to recall Brock Turner judge Aaron Persky qualifies for June ballot, Bay Area News Group. 23 January, 2018.

Greenberg, D. Memo to Obama Fans, Clinton's presidency was not a failure. (12, Feb, 2008).

Griffiths, J. Trump says he considered 'this Russia thing' before firing FBI Director Comey. CNN (12 May 2017).

Grimm, M. (1998). Floodplain management. Civil Engineering, 68(3), 62.

Gross, Terry "Mueller's Reputation In Washington Is 'Stunningly Bipartisan,' Journalist Says". NPR. 1 February, 2018.

GSW investor gets 1-year ban for shoving Lowry. ESPN News Services, 6 June, 2019.

Gurman, S. FBI probing Clinton Foundation corruption claims. Associated Press, 5 January, 2018.

Hafner, J. Judge finalizes $25 million Trump University settlement for students of 'sham university'. USA Today, 10 April, 2018.

Hahn, P. How Jimmy Carter lost Iran: The politics behind Carter's biggest blunder (22 Oct, 2017).

Hale, J., Hale, D., & Dulek, R. (2006). Decision processes during crisis response: An exploratory investigation. Journal of Managerial Issues, 18(3), 301.

Halper, Evan. Ben Carson made it clear that he was too inexperienced for a

Cabinet job. Now Trump says he's considering Carson for one. Los Angeles Times. (22 November, 2016).

Harry S. Truman Presidential Library and Museum
https://www.trumanlibrary.org/speaks.htm

Harris, S., Miller, G., Dawsey, J. CIA concludes Saudi crown prince ordered Jamal Khashoggi's assassination. The Washington Post, 16 November, 2018.

Heads, TV Talking (December 13, 2016). "What 29 TV Shows Have Been #1 in the Annual Nielsen Rankings?" TV Talking Heads. Archived from the original on March 17, 2017. Retrieved March 17, 2017.

Hennessy-Fiske, M. Ft. Hood shooter received glowing evaluations before attack. (24, August, 2013).

Hambrick, D. (1981). Strategic awareness within top management teams. Strategic Management Journal, 2(3), 21–37.

Hambrick, D., Finkelstein, S., & Mooney, A. (2005). Executive job demands: New insights for explaining strategic decisions and leader behaviors. Academy of Management Review, 30(3), 17–28.

Hammond, J., Keeney, R., & Raiffa, H. (1998). The hidden traps in decision making. Harvard Business Review, 76(5), 47–58.

Hansen, J., & Patton, M. (1994). The Joint Committee on Standards for Educational Evaluations (2nd ed.). Thousand Oaks, CA: Sage.

Hayes, C. Kelly Sadler, White House aide who reportedly mocked John McCain, is out. USA Today, 6 June, 2018.

Hazy, J. (2006). Measuring leadership effectiveness in complex socio-technical systems. E:CO Issue, 8(3), 17.

Herrera, J. Kirstjen Nielsen's Role in Family Separation: A Timeline. Pacific Standard, 10 April, 2019.

Hersey, P., & Blanchard, K. H. (1969). Life-cycle theory of leadership. Training and Development Journal, 23(2), 26–34.

Hersey, P., & Blanchard, K. H. (1982). Management of organizational behavior: Utilizing human resources (4th ed.). Englewood Cliffs, NJ: Prentice-Hall.

Higgins, S. (2005). Wal-Mart is lauded for fast relief aid to Katrina victims. Investor's Business Daily, 10(3), 15.

Higgs, R. (1997). Crisis and leviathan: Critical episodes in the growth of American government. New York: Oxford University Press.

Hillson, D. (2004). Effective opportunity management for projects. Boca Raton, FL: CRC Press.

Hines, A. (2006). On risk and disaster—Lessons from Hurricane Katrina. Financial World, 24(8), 19–21.

Hinnebusch, R. The American Invasion of Iraq: Causes and Consequences (2007).

Ho, C. From Ukraine to Trump Tower, Paul Manafort unafraid to take on controversial jobs. (7 April 2016).

Hohmann, J. Poll: Jimmy Carter takes big hit (12/06/2010).

Holder, R. W. (2008), "useful fool", Oxford Dictionary of Euphemisms, Oxford University Press, p. 394, ISBN 978-0199235179, useful fool – a dupe of the Communists. Lenin's phrase for the shallow thinkers in the West whom the Communists manipulated. Also as useful idiot.

Holland, J. Black Americans aren't buying Omarosa's turn against Trump. Associated Press, 15 August, 2018.

House Ways and Means Committee Republicans Vote to Keep Trump Personal & Business Tax Returns Secret. Press Release (7 Sep, 2017).

Hruby, D., Dean, S. Austria's Chancellor Kurz calls for early elections after vice chancellor resigns over alleged corruption video. CNN, 20 May, 2019.

Huang, Z. Donald Trump has more than 100 trademarks in China, including 35 granted pre-approval since he became US President. Quartz, 10 March, 2017.

Hudson, J., Dawsey, J. Putin out-prepared Trump in key meeting, Rex Tillerson told House panel. The Washington Post, 23 May, 2019.

Huff, A. S., & Reger, R. K. (1987). A review of strategic process research. Journal of Management, 13(6), 31.

Hundreds of priests shuffled worldwide, despite abuse allegations. USA Today. Associated Press. 20 June 2004.

Hutzler, A. Fox News Reporters Leave, Saying Donald Trump has Skewed the Network. Newsweek, 25 August, 2018.

Hurtado, P. Smythe, C. 'Wolf of Wall Street' Jordan Belfort Isn't Paying His Debts, U.S. Says (16 May 2018).

Ignatius, D. Foreign adversaries have figured Trump out. The Washington Post, 14 May, 2019.

Immelman, A. The Leadership Style of U.S. President Donald J. Trump Aubrey St. John's University / College of St. Benedict, 20 January, 2017.

Inducing Panic Law and Legal Definitionhttps://definitions.uslegal.com/i/inducing-panic/

In Fight with 'Chuck And Nancy,' Trump Says He'd Be 'Proud' To Shut Down Government. NPR, 11 December, 2018

Ingram, D. Key facts in 'Fast and Furious' gun-probe controversy. Reuters (19 September, 2012).

Ink, D. (2006). An analysis of the House Select Committee and White House reports on Hurricane Katrina. Public Administration Review, 66(6), 800.

Iran Hostage Crisis History.com Staff http://www.history.com/topics/iran-hostage-crisis (2010).

Itkowitz, C., DeBonis, M. Former Bush official puts Trump on the couch: a '10 out of 10 narcissist'. The Washington Post, 15 May, 2019.

Jacobson, G. The Triumph of Polarized Partisanship in 2016: Donald Trump's Improbable Victory Science Quarterly Wiley-Blackwell (2016).

Jaffe, A. Colin Powell: Invasion of Iraq 'Badly Flawed' (6 Sep, 2015).

Jamal Khashoggi: All you need to know about Saudi journalist's death. BBC, 11

December, 2018.

Jan, T. Ben Carson's HUD: Political loyalty required, no experience necessary. The Washington Post, 20 September, 2018.

Jentz, B., & Murphy, J. (2005, January). Embracing confusion: What leaders do when they don't know what to do. Phi Delta Kappan, 358–362.

Jensen, E. "Matt Lauer scandal: There may be as many as 8 victims, Lauer breaks his silence". USA Today. Retrieved 30 November 2017.

Johnson, J., British general undercuts Trump-Bolton push for war: No "increased threat" from Iran. Salon, 15 May, 2019.

Jones, J. Presidential Moral Leadership Less Important to Republicans. Gallop, 29 May, 2018.

Joskow, M. These are Fox News' leading advertisers. Media Matters, 9 May, 2019.

Josephs, L. Boeing should have disclosed automated system to pilots, FAA head says, 15 May, 2019.

Kappelman, L., McKeeman, R., & Zhang, L. (2006). Early warning signs of IT project failure: The dominant dozen. Information Systems Management, 5(4), 37–45.

Kaplan, Harold I.; Benjamin J. Sadock (1972). Modern Group Book, volume 4: Sensitivity through encounter and marathon. J. Aronson.

Kaur, H. Kanye West just said 400 years of slavery was a choice. CNN, 4 May, 2018.

Kaval, V., & Voyten, L. (2006). Executive decision making. Healthcare Executive, 21(6), 5–17.

Kelly, Elizabeth, Will the new tax plan mean the end of Social Security and Medicare as we know it? (MarketWatch, 14 Dec 2017).

Kessler, G., Kelly, M. President Trump has made more than 2,000 false or misleading claims over 355 days (10 Jan, 2018).

Kellerman, B., Bad Leadership: What It Is, How It Happens, Why It Matters (Boston, MA: Harvard Business School Press, 2004).

Kiefer, J., & Montjoy, R. (2006). Incrementalism before the storm: Network performance for evacuation of New Orleans [Special issue]. Public Administration Review, 66.

Kiley, D. Harley-Davidson Complains Of Trump Tariffs In Reporting Big Sales Decline. Forbes, 23 April, 2019.

King, G. (2002). Crisis management & team effectiveness: A closer examination. Journal of Business Ethics, 41(3), 235.

King, J. Bush calls Saddam 'the guy who tried to kill my dad' CNN (27 Sep, 2002).

Kirkpatrick, D. (2005, September 15). Ex-FEMA chief tells of frustration and chaos. New York Times, pp. A1–A3. Retrieved November 18, 2008, from www.nytimes.com/2005/09/15/national/national special/15brown.html.

Knabb, R. D., Rhone, J. R., & Brown, D. P. (2005). Tropical cyclone report, Hurricane Katrina. Miami, FL: National Oceanic and Atmospheric Administration National Hurricane Center.

Konnikova, M. Trump's Lies vs. Your Brain January/February 2017.

Kotter, J. (1990). What leaders really do. Harvard Business Review, 79(11), 85–96. Retrieved November 15, 2005, from Capella University database.

Kottler, J. What REALLY Leads to Change in People's Lives? Psychology Today, 24 July, 2013.

Krane, D. (2007). The unavoidable politics of disaster recovery. The Public Manager, 36(3), 31.

Krogstad, J., Radford, J. Education levels of U.S. immigrants are on the rise. Pew Research Center, 14 September, 2018.

Kruzel, J. Is WikiLeaks Russia's 'useful idiot,' its 'agent of influence,' or something else? Politifact, 18 March, 2019.

Kushell, E., Ames, M., Heide, D., & Bosserman, N. (2003). On the folly of leading people to do A while hoping they will do B. Business Forum, 26(3/4), 12–17.

Kumar, A., Orr, G. All for nothing': Trump's wall retreat bewilders allies. Politico, 25 January, 2019.

La Ganga, M. Ex-Montana judge to get bar association award despite censure over rape comments. (24 Apr 2015).

Landay, J., Young, A., & McCaffrey, S. (2005). Chertoff delayed federal response, memo shows. Retrieved December 10, 2008, from www.realcities.com/mld/kr Washington/1263712.htm.

Lattin, Don (17 July 1998). "$30 Million Awarded to Men Molested by 'Family Priest' / 3 bishops accused of Stockton coverup". San Francisco Chronicle. Retrieved 23 July 2012. Attorney Jeff Anderson said the Howard brothers were repeatedly molested between 1978 and 1991, from age 3 to 13. Reverend Oliver O'Grady later confessed to the abuse of many other children. The documentary Deliver Us from Evil explored his story and the cover-up by Diocesan officials.

Lawrence, C., & Lavander, E. (Executive Producers). (2005, September 6). *CNN* [Television broadcast]. Retrieved January 10, 2009, from www.cnn.com/2005/WEATHER/09/07/katrina.impact/.

Leadership Lessons from Donald Trump, How should a President lead? Psychology Today, 28 October, 2018.

Lee, M. Fact Check: Has Trump declared bankruptcy four or six times? The Washington Post, 26 September, 2016.

Lester, W. (2007). Transformational leadership and NIMS. The Public Manager, 36(3), 11.

Leetim, T. Mark Zuckerberg is in denial about how Facebook is harming our politics. Vox (10 Nov 2016).

LeTourneau, N., Trump Is Spreading Incompetence Throughout the Federal Government. Washington Monthly, 2 October, 2018.

Levenson, E. Michigan State University reaches $500 million settlement with Larry Nassar victim. CNN (16 May 2018).

Levenson, E., Cooper, A. Bill Cosby guilty on all three counts in indecent assault trial CNN (26 Apr 2018).

Lichtman, Allan J. The Keys to the White House: A Surefire Guide to Predicting the Next President 2008 ed. (New York: Rowman and Littlefield Publishers,, Inc. 2008), ix

"License for Nidal Malik Hasan, MD". Virginia Board of Education. Retrieved November 5, 2009.

Lincicome, S. Here Are 202 Companies Hurt by Trump's Tariffs Tariff Tracker, 2 May, 2019.

Linton, C. Justin Amash, Michigan congressman, becomes first GOP lawmaker to call for impeachment. CBS News, 19 May, 2019.

Lipscomb, D. Promotion Eligibility for U.S. Army Officers. Chron. Retrieved, 7 June, 2019.

Lipman, V. The 4 Principles Of President Trump's Deceptive But Effective Communication. 15 June, 2018.

Long, H. Trump's steel tariffs cost U.S. consumers $900,000 for every job created, experts say. The Washington Post, 7 May, 2019.

Lopez, G. Most Americans agree Trump has made race relations worse, Vox, 9 April, 2019.

Love, D. Comey is exactly right about Trump being like a mob boss. CNN, 13 April 2018).

Lussier, R., & Achua, C. (2004). Leadership: Application, theory, and skill development (2nd ed.). New York: Thompson.

MacGillis, Alec. Is Anybody Home at HUD? collaboration between New York and ProPublica, (22 August, 2017).

Madison, L. (2012, January 26). CBS News. Interview with Warren Buffett.

Maddaus, G. The Weinstein Co. Declares Bankruptcy (19 march 2018).

Majors, S. (Executive Producer). (2006, August 29). MSNBC [Television broadcast]. Retrieved September 23, 2008, from www.dailynightly.msnbc.com/faces_from_The gulf/index.html.

Manfred, T. Here Are All The Shockingly Awful Donald Sterling Stories That The NBA Ignored For Years. Business Insider, 28 April, 2014.

Mangan, D. Trump had revenue of at least $434 million in 2018, saw drop in Mar-a-Lago money, new filing reveals. CNBC, 17 May, 2019.

Marlow, I., Slatter, M., & Wozniak, T. (2006). The fury. Risk Management, 53(5), 10.

Margin Call script, (2011) https://www.springfieldspringfield.co.uk/movie_script.php?movie=margin-call.

Marcin, T. Boeing Didn't Want to Ground the 737 MAX Even After Pilots Urged Them To, Vice News, 15 May, 2019.

Marcus, A., Oransky, I. Why scientific fraud hurts people. STAT, 18 March, 2016.

Margolin, E. Watch: 3 memorable moments in election night history. MSNBC, 7 November, 2013.

Martin, A. Tagg Romney Whispered an Apology to Obama for Wanting to Punch Him. Intelligencer, 23 October, 2012.

Martin, R. (2007, August). Battle-proven military principles for disaster leadership. Fire Engineering, 69–71.

Mason, J. Why John McCain lost the White House (5 Nov, 2008).

Maxwell. S. Candidate caught with fake diploma calls it fake news — until she's forced to exit race. Orlando Sentinel, 14 August, 2018.

McBride, J., Chatzky. What Is the Trans-Pacific Partnership (TPP)? Council on Foreign Relations, 4 January, 2019.

McCarthy, N. The Government Shutdown Cost The U.S. Economy $11 Billion [Infographic]. Forbes, 30 January, 2019.

McCain, J. Salter, M. The Restless Wave Good Times, Just Causes, Great Fights, and Other Appreciations (2018).

McChesney, J. Army Recruiter Suicides Prompt Investigations. NPR, 2 January, 2009.

McDonald, S. North Korea Test Fires New Tactical Guided Weapon One Month After Trump-Kim Talks Broke Down. Newsweek, 17 April, 2019.

McGoff, C. Why do scientists commit misconduct? Retraction Watch https://retractionwatch.com/2016/08/29/why-do-scientists-commit-misconduct/

Mckinley, James C.; DAO, James (November 8, 2009). "Fort Hood Gunman Gave Signals Before His Rampage". The New York Times. Retrieved March 16, 2012.

McNamee, W. Report reveals staggering deficiencies at VA hospital in D.C. CBS News (8 March, 2018).

McPhate, M. A California arson investigator was regarded as a sage. But it was him all along. California Sun https://www.californiasun.co/stories/a-california-arson-investigator-was-regarded-as-a-sage-but-it-was-him-all-along/

McQuaid, J. (2005). Anatomy of a disaster. Retrieved December 18, 2008, from www.unchs.org/pmss/getElectronicVersion.asp?nr=2101&alt=1.

McQuaid, J., & Schleifstein, M. (2006). Path of destruction: The devastation of New Orleans and the coming age of superstorms. Boston: Little, Brown.

Menzel, D. (2006). The Katrina aftermath: A failure of federalism or leadership. Public Administration Review, 66(6), 808–812.

Merica, D. Officials from four countries discussed exploiting Jared Kushner. CNN (28 Feb, 2018).

Merica, D. Women detail sexual allegations against Trump CNN (10 May 2018).

Merle, R., Helderman, R. Chicago bank CEO accused of bribing Manafort for administration job. The Washington Post, 23 May, 2019.

Merna, A., & Merna, T. (2004). Development of a model for risk management at corporate, strategic business, and project levels. The Journal of Structured and Project Finance, 10(1), 79–85.

Michael, G. Praying for Time. Praying for Time lyrics © Warner/Chappell Music, Inc.

Michel, C. NRA spokeswoman confronted with the facts on the assault weapons ban. She had no answers. 25 Feb, 2018.

Miller, Z. 14 Questions You Were Too Embarrassed to Ask About Blocking Donald Trump at the GOP Convention. Time. 9 March, 2016.

Miles, M., & Huberman, A., M. (1994). Qualitative data analysis: An expanded sourcebook (2nd ed.). Thousand Oaks, CA: Sage.

Miles, M., & Huberman, A. (2002). The qualitative researcher's companion. Thousand Oaks, CA: Sage.

Mintz, A., Wayne, C. 'The Polythink Syndrome: U.S. Foreign Policy Decisions on 9/11, Afghanistan, Iraq, Iran, Syria, and ISIS'. Stanford: Stanford University Press, 2016.

Moffett, S. (2004, October 24). After Japan's latest earthquake, government's response improves. The Wall Street Journal, p. A17. Retrieved November 19, 2008, from ProQuest database.

Montanaro, D. Here's Just How Little Confidence Americans Have In Political Institutions. 17 January, 2018.

Montgomery, N. After 2 decades of sexual assault in military, no real change in message. Stars and Stripes, 7 July, 2013.

Moran, K., & Lezon, D. (2005, August 30). Devastating storm leaves dozens dead. Houston Chronicle, pp. 2–3. Retrieved December 17, 2008, from ProQuest database.

Morgenstern, M. So, What's a Major Reason Why Military Commanders Are Fired? The Blaze. 20 January, 2013.

Moorhead, M. Mitt Romney says 47 percent of Americans pay no income tax. 18 September, 2012.

Morris, G. (2005). Turning risk into reward: Navigating a new course toward a return on risk. Risk Management, 52(8), 24.

Morris, R. (1987). Contingencies: A good disaster plan is hard to find. Industrial Management, 29(6), 2.

Morgenstern, M. So, what's a Major Reason Why Military Commanders Are Fired? The Blaze (20 January, 2013).

Mortlock, M. (2005). Hurricanes and learning organization obsolescence. The Public Manager, 34(3), 2.

Mukunda, G. Why Staff Turnover in the White House Is Such a Bad Thing — Especially For President Trump. 6 April, 2018.

Mukherjee, S. The GOP Tax Bill Repeals Obamacare's Individual Mandate. Here's What That Means for You. 20 December, 2017.

Murray, S. Putin: I wanted Trump to win the election. Politico, 16 July, 2018.

Murdock, D. The Night Chris Christie Killed the Romney Campaign. The National Review. 4 February, 2016.

Muskal, M. Bill Clinton: 'I could have killed' Osama bin Laden in 1998. 1 August, 2014.

Myers, M. Longer hours, Saturdays at work could be on tap for some Army recruiters. Army Times, 10 May, 2018.

Nader, Ralph. Why run for President if you don't have a real chance? 15 May, 2015.

Naglewski, K. (2006, Spring). Are you ready to make effective decisions when disaster strikes? Journal of Private Equity, 9(2), 45.

National Oceanic Atmospheric Administration. (2007). FAQ: Hurricanes, typhoons, and tropical storms. Retrieved August 15, 2008, from www.aoml.noaa.gov/hrd/tcfaq/tcfaqA.html.

National Coalition for Parent Involvement in education. 2006. Research Review and Resources. Retrieved September 16, 2011, from www.ncpie.org/WhatsHappening/researchJanuary2006.cfm

Neely, B. Trump Doesn't Own Most Of The Products He Pitched Last Night. NPR. 9 March, 2016.

Nelson, L. "Why we voted for Donald Trump": David Duke explains the white supremacist Charlottesville protests, Vox. 12 August, 2017.

Nelson, S. Bill Clinton 15 Years Ago: 'I Did Not Have Sexual Relations With That Woman' (25 Jan 2013).

Neufeldt, V. (Ed.). (1988). Webster's new world dictionary of American English (3rd ed.). New York: Simon & Schuster.

Newport, F. History Shows Presidential Job Approval Ratings Can Plummet Rapidly GALLUP NEWS SERVICE. 11 February,1998.

Nguyen, T. Judge Andrew Napolitano's Lonely, One-Man War Against Trump. Vanity Fair. 7 June, 2019.

Nichol, H., & Abel, C. (2007, December). A critical analysis of emergency management. Administrative Theory & Praxis, 29(4).

Nixon and Khrushchev have a "kitchen debate". History.com Editors, Access Date, 30 May, 2019. https://www.history.com/this-day-in-history/nixon-and-khrushchev-have-a-kitchen-debate

Northouse, P. (2004). Leadership theory and practice (3rd ed.). Thousand Oaks, CA: Sage.

Nuwer, R. Scientific Misconduct Should Be a Crime, It's as bad as fraud or theft, only potentially more dangerous. Slate, 14 September, 2014.

Nylenna, M.; Andersen, D.; Dahlquist, G.; Sarvas, M.; Aakvaag, A. (1999). "Handling of scientific dishonesty in the Nordic countries. National Committees on Scientific Dishonesty in the Nordic Countries". Lancet. 354 (9172): 57–61.

O'Connell, J., Marimow, A., Leonnig, C. Congressional Democrats' emoluments lawsuit targeting President Trump's private business can proceed, judge says. The Washington Post, 30 April, 2019.

Office of Emergency Services. (1993). Earthquake mitigation success stories. Retrieved November 18, 2008, from www.oes.ca.gov/WebPage/oeswebsite.nsf/

Olen, H. Betsy DeVos's disastrous interview shows the limitations of being rich. The Washington Post, 12 March, 2018.

Oreskes, N. "Beyond the Ivory Tower: The Scientific Consensus on Climate Change," Science Vol. 306 no. 5702, p. 1686 (3 December 2004); DOI: 10.1126/science.1103618.

Osborne, D., & Gaebler, T. (1992). Reinventing government. Reading, MA: Wesley.

Owen, S. Surveys show wide disagreement on number of rape-related pregnancies per year. Politifact (15 August 2013).

Pamela McGee sports-reference.com.

Pane, L. Mass school shootings mostly happening in small-town, suburban America. Associated Press, 22 May, 2018.

Parajon, E., Peterson, S., Powers, R., Tierney, M. Snap Poll: What Experts Make of Trump's Foreign Policy, International relations scholars evaluate two years of U.S. foreign policy. Foreign Policy, 7 December, 2018.

Parker, A., Denyer, S. Still angling for a deal, Trump backs Kim Jong Un over Biden, Bolton and Japan. The Washington Post, 27 May, 2019.

Pascrell, B. Statement on Trump Tax Returns Petition Going Ignored. Press Release (28 Feb, 2018).

Paulson, Michael (8 April 2002). "World doesn't share US view of scandal: Clergy sexual abuse reaches far, receives an uneven focus". The Boston Globe. Retrieved 17 July 2012.

PBS News Hour. 57 percent of voters say they won't support Trump in 2020. 17 January, 2019.

Pearson, C. M., & Clair, J. A. (1998). Reframing crisis management. Academy of Management Review, 23, 60.

Pennycook, G., Cheyne, J., Barr, N., Koehler, D., Fugelsang, J. It's still bullshit, Judgment and Decision Making, Vol. 11, No. 1. January 2016.

Pennycook, G., Cheyne, J., Barr, N., Koehler, D., Fugelsang, J. On the reception and detection of pseudo-profound bullshit Vol. 10, No. 6. (November 2015).

Peters, T. (2004). Leaders. Office Solutions, 21(2), 27. Retrieved November 23, 2008, from Business Source Premier database.

POLITICO STAFF Full transcript: Mitt Romney's remarks on Donald Trump and the 2016 race (3 Mar, 2016).

Prahaled, C. K., & Bettis, R. (1988). The dominant logic: A new link between diversity and performance. Strategic Management Journal, 7(5), 27.

Priest, Dana (November 10, 2009). "Fort Hood suspect warned of threats within the ranks". Washington Post. Retrieved November 10, 2009.

President Trump Directed His Attorney Michael Cohen To Lie To Congress About The Moscow Tower Project. BuzzFeed, 17 January, 2019.

Press, B. Press: Trump wastes 35 days for nothing. The Hill, 28 January, 2019.

Quarantelli, E. (1988). Disaster crisis management: A summary of research findings. Journal of Management Studies, 25(4), 373–378.

Quotation from page 6: "The number of papers rejecting AGW [Anthropogenic, or human-caused, Global Warming] is a miniscule proportion of the published research, with the percentage slightly decreasing over time. Among papers expressing a position on AGW, an overwhelming percentage (97.2% based on self-ratings, 97.1% based on abstract ratings) endorses the scientific consensus on AGW."

Quotation from page 3: "Among abstracts that expressed a position on AGW, 97.1% endorsed the scientific consensus. Among scientists who expressed a position on AGW in their abstract, 98.4% endorsed the consensus."

Ramsey, E. For the 'Cause of Christ,' Liberty Alumni Return Diplomas. Red Letter Christians, 27 October, 2017.

Ramsey, R. (2006). Top ten lessons for supervisors from last year's hurricanes. SuperVision Journal, 67(10), 9.

Rand Corp. The Future of U.S. Health Care: Replace or Revise the Affordable Care Act? https://www.rand.org/health/key-topics/health-policy/in-depth.html.

Relman, E. It's Chris Christie's last day in office — here's how he became the least popular governor in New Jersey history. 16 January, 2018).

Reints, R. Ivanka Trump's Brand Received Five New Trademarks From China This Month. Fortune Magazine, 21 January, 2019.

Relman, E. A Fox News contributor quit the network, calling it a 'propaganda machine for a destructive and ethically ruinous administration'. Business Insider, 21 March, 2018.

Report on the Firefighter Arson Problem: Context, Considerations, and Best Practices National Volunteer Fire Council. 2011.

Retracted autism study an 'elaborate fraud,' British journal finds. CNN Wire Staff, 5 January, 2011.

Reynolds, P. D. (1979). Ethical dilemmas and social science research. San Francisco: Jossey-Bass.

Reuters. Senator Rubio says US workers get little benefit from tax reform: Report (30 April 2018).

Rike, B. (2003, May/June). Prepared or not . . . that is the vital question. The Information Management Journal, 25–32.

Rising, D., Jenne, P. Ousted by parliament, Austria's Kurz vows to win job back. Associated Press, 27 May, 2019.

Riotta, Chris GOP Aims To Kill Obamacare Yet Again After Failing 70 Times, July 29, 2017.

Robinson, C. (2005, January). Preparing for the unexpected: Teamwork for troubled times. The Journal for Quality & Participation, 1, 17.

Roberts, D. The "Trump effect" threatens the future of the Paris climate agreement. Vox, 12 December, 2018.

Robert S. Mueller III (1990–1993)". United States Department of Justice. August 10, 2016.

Robson, C. (2002). Real world research (2nd ed.). Malden, MA: Blackwell.

Roig-Franzia, M., & Hsu, S. (2005, September 5). Many evacuated, but thousands still waiting. Washington Post, pp. A1–A2. Retrieved October 7, 2008, from www.washingtonpost.com /wpdyn/content/article/2005/0905.html.

Rome, H., Why Iran Waits: Staying in the Nuclear Deal Is Its Worst Option, Except for All the Others. Foreign Affairs, 10 January, 2019.

Romm, T., Harwell, D. White House declines to back Christchurch call to stamp out online extremism amid free speech concerns. The Washington Post, 15 May, 2019.

Rosenberg, E., Leaving the Iran Nuclear Deal Will Have Unintended Consequences. Foreign Policy, 15 May, 2019.

Ross, J. The brief rise and lengthy fall of Sarah Palin (23 January 2016).

Rothschild, M. Atrocious Things That Happened Because of Bernie Madoff. Ranker https://www.ranker.com/list/bernie-madoff-scandal-casualties/mike-rothschild

Rucker, P., Dawsey, J. 'We fell in love': Trump and Kim shower praise, stroke egos on path to nuclear negotiations. The Washington Post, 25 February, 2019.

Ruiz, Rebecca R.; Landler, Mark (May 17, 2017). "Robert Mueller, Former F.B.I. Director, Is Named Special Counsel for Russia Investigation". The New York Times. ISSN 0362-4331. Archived from the original on May 17, 2017.

Rupar, A. Rudy Giuliani lied about a Trump Tower Moscow letter of intent. CNN has receipts. Vox, 19 December, 2018.

Rupar, A. This video of Trump saying he knew nothing about Stormy Daniels payment is very awkward now. Vox, 27 February, 2019.

Safire, William (12 April 1987). "On Language: Useful Idiots Of the West". The New York Times. Retrieved 19 July 2017.

Salierno, D. (2004). Many U.S. firms unprepared for disaster. The Internal Auditor, 6(6), 2–8.

Samuels, B. Cohen says Trump directed him to lie about hush money payments. The Hill, 27 February, 2019.

Santoro, G. Fred Greenstein, an expert on comparative styles of Presidential leadership American History (2010).

Schiefter, B. (Executive Producer). (2006, February 15). CBS Evening News [Television broadcast]. New York: Central Broadcasting Service.

Schneider, S. (1992). FEMA, federalism, Hugo, and Frisco. PUBLIUS: The Journal of Federalism, 32(2), 3.

Schneider, S. (1998). Reinventing public administration: A case study of the Federal Emergency Management Agency. Public Administration Quarterly, 22(1), 35.

Schneider, S. (2005). Administrative breakdown in the governmental response to Hurricane Katrina. Public Administration Review, 65(5), 515–516.

Schlesinger, Jr., A Forward to Thirteen days. In R. F. Kennedy, Thirteen days (pp. 7–15). New York: W.W. Norton. (1999).

Schultheis, H., Frederick, R., Altiraifi, A.5 Ways the Trump Shutdown Is Harming Struggling Workers, Families, and Communities. Center for American Progress, 17 January, 2019.

Scott, E., Michael Cohen's claims about Trump's racism say more about him than the President. The Washington Post, 27 February. 2019.

SecurityDegreeHub.com
https://www.securitydegreehub.com/what-is-a-security-clearance/

Sementelli, A. (2007, December). Toward a taxonomy of disaster and crisis theories. Administrative Theory & Praxis, 29(4), 497.

Senge, P. M. (1992). The fifth discipline. New York: Doubleday.

Serjeant, J. Kanye West's meeting with Trump provokes scorn, sadness, support. Reuters, 11 October, 2018.

Seymour, M., & Moore, S. (2000). Effective crisis management: Worldwide principles and practice. New York: Cassell.

Sharman, R. (2002, May/June). Enterprise risk management—The KPMG approach. The British Journal of Administrative Management, 31, 26.

Sherman, J., Palmer, A., Lippman, D. NEWT ups his speaking fees, agency cites 'insight' into Trump -- Clinton, Trump Politico (12/02/2016).

Shelbourne, M. Russia says it stopped Mitt Romney from becoming secretary of State: report (3/3/18).

Shoop, T. (2006). Embracing bureaucracy. Government Executive, 38(5), 82.

Shughart, W., II. (2006, April). Katrinanomics: The politics and economics of disaster relief. Public Choice, 127(1–2), 317.

Sit, R. Donald Trump Is an Embarrassment to Most Americans, Who Don't Want Him as a Role Model to Their Children: Poll. Newsweek, 25 January, 2018.

Skowroneck, S. The Politics Presidents make. Cambridge, MA: Harvard University Press. (1993).

Smith, M. (Executive Producer). (2005, October 12). Frontline [Television broadcast]. Arlington, VA: Public Broadcasting Service. Retrieved January 21, 2009, from www.pbs.org/wgbh/pages/frontline/storm/interviews/blanco.html.

Smith, A. Poll: More Virginia voters want Gov. Northam to stay than quit. NBC, 20 February, 2019.

Smits, S., & Alley, E. (2003). Thinking the unthinkable—Leaderships role in creating behavioral readiness for crises management. CR, 13(1), 23.

Snyder, B. What Took Facebook So Long? Reuters. 18 March, 2018.

Sobel, R., & Leeson, P. (2006). Government's response to Hurricane Katrina: A Public Choice analysis. Public Choice, 127(55), 73.

Spinetto, J., Millard, P., Wells, K. (2013). How Brazil's Richest Man Lost $34.5 Billion, Bloomberg BusinessWeek.

Squitieri, J. Republican member of House Intel Committee says it has 'lost all credibility'. CNN (13 March, 2018).

Stake, R. E. (1995). The art of case study research. Thousand Oaks, CA: Sage.

Steinberg, B. (November 29, 2017). "Matt Lauer Responds to Harassment Claims: 'There Is Enough Truth in These Stories'". Variety. Retrieved November 30, 2017.

Stewart, E. Donald Trump Rode $5 Billion in Free Media to the White House. The Street, 20 November, 2016.

Stephens, Scott "Catholic sexual abuse study greeted with incurious contempt". ABC Religion and Ethics, 27 May 2011.

"Sterling settles housing bias lawsuit". ESPN. Associated Press. 3 November, 2009.

Stewart, E. Watch John McCain defend Barack Obama against a racist voter in 2008. Vox, 1 September, 2018.

Stewart, E. Mick Mulvaney says in Congress, he only talked to lobbyists who gave him money Vox, 25 April, 2018.

Stewart, E. Donald Trump Rode $5 Billion in Free Media to the White House

(20Nov, 2016).

Stogdill, R. M. (1974). Handbook of leadership: A survey of theory and research. New York: Free Press.

Stracqualursi, V. Watchdog: Housing department broke the law with $40,000 furniture purchase for Ben Carson. CNN, 17 May, 2019.

Stracqualursi, V., Marquardt, A. White House security official files whistleblower complaint against boss. CNN, 1 April, 2019.

Strauss, V. So what is the DeVos-Trump record on special education funding anyway? The Washington Post, 28 March, 2019.

Sullivan, A., Stephenson, E., Holland, S. Trump says won't divest from his business while President. The Washington Post, 11 January, 2017.

Sullivan, K. New York Times: Tax documents show Trump businesses lost more than $1 billion in a decade. CNN, 8 May, 2009.

Sulzberger, A.G. I Am Part of the Resistance Inside the Trump Administration. The New York Times, 5 September, 2018.

Schwartz, D. This Valedictorian Tricked His Trump-Loving Town into Cheering Obama. Vice (4 June 2018).

Takada, A. (2000). Transformation of an internal model under crisis management. The Japanese Economy.
Takada, M., & Helms, M. (2006). Bureaucracy, meet catastrophe: Analysis of Hurricane Katrina relief efforts and their implications for emergency response governance. International Journal of Public Sector Management, 19(4), 397–411.

Tan, M. 129 Army battalion, brigade commanders fired since 2003. 2 Feb, 2015.

Tani, M. Jimmy Carter: I have one big regret from my time as President. 20 August, 2015.

Tay, S. The US slipped to third place in a ranking of most competitive economies. CNBC, 30 May, 2019.

Terry, L. (1995). Leadership of public bureaucracies: The administrator as conservator. Thousand Oaks, CA: Sage.

The CEO of Salesforce Found Out His Female Employees Were Paid Less Than Men. His Response Is a Priceless Leadership Lesson. Inc., 26 July, 2018.

The Innocence Project, False Confessions & Recording of Custodial Interrogations https://www.innocenceproject.org/false-confessions-recording-interrogations/

The Institute for Civility in Government https://www.instituteforcivility.org/who-we-are/what-is-civility/

The United States Postal Service Commission Report On A Safe And Secure Workplace (2000). The National Center on Addiction and Substance Abuse at Columbia University.

The U.S. has 1 million more job openings than unemployed workers. The Associated Press, 15 March, 2019.

The Week. 8 times Trump denied doing business in Russia. 30 November, 2018.

Thompson, M. Fort Hood: Were Hasan's Warning Signs Ignored? Time. 18 November, 2009.

THE FINANCIAL CRISIS INQUIRY COMMISSION (2011). The Financial Crisis Inquiry Report.
Tice, J. 20 percent of screened Army captains booted by retention board. Army Times, 11 February, 2016.

Tiron, R. Obama outscores McCain in veterans' group's report card. The Hill, 7 October, 2008.

Tracey, J., & Hinkin, T. (1998). Transformational leadership or effective managerial practices? Group & Organization Management, 23(3), 3.

Trimble, M. Trump Foundation to Shut Down. Digital News Editor, 18 December, 2018.

Trochim, W., & Kane, M. (2006). Concept mapping for planning and evaluations. Thousand Oaks, CA: Sage.

Trofino, J. (1995). Transformational leadership in health care. Nursing Management, 26(8), 18.

Trotta, D. Iraq war costs U.S. more than $2 trillion: study. Reuters. (14 March,

2013).

Trump's businesses take a hit as the brand 'has lost its mojo'. Market Watch, 23 December, 2018.

Trump backs off cutting Special Olympics funding. ESPN News Services, 29 March, 2019.

Tuttle, I. Yes, Trump University Was a Massive Scam. National Review, 26 February, 2016.

Ulmer, R. (2001). Effective crisis management through established stakeholder relationships. Management Communication Quarterly, 14(4), 25.

Useful Idiot. Oxford English Dictionary. Oxford University Press. 2017.

U.S Bureau of Labor. (2007). Business statistics. Retrieved 5 June, 2019.from www.bls.gov/search/osmr/htm.

U.S. Department of Homeland Security. (2004). National Response Plan. Retrieved September 18, 2008, from www.dhs.gov/xlibrary/assets/nrp_fulltest.pdf.

U.S. Department of Homeland Security. (2005, August 31). Chertoff states that he is pleased with Katrina response [News release]. Retrieved January 5, 2009, from www.dpc.senate.gov/dpc-new.cfm?doc.

U.S. Government Accountability Office. (1993). Disaster management: Improving the national response to catastrophic disasters. Washington, DC: Government Printing Office.

U.S. Government Accountability Office. (2006). Preliminary observations on hurricane response. Retrieved September 25, 2008, from www.gao.gov/new.items/d06934.pdf.

U.S. House Select Bipartisan Committee to Investigate the Preparation for and Response to Hurricane Katrina (2005a) (testimony of Kathleen Blanco). Retrieved December 15, 2008, from www.katrina.house.gov/full_katrina_report.htm.

U.S. House Select Bipartisan Committee to Investigate the Preparation for and Response to Hurricane Katrina (2005b)(testimony of Michael Chertoff). Retrieved December 10, 2008, from www.katrina.house.gov/full_katrina_report.htm.

U.S. House Select Bipartisan Committee to Investigate the Preparation for and Response to Hurricane Katrina. (2006a). A failure of initiative. Washington, DC: Government Printing Office.

U.S. House Select Bipartisan Committee to Investigate the Preparation for and Response to Hurricane Katrina (2006b) (testimony of Michael Brown). Retrieved January 5, 2009, from www.katrina.house.gov/full_katrina_report.htm.

Us Weekly Staff (November 29, 2017). "Matt Lauer Allegedly Sexually Harassed Colleague during 2014 Sochi Olympics". Us Weekly. Retrieved December 4, 2017.

Valverde, M. What you need to know about the Trump administration's zero-tolerance immigration policy. Politifact, 6 June, 2018.

Van Wart, M. (2004). A comprehensive model of organizational leadership: The leadership action cycle. International Journal of Organization Theory and Behavior, 7(2), 173.

Vardi, N., (2013). Ten Ways Twitter's IPO Didn't Turn Out To Be Like Facebook's IPO.

Vermeer, P. Religion and Family Life: An Overview of Current Research and Suggestions for Future Research Faculty of Philosophy, Theology and Religious Studies, Radboud University, Nijmegen, PO Box 9103, Nijmegen 6500 HD, The Netherlands; Published: 13 April 2014

Vera, A., Michigan's top public health official to stand trial for 2 deaths connected with Flint water crisis. CNN, 23 August, 2019.

Vogelaar, A. (2007). Leadership from the edge: A matter of balance. Journal of Leadership and Organizational Studies, 13(3), 18–32.

Wagner, k. Molla, R. Facebook has disabled almost 1.3 billion fake accounts over the past six months (15 May 2018).

Walker, S. Edgar Maddison Welch of Salisbury sentenced to four years in prison for 'Pizzagate' shooting in Washington. Salisbury Post (23 June 2017).

Wanasika, I., Adler, T. Deception as Strategy: Context and Dynamics. JOURNAL OF MANAGERIAL ISSUES Vol. XXIII Number 3 Fall 2011: 364-378

Watkins, E. Foran, C. EPA chief Scott Pruitt's long list of controversies. CNN (5

July 2018).

Watkins, E. Trump signs resolution condemning white supremacy, CNN, 14 September, 2017.

Waugh, W., & Streib, G. (2006, December). Collaboration and leadership for effective emergency management. Public Administration Review, 66, 131.

Webb, A. (2013, September). California Car Dealers Say Tesla Is "Misleading" Consumers.

Wehner, P. What I've Gained by Leaving the Republican Party, I'm more willing to listen to those I once thought didn't have much to teach me. The Atlantic, 6 February, 2019.

Weiss, R. (2002). Crisis leadership. American Society for Training & Development, 56(3), 28.

Weiss, W. H. (2007). Effective leadership: What are the requisites? SuperVision, 68(2), 6–7.

What Research Says About Parent Involvement https://www.responsiveclassroom.org/what-research-says-about-parent-involvement/

Wheatley, M. (2006). Real leadership. Leadership Excellence, 23(10), 8.

Whitaker, B. (Executive Producer). (2005, August 30). CBS News [Television broadcast]. Retrieved December 15, 2008, from www.cbsnews.com/stories/2006/02/13/katrina/main1308008_page2.shtl.

Whitten, S. Yen L.Papa John's founder John Schnatter resigns as chairman after apologizing for N-word comment, shares surge. CNBC, 11 July 2018.

White House. (2006). The federal response to Hurricane Katrina: Lessons learned. Retrieved December 12, 2008, from www.whitehouse.gov/reports/katrina-lessons-learned.

Wike, R., Stokes, B., Poushter, J., Silver, L., Fetterolf, J., Devlin, K. Faith in the U.S. President remains low. Pew Research Center, 1 October, 2018.

Williams, K. (2005). How is your company managing risk? Strategic Finance, 87(3), 21.

Wise, C. (2006). Organizing for homeland security after Katrina: Is adaptive management what's missing? Public Administration Review, 66(3), 302.

Wolfe, J.F. 10 Surprising Sports Heroes Of The Civil Rights Movement. Listverse, 16 February, 2015.https://listverse.com/2015/02/16/10-surprising-sports-heroes-of-the-civil-rights-movement/

Wolff, M. Fire and Fury. Henry Holt and Company, 5 January, 2018.

Woodward, B. Bush at war. New York: Simon and Schuster. (2002).
Xavier, S. (2005). Are you at the top of your game? Checklist for effective leaders. The Journal of Business Strategy, 26(3), 6–13.

Yeakey, G. (2002, January/February). Situational leadership. Military Review, 72–79.

Yglesias, M. The Bullshitter-in-Chief. Vox, 30 May, 2017.

Yin, R. (2003). Applications of case study research (2nd ed.). Thousand Oaks, CA: Sage.

Zhang, Z. The $1.4 Trillion U.S. 'Surplus' That Trump's Not Talking About. Bloomberg News, 11 June, 2018.

Zillgitt, J. Adam Silver gives Donald Sterling lifetime ban from NBA. USA TODAY, 29 April, 2014.

Zunes, S. Why the U.S. Did Not Overthrow Saddam Hussein. 1 Nov, 2001).

Dr. Gregory L. Cotton

ABOUT THE AUTHOR

Dr. Gregory L. Cotton is the President & CEO of COTTON7 Global Enterprises. He has over 35 years of military and corporate leadership experience, and attained the rank of First Sergeant with the U.S. Army. Dr. Cotton holds a doctorate degree in Organization and Management with a specialization in Leadership, and a Master's degree in Business Administration.

Dr. Cotton is widely considered a Subject Matter Expert (SME) in the areas of Leadership, Risk Management, Business Logistics, Anti-Terrorism, and Global Business Development. Dr. Cotton volunteers his time with the Junior Achievement organization, outreach centers, high school sports and intern programs, as well as educational and infrastructure development programs in Africa and India.

Dr. Cotton is also a prominent speaker at conferences, business gatherings, and educational institutions. He has participated on many panels, including at The White House during the Obama Administration. Dr. Cotton has earned numerous military, commercial, and volunteer awards over the years.

Some of Dr. Cotton's most significant awards include three Presidential Meritorious Service Medals, Sergeants Major of the Army Gold Medallion, Mentor of the Year, the President George H. W. Bush "Daily Point of Light Award", Department of the Army's "Outstanding Volunteer" medal, and was presented with the Mahatma Gandhi Award for Social Good on three separate occasions.

www.ingramcontent.com/pod-product-compliance
Lightning Source LLC
Chambersburg PA
CBHW081343280526
45788CB00009B/2760